The Making of an Accidental Nun

Author

Anne Victoria

The Seriously Light Trilogy ©

Oregon

Website for information about book events, media and lectures,
Or to order books:
www.seriouslylighttrilogy.com

Available at www.Amazon.com

Cover photo: in memory of Alan Anthony Young, surf at Stinson Beach, California
Anne's photo by Melissa Barker, Eugene, Oregon
Book cover design by Anne Victoria, Oregon

DEDICATION

This book is dedicated to my dear Angel friends, my family and friends whom have taught and comforted me- I love and cherish you! Also, to the life saving and wise teachers whom I have been graced with knowing, and for their love and brilliance. A special Thanks to Gloria Doyle, this book is dedicated to you, with eternal gratitude.

ACKNOWLEDGEMENTS

I am gigantically thankful to Melinda Booth-Lea and Larry Hayes for lovingly coming to my aid with their expert help I critically needed to write this book. Melinda and Larry gave me tender care while they edited, proof read, and shared their heartfelt concerns with me. They gave me countless hours of their time and taught me many priceless literary gems. My gratitude for you both will only magnify as I write my next two books…You're truly my Earth Angels.

There are a few very good friends whom I am especially thankful to, my sister being one, who have listened to me while I was undertaking this book writing task, and showered me with their loving support: Kathy, Leslie, Nichetta, and Judy- I Love You and Thank-You All!

Chapter Contents

Introduction

This is the story of the first 19 years of my life, full of twists and turns worthy of an Alfred Hitchcock movie. I was born incapable of understanding why anyone should have power over me. I thought I was free to live my life however I wished. It took miracles to survive those treacherous years.

I was also born with a powerful sensitivity to "out of body" spirits, from earth as well as other realms. The struggles began early in life, making me so different from other kids that I became a target for abuse.

I quickly developed survival skills and a hardened attitude. The craziness of the streets and my insatiable craving for excitement had serious consequences. I was bold and, I thought, a force to be reckoned with. My parents were utterly unable to help me or steer me away from the self-destructive course I had set for myself. I am lucky to have lived through it.

Then came an opening of sorts, like the pulling back of a veil to reveal the spirit world, and my clairvoyant gifts sprang to life. Lacking a teacher, my progress was tainted by my eighteen-year old whims, leaving me terrified and desperate. Only Angelic serendipity could change the way I lived. I took a wrong turn, and an Angel appeared, instructing me to do something uncanny. With no other choices and nothing left to lose, I found the courage to trust this Angel and make the leap of faith. From a dire situation that could have meant jail time, murder or worse, I was rescued and set free. This book is actually a message from "My Last Minute, Angel," describing what I was asked to share.

This volume of the Seriously Light Trilogy concludes in 1981. Since that time I have lived according to the direction of my Angel friends of the Divine Light. In 1987, they told me about the books that I would write one day. Here, at last, is the beginning of my story. Despite my remarkable history, I never thought of myself as a writer before. Given that, I hope you enjoy your reading despite, or perhaps even because of my unrefined and sometimes raw style.

The only way to tell this story was simply and purely, in the chronological order that it unfolded. I avoided injecting my present-day thoughts, and wrote with the perceptions I held during those times. My current understanding about my history will be shared when I write about self-discovery and reflection in future volumes. The Seriously Light Trilogy is the story of my first fifty-year journey: flowing through that time with Angelic guidance and care. My Angel friends have arranged many opportunities for healing, education, spiritual growth, and forming the perspectives and beliefs that I now hold. Looking back, I can say that I am eternally grateful for my unique and exciting education. Thank-goodness, I listened to the Angels at critical moments. They graced me with invaluable spiritual insights, love, and comfort, and guided me to happiness and spiritual fulfillment through being of service. I believe that anybody can be saved by Angels of the Light, as I was. Nurturing my awareness and using my extrasensory gifts for the highest good of the planet are my earthly jewels.

My hope is that you take away from this book as much inspiration, wonder, and peace as my life has given me. I know a loving intelligence, with awesome power, is watching over us, that we are all connected, and ultimately made of Divine Light-Love! Your prayers are being heard, and where you focus your energy is vital, for that is what you will manifest. I pray that everyone will make decisions based on the highest good of All.

We are All, born with a miraculous sense of intuition, each with our unique way that our angelic friends can communicate with us. Living with the guidance of my Angel Friends has given me constant opportunities to spread love, health, and divine happiness.

The decision I made, at 19, has graced me with joys beyond the scope of my imagination. Multitudes of magnificently Angelic people have blessed my life and continue to do so everyday.

I surrendered my life to divine orchestration and communicate with my Angel friends through all my senses: hearing, seeing and feeling them. Then, the truly remarkable miracles, world travels, inner growth, otherworldly interactions and healthy, wild adventures began.

With All My Love and Thanks,
Anne Victoria

CHAPTER 1
MAKING SENSE OF IT ALL

In reading these first words, you begin a journey through the first nineteen years of my life, as best remembered, to be the truth. Although I changed everyone's names, the events themselves remain as correct as humanly possible. I have written through the eyes of the moments, my emotional and mental understanding at that time, with the purest of recollection. This is the miraculous the story of my childhood; without comment from my present thoughts about the occurrences, the lessons learned, and the myriad of ways I hurt and helped people. Simply put, I begin at the beginning, with the experience of a three year old, in Upstate New York. Having grown up with a loving mother who was also a labor and delivery nurse and childbirth educator, and happening to be a preachers daughter, with both of them being Activists was perfect for a spirit like me. Especially being born with a spirit sensitivity that grew into mediumship. The spirit encounters I had as a young child had a lasting effect on me; then knowing there is more going on here than what, us, humans commonly witness. My family also included, my sister, four years older than me, and my brother, a year older than me.

My first memory was, also my first power-struggle, when my Mom had worked the night shift and left Dad to prepare our dinner. He was not a chef by any means, having only a few things in his bag of tricks, chipped beef on toast being his staple. This particular dinner memory sticks in my mind for a few reasons, probably because I was traumatized. Dad was making dinner and I was hoping that he would burn the canned peas so we would not have to eat them, but he didn't. I could not even swallow canned peas; both the texture and taste was nauseating. My Dad was not only an Episcopalian Priest, he was a former Marine and an authoritarian who decided to show me who was in charge. I was ordered to sit at the table until I ate all my peas. He sat at the table and glared at me for hours, so I had no chance of hiding the peas anywhere. When my mother returned she was demonstrably mad at my dad for making me stay at the table and not letting me go to bed. I rarely heard her scold him but this night she gave him an ear full: 'He was ridiculous with his controlling ways, more than once.' I felt that my mom rescued me from being left there all night and even into the next day if those peas were still on my plate. He swore that I would be eating those peas at breakfast but, thankfully, my mom threw them away. The problem between my dad and me is that I had inherited as much stubbornness as he had, maybe more. I was only three years old, but the power clashes with my dad began that night.

Our family moved from a duplex to our own home, just three blocks down and over a steep hill. Being so young, I do not have many memories of our duplex home and the move. I was happy about our new home and especially the big backyard. We moved into a two story home with a basement and huge attic.

I remember sitting on the living room floor, in front of the television, when a Special News Announcement came on the screen. This was the announcement that President Kennedy had just been shot and killed in Dallas, Texas. I could feel the intensity of my parents' reactions to the news and it chilled me. The odd thing is that without being old enough to understand what was truly going on; the news gave me a strong gut feeling that some things are seriously wrong with the world around me.

Not long after, a lively party was thrown in our backyard and it was well attended. There was a lot of laughter and people hugging on this warm, sunny day. I remember seeing two Nuns walking down our driveway, arm and arm, giggling and swaying from side to side. Later in my life, I learned that this lively party was to celebrate these people, Dr. Martin Luther King and my father included, traveling to Selma, Alabama to march for Human Rights. They were about to depart to one of the last marches before Dr. Martin Luther King was shot and killed. Dr. King hugged me and I feel blessed every time I remember this. My Father, commonly called The Reverend, is also an Episcopalian Priest. Apparently, my Father's protesting got him arrested and landed him in a Southern jail. I certainly did not miss him, or really notice him missing as he was released fast. My parents knew better than to tell us kids about

Dad's arrest until we were in our early twenties. I surely would have used his arrest against him while he was trying to discipline me in my teenage years.

At first the thought of this next memory was weird, yet it became understandable as I grew up. I was riding my tricycle in front of the house; having a great time until I fell over and skinned my knee. Screaming, I went running towards the front door of the house where my father was standing with his arms opened wide, ready to comfort me. I pushed him aside and went inside to find my mother. I wouldn't let him near me and wanted him to get out of my way forever, no buts about it.

The neighborhood we moved to was a fun place to be a kid. There were many children living on our street and each entertaining in their unique ways. Cliques of kids formed and I roamed from clique to clique since I didn't fit in well with any of them. The outdoors was where the adventures were: kickball, capture the flag, or something else exciting was always happening. Weather permitting, I was out in the neighborhood and did not like being inside the house much. Watching television and reading books were not exciting for me, with the exception of the Saturday Monster Movie matinee.

My brother, sister and I were sitting on the couch when my mother broke the shocking news to us. We were going to get a little brother soon. The first thoughts us kids had were around how this would affect our play areas. Could a fourth kid fit in? For example, when we would be jumping on the couch, us three kids barely fit. Once our little brother arrived home, we all decided that he was a great! He was the cutest little guy and I adored the moments when my mother let him sit on my lap. Now we were four children and quite a handful for our parents. Luckily, Mom was creatively resourceful when it came to finding ways to keep us entertained. I shared a bedroom with my sister at this point, which seemed logical at first.

One afternoon, I came home to find a very handsome man sitting in our living room. The man told me he was "Batman." Batman was my hero, so I was impressed and quickly planted myself on his lap. I did not budge from there until the enchanting "Batman" left. He showed me his badge, and told me he needed to go meet Robin. That was the only time I ever saw this man, but he left an enormous impression on me. I told all the kids on the block that Batman had been in our house, that he was my friend, and that I had sat on his lap. Nobody believed me. They laughed at me, and said I was a liar. I couldn't understand why they wouldn't believe me. I came to learn that he was from the Federal Bureau of Investigation.

✵

I had my first heartbreak when my best friend, Frankie, moved away. I was only three years old, and couldn't understand why his family took him from me. Missing him left a big hole in my life and my days were empty without him. I tried to play with the girls on the block, but thought their games were stupid. I didn't have any interest in dolls or playing house. They weren't thrilled with me either.

I wanted to climb trees, build forts, make things in the dirt, and wrestle. I thought that if I wished hard enough, I could grow up to be a boy. I prayed, many times, every day, for this. I wore my brother's clothes, started calling myself Elliot, and refused to answer unless my family used my new name. I explained that I was wishing and praying to become a boy. Surprisingly, no one laughed at me, but they looked at me as if I were an alien or nuts.

✵

We were sitting in front of the television and eating popcorn with my dad. Mom was working the night shift at the hospital. I held popcorn kernels in front of my mouth and practiced sucking them in. Suddenly a kernel got stuck in my throat and I started choking. My father flipped out, told my siblings not to open the door for anyone, threw me, upside down over his back and drove like a madman to the hospital.

I was blue by the time we got there, and the doctor put me on the exam table. My father said that when the doctor looked at me, he saw that the kernel had dislodged and I began breathing again. I was too young to remember this event, but my parents told me about it in my later years. I can only imagine how scared my family was. There would be no more slurping popcorn for me.

CHAPTER 2
TOMBOY GROOVE

I was walking to school for my first day of kindergarten. There were many of us walking together, moms and kids. I was glad my mom was going to walk me to class; it was a big deal for me. The day was beautiful, and I was excited to be going to school. As we entered the building, my stomach tightened up and I was filled with panic. Mom and I looked through the window at the class for a few minutes. She was trying to calm me down, telling me about the fun I was going to have.

The teacher came to the door and greeted us, and my heart sank. My mom introduced us and I threw a temper tantrum in the hallway and received a pep talk from my mom. I couldn't believe I was going to be left there to spend the rest of the day with all these kids. I was in shock, but managed to enter the classroom. It took a while for me to relax and adjust. I did a lot of watching and ended up having a great time.

Summers were fantastic and filled with fun times. Our family spent a few weeks at a camp in the Adirondack Mountains that was owned by our church diocese. The camp had a big lodge where family-style meals were served and special events happened. It was a huge camp, with hiking trails and a lake. There were boys' and girls' campgrounds, with big tents on wooded platforms, places for the arts and crafts, an archery range, and canoes.

We all loved going to the camp, and made friends with many other families there. I spent most of my time swimming and sunbathing. I am a fish through and through, a double Pisces, and there was no keeping me from the water. I have many happy memories of singing around the campfire, roasting marshmallows, laughing and feeling loved by my mother. My mother was cuddly and liked to hug me around the campfire. She's like a Big Hug of Sunshine on two legs.

Because my mom was the lifeguard and camp nurse, I was a "staff brat," with special privileges. I had more freedom than the other kids. When I was a little older, I could hike by myself, take out canoes, and roam through the kitchen asking for goodies. When I wasn't swimming, I had fun making artwork and learning new crafts. Archery grabbed my interest, and I practiced for hours on end. I got to be a good shot, too.

Swimming was still my favorite activity, and I took to the lake like a fish. I wouldn't stop swimming, even when my lips turned blue and my teeth were chattering from the cold. I was having such a great time that I didn't notice things like goose bumps. My Mom would finally make me come in, wrapping me in a warm towel and fluffing me up to put a stop to my blue lips and shivers.

Nobody doubted that I was a true tomboy. Now, in the first grade, I mostly played with the boys. Being taller than most of the kids, and pretty darn tough, I was a favorite team pick for lunchtime football. I could throw a powerful and accurate spiral that surprised me as much as it impressed the boys. I was invited to join a "club" of boys, just four of us really. We were not the type of club that might come to mind; we were mostly good, kids, playing behind our houses. Many of our garages became our clubhouses, mine included. The worst thing we ever did was to sneak cookies from our homes.

I had a favorite boy, the class clown, bold and always laughing. He liked me too, and he was the boy who invited me to be in the "Club". Often, when the teacher turned her back to us, he would make birdcalls and farting noises. I would crack up laughing at his silly goofing around. Although happy to have met some boys to play with at school, I was still determined and praying to become a boy.

Drawing pictures was a favorite pastime for me and in the first grade we got to draw often. I would pile up the colorful crayons and was free to create. Somehow all my drawings had the same theme; a cute house, rolling hills, bright yellow sun, flowers and a big rainbow. Rainbows filled me with happiness when I envisioned them.

I was supposed to meet up with my brother and sister after

school, out in front, to walk home together. One day, I came out of the school before my siblings and decided to set out on my own, without a care. Although the way home had many turns to it, finding my way was easy. My mom was happy that I made it home although she seriously scolded me for leaving school without my sister and brother. I did not want to have to wait around for them; I wanted to do my own thing. Rules were entering my life now, left and right. I did not know until years later that my mother's extra concern was because of threats against our family. It seemed that my father's activism drew the attention of the John Birch Society and they meant bad news. The Birch Society wanted my father dead, because of his friendship with Dr. Martin Luther King.

My big sister and I shared a bedroom and we were very territorial. She was bigger than me and was scary when she was angry. There were times when she would catch me wearing her socks, or shirt on and go insane with fury. We screamed and chased each other, always ending up with one of us hurt and crying. My mom broke up our squabbles, but our vengeful thoughts remained. My sister and I rarely played together, as she was living in a different world than me. My passion was outside with the boys in the neighborhood climbing trees and playing sports. My older brother was a book-worm and my younger brother, well, he was younger. I just didn't get my boy fix from my brothers.

A family moved in down the block and they had two young boys with great toys. I quickly became friends with the older one, my age. One afternoon, we were playing in his bedroom. He wanted to show me something fascinating and in his closet. Innocently, he wanted to show me what he discovered his penis could do. He pulled his pants down and showed me his erection. It was truly fascinating, like he said. I was looking at his penis and wishing that I had one of those, when his mother opened the closet door. She was mortified and started yelling, " You are bad kids!" I couldn't understand why she was that upset. She said, "You are too young for this behavior", pointing her finger in my face. I told her that it was OK because I was in the third grade. She became madder and called me a liar. She told me that I was in the first grade and never come back. She kicked me out of the house and called my mother. My mother scolded me but was more concerned about my lying than the curiosity of six year olds.

✷

Every day, I prayed about my disturbing dilemma of being a boy trapped in a girls' body. I was realizing that my prayers were not changing me into a boy. I was furious about it. Wearing only boys clothing helped to hide my dissatisfaction. Girls-Yuck!

Several occasions came and went where a little girl should be dressed as such; Easter and Christmas Church Services being just two. When these holidays came up I waited until the last minute before we had to be in the car to get to church on time and I would show up in my brother's clothes. My parents tried everything to get me to change into girls' clothes, but with no success. My temper tantrums could be heard down our street and tears poured from me, like Niagara Falls. At some point in my childhood, my parents decided that I could wear boys' clothes. I think they came to the conclusion that it was not worth putting the family through the scream-filled drama anymore. I would never be asked to wear a dress again! My life was looking up. I was even allowed to bring my blue jeans to church and promptly change from slacks after the service. My favorite clothes happened to be my brother's Cub Scout uniforms and a constant topic of my reprimand. It seemed that I was being scolded for refusing to be treated as a girl.

✷

I teamed up with a few boys on my block and went to war against some boys whom lived on the block behind us. We had fun throwing crab apples at each other and we were ferocious about it. Sometimes an enemy boy was captured, tied to a ladder, and bombed with crab apples, which left huge welts. This day was different from others, because we were fighting each other with a fence separating us. The fence was made from slatted wood, making it impossible to see the other side. We bombed each other with the apples and stones, loving every minute of it.

I picked up a brick and, without thinking about the consequences, I flung it over the fence. I was so proud, knowing "this" would really get them. I heard a scream and the other boys yelling for help. Instantly, I knew that I was in big trouble this time. I ran into my house, up to my bedroom, and dove under the sheets. My plan was to deny everything and say that I was taking a nap and not even there. The brick hit a boy in his head and he had to get some stitches so his mother was angry. The kids told on me, and this boy's mother came to our house to speak with my mom. I was called downstairs to face the music. I denied being there and was punished anyway. It was obvious that I was guilty, plus, I never took naps. I was punished by not being allowed to leave our yard for two weeks. My mother was trying to understand why I lied to her, would do such a terrible thing, and not care about hurting the boy.

My Grandparents on my Dad's side were lots of fun and we always visited them during our summer vacations. They lived next door to the Cleveland Zoo; a kids' dream come true! They saved their change all year and divided it up between us kids. We had plenty of money to buy our amusement ride tickets and treats. The Zoo was an adventure for us, especially the Animal Petting Area. I loved touching the animals. As far as amusement rides went, scarier the better. I was a "Dare Devil".

My Grandmother on my mother's side lived in Cleveland too. She was lovely and kind hearted. She lived alone as long as I remember, Grandpa died when I was only 6 months. There were many more kids to play with at this Grandma's, but I never became close with any of them. My dad's parents lived on the top of a duplex and the porch was screened in and filled with toys! My mom's mother also lived on the upper story of a duplex on the opposite side of the city. Spending time with all of our grandparents was always a lot of fun. My moms' mom had a big attic; a large area that held three twin beds and another bedroom off the main area. The attic was a little spooky and smelled of the old wood and the ages. This Grandmother was an artist: expert seamstress and painter of realism with oil paints. She made a substantial part of her income from sewing elegant dresses for her private clientele. All was going great in my world.

CHAPTER 3
GHOST TROUBLE

The first of the terrifying hauntings began not long after I started second grade, blowing my beliefs apart with a living nightmare. It all started on a crisp and sunny Fall day, when I was walking home from the park. The park was four blocks away from my home, but it seemed like miles this afternoon. I was walking along, enjoying myself when I first heard it, deep breathing right beside me. The breathing kept getting louder and louder. Then, I saw how the grass beside me was being squished down in the shapes of foot prints. An invisible man was walking next to me breathing very hard into my ear. The hair on the back of my neck stood up straight and I bolted towards my house in terror. I ran so fast I felt like I was jumping out of my skin, utter terror pounded through my body. I must have been stark white when I got home. I knew just how crazy my experience would sound to my family so I kept it a secret. I had the bejeebers scared out of me by a ghost, and I knew it was a ghost. It took me awhile, but back in the safety of my home, I calmed down. I assumed this was a one-time episode, over and done with.

Just a few days later, in our backyard this time, I had another terrifying visit from the ghost. It was extra-disturbing to know that I was not safe from this haunting spirit on my family's property. I was playing by the bushes near the box elm tree, when the deep breathing returned. I could see the bushes moving to the side of me as I walked, and was filled with horror. I felt it in every cell of my body, even in my hair follicles. I ran into the house and sat in the living room pretending that everything was A-OK. I was so young that I didn't know anything about ghosts or spirits, but I knew I would sound wacko if I talked about it. Here I was living in a nightmare, scared and feeling helplessly alone.

A few days later, I was at the park and, again, the eerie breathing returned. Breathing loudly and I could feel it on my neck, while leaving its footprints in the grass beside me. Running like an

Olympian, I streaked home in total terror. I often cut through this park to get home from school and with the many kids that played there, I always felt safe. It was my favorite park, until this spooky visitor appeared. The haunting happened again, a couple of days later. Why I thought that running away was protecting me is beyond me. This horrifying spirit liked terrorizing me and I couldn't do anything about it.

I was comforted by my usual routine: going to school and playing with our pet gerbils that I loved so much. It took a few weeks before I felt safe going too far from home. Normal was Good! Almost three weeks passed since my last visit from the ghostly thing and I started to think that it decided to move on and was haunting somebody else.

I was sitting at my desk, at the end of the school day when the ghost returned; I felt sheer panic and became frozen with fear. The breathing began and was becoming deeper and louder. It was coming from where our coats were hanging, in the closet near the door at the back of the room. I was getting up the courage to walk towards it and get my coat, knowing I would have to keep cool. When the dismissal bell rang it startled me, highlighting the reality of the horror I was feeling. It signaled that it was time to get my coat. Even frozen with fright, I managed to grab my coat, and run out of there.

Every cell of my body was screaming, 'NO! There is a Monster in there!' I had to make sure that nobody found out that I was scared of an invisible "something". I could never live that down. Kids are extremely cruel, especially to the strange kids; which I was labeled due to pretending to be a boy. I walked home with the neighbor girl, Eileen, and never said a word to her about the ghost. The walk seemed to take forever and I was soaked in nervous sweat the whole way while praying that this haunting spirit would not follow me and go away, again. I could not wait to be back in the safety of my home!

My personal, other-worldly nightmare went on for at least three long months. It was preoccupying whenever I was outdoors, my favorite place to be. I was a nervous wreck. Maybe the haunting creep knew I was at wits end, gave me mercy and moved on. Three weeks passed without a sign of the Ghost and I was getting back to some semblance of peace, whew. Looking into the mirror, I saw that my color was coming back, I had been white in my own right. My studies were getting interesting again; my concentration having waned during the haunting months.

Then, after finally feeling safe again, my comfort zone got blown apart. My world came crashing down on me. I was sitting in my usual spot behind a living room chair, huddled up over the heat vent. During the cold months the spot behind the chair was where I got warm from the heat vent yet could still watch the television and be privy to the goings-on with the family. I mistakenly believed that the ghost would not be able to haunt me inside the home. I was sitting behind the chair and the deep breathing started across the room in the corner to the left where my mother was sitting. The breathing was coming from behind her chair and I was sure that she could hear it, too. I was so freaked out that this Thing could enter the living room and was near my mom that I could barely breathe.

Although certain that I turned white instantly and that panic was in my voice when I asked, "Mom, don't you hear the breathing coming from behind your chair?" She laid the newspaper she was reading on her knees and looked at me. She said that it is only the wind and no big deal. I insisted, "Mom, don't you hear it? It is coming from behind your chair. It is breathing loudly!" Again, she repeated, "It's just the wind", and picked up her newspaper. I said, "You know it is not the wind, it is a ghost of some sort." From behind the newspaper she said, "It really is the wind or just your imagination".

What was I supposed to do now? This thing breached my security-blanket; so to speak, I was only eight years old, after all. I had no safe place in the world from this haunting spirit and it scared me all the way to the center of my bones. My mom thought it was the wind or the imagination of an eight year old. I should be happy that she did not get me speaking about my terrifying encounters with this spirit or she might have had me heavily medicated.

Thank-goodness that, after those long months, the haunting spirit, ghost thing laid off and my sanity came back. A dim sense of some personal safety returned and my outdoorsy nature was reclaimed. Hurray!

CHAPTER 4
"NO I WON'T!" AND PLAYED HER DRUM

This particular summer at Camp was outstanding as far as my pure joy goes. A stray dog, we all thought a Beagle, showed up at camp. Immediately, I adopted the dog and he became my best friend. He went everywhere with me, even slept in my bed. I loved my new dog and he became my hiking buddy. I recall more than once holding him in my arms while I scaled precariously down the front of these huge rock cliffs to get back to the main camp area. We came close to slipping a couple of times and I knew we were in a dangerous situation. It is a wonder I survived camp at all, when I think back on the many treacherous moments.

My parents were nice enough to let the dog sleep in the library with me, but I was curious about the dog coming home with us. What would the current occupant, an indoor, blue Persian cat think? It was not used to anything disruptive. But I loved my dog and could not bear the thought of leaving him behind.

He loved hotdogs, that doggy of mine! One day I tied him up to a tree near the dining hall while I ate dinner, like I always did. After dinner I found that he was gone, missing, and I screamed. I was heartbroken and wondering if the camp workers took him off his rope, trying to separate us. I hoped that he ended up in a very loving home because he was the best doggy. I got over my longing for my mysterious dog friend by the time we returned home.

Playing in the neighborhood gave me a chance to explore and pretend! One day I wanted to show off how cool I was to a neighbor boy, so I decided to show him something exotic. I took a steak knife that was adorned with silver filigree accents and looked like it could

have come from the Arabian Nights from our house. I was showing
him the knife when a neighbor saw me from her kitchen window and
came outside. She asked me where I got the knife. I told her that it
was my parent's knife and I was just showing him. She told me to go
home, then called my mother and told her about the knife. My
mother punished me, but I didn't understand what I did that was
wrong.

Third grade started out as bad as it could get for a "Tomboy."
The school authority was clamping down on my style, in a big way! I
was a Boyish Being and did not care one bit what anyone had to say
about it. A "Dress Code" was implemented at school saying that
girls had to wear dresses. Talk about NO WAY! Not only was I not
wearing a dress, we have sub-zero, snow blizzards where I grew up;
were they crazy?

Marching to the tune of my own drummer I ignored the dress
code. I was finished with their dumb rules. I decided that no person,
rule, or law, could tell me what to wear so I hid my blue jeans in the
garage each night. Every morning before school I would leave the
house in a despised dress, dash to the garage, and change my clothes.
Kids would look at me in a pathetic way but I didn't care, feeling
thoroughly comfortable with my appearance.

My teacher, of all people, led the public ridicule and tried her best
to humiliate me. At Roll Call the teacher would get to my name and
I would say, "Here." I was then instructed to stand while she told
the class to look at my camping clothes and they laughed at me. I
became angry with my teacher and irritated that my clothes were
other people's business. I was sent to the principal's office for
reprimand many times, for my indifference to the dress code or any
other of their ridiculous rules. Day after day I left the office in tears
and never wanted to come back to school.

Beside my teacher being mean and hurtful, she also called my
father in for a meeting. My dad was not the warm and fuzzy type;
that he was abrasive would be an understatement. By then I had no
respect for my teacher and I loudly expressed myself when
confronted. I tried to be the best student that I could, but felt she
was picking on me. When my father arrived for the meeting I was
writing on the blackboard 100 times, "I will obey the rules."

The two of them sat at the teacher's desk and discussed Me. I overheard a statement that made me freeze with fear and I stopped writing. I could not understand the full potency behind what my father said at the time: "Nobody is going to break her spirit, except for me." The teacher got in a huff and we left. As the story continues, my father spent many years trying to do just that, Break Me Down! The rule stood that I was to wear a dress to school, but there was just no way that I was going to let these people tell me what I should wear. I was angry and frustrated, yet fearless at the same time. I did not understand why their dress code applied to me and so I rebelled.

As the weeks slowly crept onward, I held my ground about the dress code. My teacher was finally letting up some on trying to embarrass me. On this extra fine day, I was speaking with a black girl that was bussed to the school from the Southside. This was the very first year of school desegregation and I witnessed many race riots. This girl told me that where she went to school the kids could wear anything they wanted to. Hearing her gave me hope and I was off and running with this exciting news. I announced at the dinner table that I would like to start the next school year being bused to school on the Southside. I grew up in a home that supported Civil Rights, Human Rights and Equality, so thought my idea would be OK with my parents.

My parents led me to believe that they would look into it for me. It took two weeks for me to realize that my parents were just plain not calling the school to arrange for anything. I took the situation into my own hands, called the school myself, and set up an appointment to interview and tour the school with my parents. I made the school appointment announcement at the dinner table. My parents stopped what they were doing, mid-bite, and looked at each other for a moment. Then my Father said, "Alright, we will go". Talk about thrilled, just the thought of wearing whatever I want to school was a dream-come-true! Our time at the school went great and it sounded as if I would be able to attend; yippee!

My present, third grade, class was a real sight to behold. The girl who sat two desks in front and on the adjacent row from me would often pick her nose and eat her boogers. She would hold each booger out in front of her, gaze at it, and eat it. When her nose was cleaned out, she would eat the erasers off of her pencils. I think I was more amazed than grossed out by her habits and had to tease her about her booger/eraser-eating habit, at least once a week. I was such a brat to her and was probably only acting out over the dress code and whole stupid school.

I did make a few friends at school, Cathy and Betty. We joined the YWCA together and had fun times swimming, I learned to dive too. One day, when we were leaving the YMCA, I witnessed my first solar eclipse with them. The sky and stars caught my attention and imagination as I gazed up and I wondered about life for hours afterwards.

Cathy had a fascinating birthday party: we piled into her family station wagon and went to the glorious Howe Caverns. As the elevator descended deep into the stalagmites and stalactites the temperature dropped quickly. This birthday party made me into a cave lover! Beauty like I never saw before and ever since I have adored collecting rocks and crystals.

My becoming aware that there are youngsters and adults that wanted what is between my legs was awful. At the beginning of learning this fact of life it came as surprise, nobody warned me. It was hard for me to understand how I could have nearly been raped in a public place with my mother only a few feet away. I didn't know the word rape at that the time, but it was clearly my vagina that they were after. My mom was sunbathing at the side of the neighborhood pool while I was swimming in the pool, which was filled with people. Suddenly there were three boys pulling on me and trying to get my swimsuit off. The boys were only about 9 years old but were very aggressive. I fought and screamed for my mom at the top of my lungs and frightened them off. The attack went on for minutes and scared the crap out of me, plus I was being drown. It was a close call! I am sure that my mom didn't fully grasp how serious the situation was.

Around this same time period and at church of all places, I had another close call when my father told me to go outside and play in the playground at the side of the church. His church was located on the edge of the university district and a big housing project. I was playing in and around a big cement culvert put in the playground as a jungle gym-type play piece. Out of nowhere, two boys appeared and tried to pull me behind the cement tube which was hidden, out of sight of the street. I knew this was super bad. I fought with everything I had in me to get away, screaming the whole time. I think it was the screaming that got them to let go of me, but I kicked, punched, bit and scratched my way free. There was no doubt in my mind that they were going for my crotch. My father was clueless about keeping his daughters safe. In fact my sister has a similar story from the same church playground. I started walking through life with more awareness of my surroundings, paying closer attention.

There was a lot to be learned about the attraction to my private parts. 'What's up with that?', I thought. I did play a little "show and tell" with some kids on my block, as do most children. The oldest kid in the crowd was an eleven year old boy. Everyone else, including the girls, were between six and eight. On one occasion I was told if I undressed and let them stare at me that they would give me candy. 'Why not,' I thought. I wanted candy and did it. Letting them peek at my undeveloped feminine body did not seem like a bad act. Maybe this shows what is meant by being a "Preacher's Daughter?"

At school, Tony was one of my best friends. I thought he was the coolest boy ever. At lunchtime, we played football with his buddies every day that weather permitted. I was my happiest that these boys accepted me as their friend, let me play with them and join their "Club." The best times spent with Tony were at the cafeteria table, where he would teach me different drum rhythms that his big brother had shown him. I had a fantasy love affair with his older brother and hoped to meet him someday, though I never did. One of my first "Crushes" and with a boy I never met; that doesn't work. Tony was a brat, especially the time when we found a garter snake on the playground and he tossed it in front of the girls. I laughed so hard watching the girls screaming their heads off and running for the school door. I will never forget all the commotion from frightening a group of girls. He really was my kind of buddy.

I was thoroughly drawn to the drumming I did with Tony and I began beating out rhythms on the furniture at home. My favorite was running up and down the stairs, beating out rhythms on the wall, adding in percussion by hitting the slats of the banister. I was a one-boy band!

My parents gave me the fantastic news that I was transferring to Dr. Martin Luther King Jr. School. The only downside to me leaving that school was that I was going to miss Tony very much. However, I had no hesitation leaving school on the last day. I turned around and looked at the school for the last time and felt a deep sense of relief. The satisfaction of knowing that I would never return to this building was like losing a thousand pound ball and chain!

Eileen, who lived next door, became my close friend, once we got over our territorial hang-ups. We played outside often and were patient and caring with one another. I had so many things on my mind and she listened to every one of them. We found laughter about circumstances in our lives and understood each other. Eileen was game for any adventurous pursuit I could think up. The two of us spent many days at the "climbing tree", playing Frisbee and exploring the woods near our homes. I felt alienated by most kids on our block and was glad to have at least one friend. I think the only reason the other kids interacted with me at all, was just the mere fact that I was there.

At different times during my childhood, I spent some months at a time, being a close friend with some kid on the block. Jack, who lived up the block, was one year younger and we had many common interests. We spent a lot of time tinkering with our bicycles, exploring the neighborhood, and taking care of the fort we built in our garage. Jack was a great ally in schemes too.

Eileen, Jack and I loved to chip in our money and share a pizza, one of our biggest treats. After pooling our coins we could afford the boxed, make your own pizza kit. Preparing the pizza let us feel like we were doing a teenager type, grown up thing. Yes, it was obvious that we all thought we were mega-cool, knowing how to cook.

I fantasized and conjured up a grand scheme and decided to pull it off. I am not sure how or when it began exactly, but I could nasty. There is nothing else I can say about it, having no idea at the time how I had become capable of being so rotten and hurtful. The frightening thing about my behavior is that I did not have the slightest care about the feelings of others.

The Pizza Raffle Scam was my first, really naughty plan. I thought of it while taking a walk on a chilly Spring Day. We would forge raffle tickets to be sold door-to-door around the neighborhood. The story behind the raffle tickets went like this ... 'The raffle money is being used to fund the children's story telling hour at the library and the winner of the raffle gets a large pizza from Johnny's. I presented my scheme to Eileen and Jack and they were thrilled to help out. We planned to split up all the money that was left from the tickets . . . after we ate the winning pizza ourselves.

We gathered up our art supplies and met at Jack's house, where we made the fake raffle tickets. Ready with our bogus story, we headed out around the neighborhood. It was easy to sell sixty tickets at a dollar a piece. Sixty dollars was a "Big Score" for three eight year olds. While we were counting up the money we made I changed the rules. Instead of splitting the take evenly, I announced that since I had thought up the scam the pizza was their pay and I got all the money. I pocketed the money and left, ripping my friends off with no regrets.

What a horrible, greedy thing to do to my friends. Even though we ended up being friends again soon after, I still do not know why they would ever speak to me again. I felt absolutely no remorse.

✴

My spirits were lifted especially high this summer because of the excitement of going to a new school. I was going to be able to wear whatever I want for the rest of my life! Camp and visiting my grandparents was wonderful, topped off by the State Fair. My Mom always took us to the fair and was an expert in finding fun things for us to do and create. She had an abundant veggie garden which I loved helping her with. Summertime was always a blast and we were all sorry to have it end; but not this time for me!

We had one last hurrah for the summer. Our family spent lots of time with another family, my parents' best friends, whose kids were the same ages as us. They had purchased some land way out in the Boonies and we loved camping there. Our families and others spent a week at a pop up there and it was beautiful. Us kids ventured out and hiked down to a creek that we followed for miles. My mother found a deer antler the first time she went to the wooded property and she cherished it. Her "Mother Nature" Spirit shown then and when she collected the gorgeous plant specimens for the huge terrariums she created. Being in the country with our friends was a special treat and the moms made sure we had games and goodies. I was relaxed from the country and in the perfect frame of mind to enter my new school.

The first day at my new school was both exciting and scary. My parents decided to send my two brothers to the school with me. My little brother was starting kindergarten so he had nothing to compare the experience with. Both of my brothers seemed fine with being bused to the Southside and my parents were glad that I was not alone. I expected my older brother to be angry with me for the upheaval that I caused in his life, but he never said anything about it. He was also a bit of an outcast at school because he was one of the smartest and the nerdiest looking kid you might ever have seen. He looked so bizarre when he walked to school, waving his arms and singing happy songs. Taking the bus was a big shift for us; having to meet all the new kids. Both of my brothers were extremely sweet and gentle and I was curious about how they would get by in this tough environment. It turned out that of the three of us, I was the one being targeted for blood.

My class had more kids in it than the classes at my old school and two teachers instead of one. My teachers were both men who liked me, even to the point of sincerely worrying about me. There was one other white kid in the class, Nathan, and I thought he was wonderful. He wore his blonde hair at shoulder length and listened to rock-n-roll. We became friends in the classroom, but never outside of school.

There was a large gang of girls in the class and it soon became clear that they did not like me. These girls were so dressed up that they looked like they were going to an Easter church service. Their hair was meticulously sculpted with braids, weaving, and ribbons. Their shoes were all shined and their dresses were beautiful. The girls at my old school didn't dress like that. My clothes were a dream come true; quite comfortable in my blue jeans, t-shirt, and new sneakers. My first day in class was eye-opening, knowing nobody and realizing that I was different than any student I saw. The girls snarled at me and made it clear that I was sadly outnumbered. All in all, however, it was thrilling and I liked my new school so far.

After school the kids who rode the buses lined up in the front of the school. Feeling like the day was a success; I was waiting at the edge of a four foot high cement wall. Out of nowhere, I was grabbed by three boys and pulled down behind the wall. They started to hit me and grab at my clothes. They were trying to get my pants off and were surely intending to rape me. I was in shock and helpless to fight off three boys.

I remembered that a boy who lived up the street from me rode same bus and had been standing very close to the wall. I screamed his name, Robert, and yelled as loud as I could for help. He was a big and tough sixth grader. He came running behind the wall and threw the boys off, saving me. I think I was too rattled to show much emotion about it, but I thanked Robert for saving me. He gave me some suggestions to follow for safety. Robert told me that if I was going to survive at this school that I must never go down in the basement, never go near any of these walls (there were some on the playground too) and never be alone anywhere. I listened carefully and thanked him again.

I made no mention about the rape attempt to anyone, especially my parents. As crazy as this school transition was, it was exciting for me. I was determined to make the best of Dr. Martin Luther King Jr. School so I would never have to return to my old school. I would rather scrap for my life any day than to wear a dress.

My desk was in the back of the classroom where I could keep an eye on the gang of girls who were determined to harass me every day. Each of the girls took turns hitting me, pinching me or pulling my hair when they passed by my desk to use the bathroom. They attacked me whenever the teachers weren't watching. I did not always tell on them, but I noticed how I could get so mad that I did not feel the pain of their attacks. The pack of girl's hatred towards me grew although I gave them no reason for it.

It seems that all it took to single me out was me being a "tomboy", white and a loner. The girls began hurting me worse and even the teachers were getting concerned about me. If the teachers had to leave the room, even for five seconds, I was a victim of some painful attack. There were a few times when the teachers would leave for a moment that the girls did not attack me. I sat there anticipating the attack and so I frightened myself just the same.

Being called ugly about fifty times a day did not bother me, I was used to it from my last school. I never thought about how I look to others or if they liked me; it didn't matter much.

I learned about 'Slamming' when a person grabs your arm, twists it over their head and gets under you in the perfect manner to flip you over them and slam you to the ground flat on your back. It works every time and completely knocks the wind out of someone; besides hurting like hell. One winter day I was slammed in the classroom with the teacher standing just feet away. I gasped for air and made sure to not shed a tear. The classroom erupted in a ruckus with one teacher screaming and the other seeing if I would need an ambulance. Slamming became popular at school that year and I often saw it happen to others. Luckily, I was slammed just that once, that year.

I did not retaliate against the pack of girls, knowing that the 10 to 1 odds meant me getting my ass kicked. My pride was hurt, rage was building up inside of me and I was outnumbered. Even though I knew I would survive, thoughts of what the pack of girls might do to me next ran rampant.

The school had a brilliant strategy for keeping the peace. The policy was that anyone doing anything violent to someone else insured that Friday dancing would be cancelled. Each Friday afternoon everyone in the school went out into the hallways and we danced up a storm. Music, mostly Funk and Motown, was blasting through the school's loudspeaker system. Teachers joined in and everyone danced their fannies off. I was not a dancer and had never heard this type of music before. The music moved me and I truly loved the rhythms.

I was standing in the hallway and watching when another gang of girls threatened me with serious harm, so dangerous that I listened up. They told me that if I did not dance the "Bump" right now, that they were going to beat me up. I started to do the "Bump" right away, mimicking what I was seeing, and they laughed. I danced for my first time and took a liking to it. I practiced the Bump against the door jams at home and was going to get Funky dancing down by Friday. My family thought I was entertaining, "Getting Down" to Motown. I was determined to dance well enough to save myself from the girls' threats. My brothers were not as "different" as I was, so they were not targeted for harassment. They were not practicing their white boy dance moves for school under threats of being beaten. The dancing in the hallways was fun and it did keep the peace; at least when it came to the big stuff, like rapes.

Scrapping (one-on-one fights that get broken up and settled fairly easily) was basically overlooked. Dancing was a great deterrent to serious violence and the kids were extremely afraid to ever be the one responsible for the dancing cancelled. You had to be very bad to have the dancing cancelled, because I saw kids getting away with all kinds of violent acts.

Goings-on at home took a turn towards pure enchantment! One morning there was a big black man at our breakfast table who spoke with a strong foreign accent. He had arrived during the night and at breakfast smiled at me with genuine sincerity. Genuine sincerity, no wonder his smile felt different from everyone else's, except my loving mother's. This comforting man, Kutman is his name, stayed with our family for weeks. My Dad was a trip, to put it mildly, and got himself into the strangest situations. This time, we were hiding out this man because he was a political refuge from Africa and escaping assassination.

Well, Kutman liked the drum rhythms I played on the furniture and walls more than anybody else. One day he brought me the best present, bongo drums. Kutman was a wonderful man and had a powerful influence in my life. He met and married Claire, a family friend and a gregarious, joyful woman. After their marriage, they moved away and I never saw them again. My bongo drums kept me happy and gave me something joyful to do with myself during the brutal winter. I spent way too much time going stir crazy indoors and my bongos made it easy for me to flow with my heart and feel at peace.

My father decided that I had to be in the church choir because I am a Preacher's kid. I threw a major temper tantrum in rebellion against the order. Even with my tears and screams, I found myself standing there in my choir robe. I stood with the choir during Sunday Service with a hymnal in my hands, wondering 'how could this be happening to me'. When it came time to sing the only thing that came out of me was a stream of tears. My mouth stayed firmly closed. My father changed his mind after seeing that choir would never work. Being made to do something that I seriously did not want to do felt painful and made me mad. I wondered how much my father cared about my happiness and decided, not at all.

That winter was fantastic in such a huge way that the classroom troubles did not even matter anymore. I switched musical instruments from playing the cello to the drums. My sister, older brother, and some other relatives all played the violin. I thought I was being rebellious when I decided to take the cello instead. How silly I was, because it was playing drums that let me feel rebellious. The bottom line is that my cello instructor meant well but was boring me with the musical pieces she had me practicing. I can now see the point of starting with the basics but it was hard to be motivated by Twinkle, Twinkle Little Star, when you are crazy about the Rolling Stones and Led Zeppelin. Granted, I appreciated Twinkle, Twinkle Little Star but it frustrated me since I wanted to be playing something drastically different. Playing the drums changed my life in so many powerful ways, least of which was no longer lugging an instrument that was as big as I was on the ice in the freezing blizzards to the bus stop and then to lessons. Now, I was able to carry a pair of sticks instead that could come in handy, as weapons in my new school.

My drum class was small; only three boys in it and myself. I was thrilled to see that Nathan from my class was there. I was the first girl drum student my teacher ever had. I felt welcomed by him and the small class size meant that we had plenty of personal attention. I was given the name of the drum lesson book that I would have to buy for class along with a practice pad and drum sticks. Now I needed some money. So, the day had come when I was finally going to have to tell my parents what I did. I was hoping that changing instruments would be fine even though I did not discuss my plans with them first.

I explained to my mom why I decided to change instruments and needed the drum things, and was hoping it was OK. My mother said that she wished I had given her some notice but that it was fine. My mom was the sweetest and most supportive mom in the world. We went downtown to the music store, where there were at least three drums sets and many percussion instruments, sending my imagination wild. We picked up my drum lesson book and my new drumsticks. I got into the car, thankful for the sticks and book, but really wanting a whole drum set. My practice pad came from a boy who lived a few houses down the block. He gave up playing the drums and sold me his practice pad cheap. Rat-a-Tat-Tat, I began practicing immediately!

Martin Luther King School never stopped amazing me. Here we were, to help put an end to racial discrimination against blacks and we were the recipients of the anger. Within the black student body there were some tough kids, crazy kids, and kids that roamed in packs (not official gangs, but the same power) that all picked on the white kids. There were only a handful of white kids that were tough enough to be left alone and the rest were always concerned for their own safety. The extortion was rampant. Each day the payoffs could be seen. White kids were threatened with being beaten if they did not bring money and/or food to these black kids. These scared white kids paid up more and more; it did not end. For some reason, I was never asked to pay anyone anything, that first year. A good thing that I was not asked because I would have opted to be beaten instead of having my pride hurt.

Fights broke out almost daily so it was no mystery why there were two teachers per classroom. Each day, after lunch, we would go out onto the playground where there were never less than two fights. With only a few exceptions, I had a great time on the playground, never boring.

For two weeks before the last day of school, I was threatened daily with having my ass kicked on the last day of class. The mean pack of girls smacked me in the head when they reminded me. By the time the last day of school arrived, I was scared to death! I did not tell anyone about the threats in fear that they would beat me worse for squealing on them.

My teachers were well aware of the constant torment I was going through as they could overhear much of it. They knew that I was in real danger of being beaten at any time. That is why my teachers were so surprised when I answered their question, "What school will you be attending next year?" I was called up to their desk and was told they did not have my new school listed in their file. I told them that I would be staying at King School. They looked at each other and were obviously quite worried about me. My teacher said that he just assumed that I would be transferring away. Kind of funny how that thought never once crossed my mind.

I woke up on the last day of class and immediately thought about the mean girls threats, and decided to fake a stomachache. When my mom came in my bedroom to see why I was not eating breakfast, I told her that I had a terrible stomachache and in too much pain to go to school. My mom explained how much fun the last day of school is and how I would get to say goodbye to my friends for the summer. I let her know that I knew that but was too uncomfortable to go. She pulled up my pajama shirt and felt around my abdomen seeing if she noticed anything wrong. My mom, the nurse, asked me if different spots she was pushing hurt. She pushed a place and I yelled out, Oww!

Suddenly, my mom was helping me get dressed and said that we were going to the emergency room right this second. She told me that if it is my appendix I would need emergency surgery. To this day, I am not sure if she was calling my bluff, or really thought that it was my appendix. In any case, I told her that we do not need to go to the hospital and that I was faking the stomachache. We had a long talk about the threats and the mean pack of girls. My mom knew about these girls from altercations over the year, fights, scratches, getting slammed, and the like.

My mom did just what I was most afraid of; she drove me to school and had a meeting with the principal and my teachers about my safety. I was so embarrassed about entering the school with my mother and her telling them that I was too scared to come to school. It was dreadful to think that the kids at school would see that I was a wimp. The principal and my teachers reassured me that I was safe, and could be certain of it. The principal was a caring, muscular, and tall black man and he did make me feel safe. I went to class after exhausting every avenue to avoid it. To my surprise, the mean girls were so happy about it being the last day of school that they gave me no attention whatsoever. Glad that emotional day ended and summer vacation was here!

CHAPTER 5
UP, DOWN, INSIDE OUT

My father was assigned to a different church on an American Indian Reservation. The church experience was enchanting and the cultural exposure ended up being highly educational for me. My whole family loved it there too. It was interesting being introduced to the American Indian way of life: clans, colorful ceremonies and celebrations, strange and delicious foods, and fun friends. The people at this church were very loving, the church events were quite lively, and the air was filled with laughter and music. Playing with the Indian kids was the best. My friends on the Reservation were adventurous and taught me how to play lacrosse, use a bullwhip, and ride snowmobiles. Their energy for play seemed endless.

Being given the position of "Altar Boy" was the most exciting church assignment my father ever gave me. He was getting the idea that treating me like a boy would get him much further than trying to make me sing in the choir. I enjoyed the ceremonial rituals, pouring the wine and water, and presenting the communion wafers to my father. The Sanctuary was the only place that my father and I got along with no strife. The Altar Boy robes were even cool.

Since we still lived in the city, we drove out to the congregation every Sunday and for other events during the week. My father rented out the church rectory, where the priest and his family would normally live, to a family for next to nothing. Rectories are great for many reasons, for example, the priest is available in an emergency and having housing might somehow offset the fact that he was not paid very much. I thought the idea of living on the reservation would be so much fun that I kept suggesting it.

There were often weekday events at the church – some bake sale, wedding, celebration, or a myriad of other reasons, and I looked forward to going. If we became too tired and bored my mom would drive us home. There were many times that I was grateful that my parents drove to church separately. My father would spend many hours in meetings and assisting people with their troubles. He would do just about anything, and I mean anything, to help someone in need. However, when it came to helping us – being encouraging, supportive, just keeping the home maintenance trip together – Zippo, Nada and I am not exaggerating. Well, that is a big subject for another time and straying from the original topic a bit.

We all enjoyed the relationships we formed with people on the reservation. On one occasion, a particularly festive event was going on at the church and the flamboyant Indians were dancing their traditional dances. I was sitting in a circle of other kids, including my siblings, on the floor leaning on our hands to support us. Just my luck, of all the possible hands, my hand got danced on. I could not believe it and it hurt like crazy. Several participants were pushing my father to get me to the hospital. Since my mother was working that day, I was at the mercy of my father who did not want to take me. I was left at the mercy of an ice pack. After a few hours of me crying in the corner and some members of the congregation working on him, he relented and took me to the hospital. My fractured pinkie was put in a splint and wrapped in a bulky bandage.

That same week at school, our class broke up into groups and each group prepared a presentation that was filmed. I was mortified to see that I was holding my giant white bandage in front of my face the whole time I was filmed. I was beginning to feel like I was the underdog at class presentations. I was a flop at speaking in front of the class, terrified to be honest, and felt like I came across as weird. Maybe being treated as if I was weird daily, helped that.

During the summer, our family went to the church camp in the Adirondacks, and like always, we were all thrilled. The camp offered non-stop fun things to do. Archery was a passion of mine and the range is where I could be found when I wasn't swimming. Just a few blocks from our home was a city park where I was able to continue shooting archery during the rest of the year.

I had a lot on my mind this summer, thinking mostly about how I was going to have to defend myself this next year at school. Two male camp counselors showed me a few moves that I could use to protect myself. These men were friends of my parents and took my situation seriously. I learned one move that would stop any of these kids in their tracks before they could get me. I had confidence now and it was clear that I had developed an angry attitude to go with it.

I had put up with one injustice after another, or so that is how I thought about it. Starting with the Dress Code at my old school, kids picking on me, my father picking on me, kids trying to rape me, and now another one. At camp I slept on a cot in the library. The library was in a large cabin that also housed the nurse's office and my parents' bedroom, plus another bedroom that two male counselors shared. There was a staircase at the end of the library that led upstairs where the kitchen staff slept.

One night I awoke to a visitor sitting on the end of my cot by my head. The visitor was a man named Chuck who was one of the cooks. He had stopped by my bed on his way upstairs. He asked me how I was doing and if I wanted a backrub. I was scared and did not answer right away, I took a big breath and then I said, "No." He told me how much he liked me and then put his hand under the sheets and my shirt and started to gently rub my back. I was so terrified that I was paralyzed and my heart was pounding. I did not know what to do. He was saying something while his hand went towards my butt and I jumped. I got up my nerve and told him, "You better stop and go or I will scream out for my parents". He stopped and left in a split second, knowing my parents are just on the other side of the wall and that my father would have had him arrested on the spot. Why I never told anybody was strange, but I did not say a word about Chuck's visit to my cot. For some reason, Chuck left the camp and did not finish out the summer. Even at church camp, I did not have many chances to be a carefree kid. Did weirdo circumstances pop up in my life the same as other kids, or am I a magnet for trouble? Sometimes I had to wonder.

My mom kept the family having fun times all summer long. She was always planning something great: drive-in movies, the state fair, picnics at the lake near our home and loved us like cuckoo. A happy summer was ending and I felt ready for the new school year ahead of me. I felt refreshed and that the worst was over and life would be easier from then on.

It was the perfect chance for a last sleep-over at my friend's house before the school year began. I had become friends with a girl my age from church whose family also lived in the city. Our parents became close friends and our families spent summers together at the church camp. This is the first time I slept over at her house and she had never slept at mine, either. My mom dropped me off and our playtime commenced, but I felt a little uncomfortable. My mother sensed my trepidations and gave me an extra big hug before she left. Bedtime came and we snuggled in.

I freaked out when my friend attacked me and kept grabbing at my crotch. I couldn't believe that this little girl from church was trying to rape me. I told her to leave me alone, that I wasn't into anything sexual with her. She insisted on attacking me as if she was possessed or something. Maybe this is how sex addicts start out? I ran out of her bedroom and went downstairs to her mother's side. I lied and told her mother that I have a terrible stomachache and to please have my mother come and get me fast. My mom arrived and rescued me, but I kept the lie going about a stomachache. I have no idea why I didn't rat on the girl to my mother, but I will say that this ended our friendship!

The idea of playing sports, or even watching sports was non-existent around our home with the exception of the Olympics. My siblings never played sports, and my brother never even learned to ride a bike; but we all swam and swam well. The family swam at summer camp and at the local pool and the nearby lake. My mom was the swimmer and she made certain that we had swimming and picnic time often. Dad had an aversion to anything that might be related to exercise and never joined us swimming anywhere, ever.

I was different and a tomboy but was never a sportsy-jock type. That summer I joined the city swim team and raced in both the back-stroke and free-style. Practice was twice a week and my mom was wonderful about getting me to the swim meets and enthusiastically cheering me on. I was not the best or worst of the swimmers on the team, and I loved being part of it. The team consisted of around fifteen of us, from eight to sixteen years old. The swim practices were intense and competitive. The city swim team kept me focused on something besides my school life and my neighborhood kids. School sports did not appeal to me and it would have left me open for a lot of mistreatment, trust me. I felt healthy, strong, and in great shape just like I always have.

School started and the classroom was arranged differently than I had ever seen before. The desks were in pairs facing one another. I really liked it. I sat across from Rachelle, the Mayors' daughter. Rachelle had some Greek heritage, was tall, and showed me what garlic breath really was. I was ecstatic to be away from last year's pack of mean girls. Rachelle's friends were OK and I hung out with them on the playground sometimes. These girls lived clear on the other side of town so I only saw them at school, but I met my new best friend through Rachelle.

My new best friend, Linda, was even more of a tomboy than I was. We were both ecstatic to make friends with another tomboy. We had great, boy-ish times together. Our parents supported our friendship and would eagerly drive us back and forth to one another's home for weekend sleepovers. Linda's home was twice the size of mine and she had a huge park next to her house, with a lake and woods. We spent our time together at her house, out exploring the parks forests and ponds. Linda had a cool, dingo-looking dog that followed us everywhere. Linda started to take drum lessons at school with me and we joined the school band together. Life was fun!

The tranquility in my classroom did not last long. Soon the kids formed their cliques and sorted out their grudges. A crazy white girl was in my class, Laurie. Somehow she was in pretty tight with the mean pack of girls from last year. Only one of the mean girls was in my class this year; maybe the teachers separated them on purpose. This crazy girl, Laurie, decided that she was going to pick on me every day by hitting me in the head when she walked by my desk. Anyone can just imagine how happy I must have been about this. Her tactics of torturing me daily were much different than the other girls because she didn't say anything. There was no way I was going to take any crap this year and had my new self-defense moves for protection.

To make a very long story shorter, I will just say that I used my new moves to defend myself and it worked. I was minding my own business and working at my desk when Laurie walked by me and hit me hard in my arm. After having endured a few weeks of her picking on me, I snapped. I jumped up from my desk and hit her as hard as I could in the face. A brutal fight broke out and I ended up beating her badly. We punched and kicked each other, knocking desks out of our way. Eventually, the teachers were able to separate us. The whole class was in an uproar, shouting and jumping around so they could either get a better view or to keep out of our way. For our punishment, both of us had to stay after school and we missed the school bus. Laurie had to be picked up by her mom because she lived so far away. The teachers told her mom the details of the fight.

I, on the other hand, lived closer and was able to walk the two miles home. I did not mention the fight to my parents and was proud to have finally stuck-up for myself. I let out all the anger built up inside of me over the last year and unleashed on her. Laurie must have something seriously wrong with her, because she kept attacking me even though I brutally beat her. 'Why would she keep coming back for more?' I wondered.

The fights with Laurie went on weekly. Each time, I would jump up and beat her until the teachers could get us apart. Strangely I did not mind the fights with Laurie, they were just an annoyance.

My parents were notified after our second fight and a meeting was called. The teachers were at a loss about what to do because Laurie kept attacking me. Nevertheless, I was punished and spent many days in after school detention. I am sure that was a big drag for my teachers, too.

One day, I went into the lavatory and I was followed in by the vicious pack of girls. I exited the stall and was eye to eye with one of the girl's. She was yelling in my face, telling my how they were going to kick my ass for fighting with Laurie. I lost it and had no more patience. I shouted at her louder than she did that it was Laurie starting it and they should tell her to stop making me beat her ass!

The girls backed down but said, "You better watch it." I felt powerful and exhilarated from standing up to the pack of girls who tormented me for so long. I was happy and knew that I won some of their respect. The scary part of what was going on inside of me was that I was going to attack anyone who messed with me and was never going to back down. I was becoming hardened, but I was certain that my parents were not noticing my deep changes.

Learning and my class assignments were a joy and I liked my teachers a lot. This year the teachers were two sweet women. There was the seasoned teacher, about thirty-five years old, and a younger class assistant, a student at the University. Leaving my last school was the best thing I could have done to have re-stimulated me and improve my education. I loved learning and doing well on my exams. Many of our lessons required us to break off into small groups and I liked that a lot. King School was a pilot school for a curriculum that allowed each of us to work at our own speed. I was studying French in the fourth grade, something not offered at my last school.

Still, being in the school band and taking drum lessons with my buddy Linda were the highlights of my life. Four of the band members, including Linda and I, started eating lunch and spending our recess time in the band room with our teacher. This allowed us to experiment with playing different instruments, whichever one we wished to try. I experimented with every instrument and especially liked being able to play the full drum set. Spending lunch together, playing music and laughing was so much better than eating in the classroom and going to play on the playground.

I was safe once I was inside the band room, but getting there was a bit frightening. I did not forget my first day of school and what Robert told me after he rescued me from nearly being raped. He said, "if you are going to survive here than you must never go in corners, near the walls outside, or in the basement." The band room was in the basement. My strategy was by bending down low at the top of the steps, I could see if anyone was in the first area down there. If the coast was clear, I would run down the stairs like a bat out of hell to the band room door. The basement ceiling showed the pipes and the walls had gizmo boxes at various places giving it a creepy feeling. There were so many places for kids to hide down there and the possibility of being followed was high. The band room was kept locked, so I had to adjust my timing to account for waiting for the teacher to open the door for me.

Winter meant "Snow Days," times when school would be closed due to horrible snow storms. Being bused to school gave us kids a few extra snow days than the walkers. Snow Days meant grabbing the sleds and heading up the hill. We lived a block down from the peak of the best sledding hill, high and steep. That winter I hit a dry spot and flipped over, smashing my knee into the ice and concrete. There I was, on my side, holding my knee and crying my head off. One of the kids ran down to my house and told my mother, who arrived fast. I was placed into a red plastic boat shaped sled, put in the back seat of my mothers' car, and off we went to the hospital. The snow on me and in the sled melted and left me sitting in a cold bath by the time we arrived.

The nurse had to cut my pants off to get to my knee. Being a "tomboy" meant that I wore my brother's clothes, except that I was forbidden to do so. I happened to be wearing my older brothers Cub Scout pants that day and, boy oh boy, were my mother and brother mad at me. I cracked my kneecap and had to wear a brace for a few weeks. Talk about a snag in my sledding plans for a while.

Happiness prevailed anyway because of my excitement over band practice. The band was learning songs for a Spring Concert and we were sounding "rockin" wonderful. One of the songs we played was "Cha Cha Banana", but the drum score just did not sound right to me. Of course they were right -- it's their song -- but I brought my thoughts to my teacher. He told me that I was free to rewrite the drum parts in any way I wished. My teacher was an easy going man and very patient with us. I took the challenge he gave me and rewrote the drum parts of the song. The teacher was impressed with my drum score and let the percussion section play the song my way. The whole band was bubbling over with joy about putting on a concert for the whole school and our families.

A month later, on a Sunday morning, I was kicking a soccer ball around in the street in front of the house. All of us kids were outside in front of the house waiting for my father to take us to church. My older brother had stepped on my foot that was supposed to catch me after kicking the ball, sending me falling backwards on the street. I fractured my funny-bone of all things. I was dropped off in front of the hospital and greeted by mom, who was working there that day. My dad was angry that he had to take the extra fifteen minutes, and because he thought that I did it on purpose to get out of going to church. My arm was put into a sliced cast, wrapped in strong gauze, and supported by a sling.

My cracked elbow meant I couldn't play drums. Even worse, the Spring Concert was coming up and I was supposed to still be in my cast. One evening, a few days before the concert, I sat on my bed and thought about taking the cast off myself to see how I was doing. After a minute of thinking, I went into the bathroom and did it. I gently moved my white and withered arm around and felt no pain at all. I was so happy that I ran downstairs to show my mother that I was fine. Her eyes bugged out when she saw my arm and she ran to the telephone to call the doctor. Mom said, "I can't believe you; what did you that for?" I replied, "The Concert!"

The doctor asked her if I was in pain and I answered, "No", so he said I should just be careful. Yippee!! I was going to play in the concert after-all.

Another truly terrifying time began and terror is putting it mildly; this was like an Alfred Hitchcock movie. I was playing with my pet albino mice, George and Henry, in my bedroom after school one day, a day I will never forget. The telephone rang and my sister picked it up and called out, "It's for you." I took the call in my parents' bedroom. The voice on the other end was an adult male voice, deep and resonant, with a heavy breath.

The man told me that he was going to do these explicit sexual things to me which he described in gruesome detail. He told me he would kill me with spiders if I did not have sex with him. I hung up the phone and just stood there in shock. I knew that I must have turned pale as a ghost and chills ran through me. I went into my bedroom and tried to think of who it might have been. I thought about every man in the neighborhood but had no idea who it could be. I stood there, shivering with fright, not knowing what to do.

I was too embarrassed by the sexual things the man said to tell anyone about the call. Instead I lived in a waking nightmare. Whenever I walked to the store I stayed in the middle of the street so nobody could jump out of the bushes and grab me. I looked at every porch and window to see if anyone was watching me. I walked faster than before the terrifying phone call. As the days went by keeping myself safe became my automatic thought. The stress was almost unbearable. My heart began to pound and a strong surge of fear twisted my stomach every time I was near a man. Weeks went by and this man did not reveal himself, thank-goodness.

One night my parents announced that they were going out until about 9:30 pm and it was rare that they did that. My older sister was left to watch over us until they returned. I freaked out as soon as I heard the news! I didn't feel safe with only my siblings and the thought of the man coming for me was scary. I laid on the hallway floor, hanging on to my mother's leg in a crying, screaming frenzy of terror. I begged them not to leave; to take me with them. I was so frantic but could not convince them to stay. I really was out of my mind in fear but they thought I was making up the threatening phone call story just so they would stay home. They did not believe me and went out, leaving me crying in absolute terror.

I went up to my room, shut the door, and sat on my bed. The worst thing that could have happened did; a spider came walking across my blanket. I flipped out and ran downstairs to a spider book to look up the type I saw. I thought it looked like a brown recluse, but I was so freaked out that it could have been anything. It was probably just a garden spider. I was convinced that the man had been in the house so I locked myself in the upstairs bathroom after thoroughly inspecting it for spiders and put towels at the bottom of the door. I curled up on the bathroom floor and waited for what I did not know.

My parents returned hours later and my sister told them that I was barricaded in the bathroom. I heard them come in the house and felt a little relief, but there was no way I was going to unlock the bathroom door. My father and I yelled at each other through the door until he agreed to search my whole bedroom for spiders. My father was not considerate about my feelings as was his norm. He agreed to my terms and I came out, just to be let down. My father walked into the middle of my room, turned around once, lifted my bedspread and declared the room spider-free. I was screaming that his search was not good enough and to check everywhere. I had an emotional melt down so he looked a little closer and did find the spider, which he killed. He said, "There, now go to sleep" and walked out.

I turned on all the lights and striped my bed of the sheets, looked in every nook and cranny, and, after figuring that my spider search was sufficient, curled up on the outside corner of the bed in the smallest ball that I could make myself into. With no sheets on the bed, I could easily keep watch around me. I somehow managed to fall asleep. Checking the room for spiders became a bedtime ritual that lasted for years.

Somehow, enough time finally passed after the terrifying phone call that my fear faded and I figured it was over. I was still keenly aware of my surroundings, but thoughts of the man on the phone drifted away. This nightmare had lasted for about five long months.

A metal geodesic dome was erected in the side yard of a home three doors down the street. Us kids were fascinated by this big, new play structure, since nobody had seen one before. For the first week, many of the kids from our block and the next block up played on it.

One afternoon Paul, from the next block up, was playing on it towards the top and I was at the bottom of it. There were other kids climbing on it, too. For some reason Paul began calling me ugly and stupid. I got frustrated with Paul and felt embarrassed in front of the other kids, who were all laughing at me by this point.

I Lashed Out! I became so crazed that it surprised even me. I jumped up and grabbed onto Paul's arm, which was sticking out through the metal dome, and yanked down as hard as I could. He climbed down and went running home holding his arm, crying and screaming in pain. I did not stop there and was chasing him after rushing into my house and grabbing a baseball bat. I stood in his front yard yelling, "You better not mess with me again!"

Paul's mother was my mom's good friend. As a matter of fact our families were friends. His mom was on the phone with mine in a lightning second. I stormed back home and Paul's mom was not far behind me. My mother was shocked at how vicious I acted. I was forbidden from going outside of the yard for the next two weeks. Paul and the other kids that watched me lash out became cautious when I was around and were fearful of me now.

The next week I had another neighborhood altercation with a boy up the block. He was a year older and we were co-club members in the neighborhood. We started fighting about something and one thing led to another. The next thing I knew I was running down the middle of the street towards my house when he hurled a brick at me. He threw it as hard as he could while trying to run me down. He meant to hurt me. The brick flew by my head, missing by only an inch or two. I knew I had just had a very close call with a serious injury, maybe even death. Rattled a bit, I kept running as fast as I could into my house.

During this time my father was teaching out of town during the week and only home on the weekends; which suited us just fine. Besides being an Episcopal Priest, my father was a scholar in Sociology and Criminology and would have had doctorates in both if he could have gotten around to writing his Dissertations. He was a king procrastinator. He kept this pleasant work schedule for two years or so and I didn't miss him. He chain smoked non-filtered cigarettes and never had an encouraging thing to say to any of us. He complained about everything we did and picked through his dinner plate with an insulting look on his face. He yelled a lot, making it clear that his family was a pain in his ass.

The weekdays went smoothly and our home was tranquil. My father had the weekends to rule over his family. He probably wondered how seriously we took him. None of us needed to say anything; we all knew we were much happier when dad was away. It did not matter what either of us wanted to do; the answer from dad was always an abrupt NO. It was a good thing that I did not care what he thought of me and ignored him as much as possible. For some reason my dad made a point of picking on me and trying to break my spirit. My siblings would probably say that I was born into being at war with this man and that he was determined to triumph.

Thank goodness for the climbing tree, a place I would go and spend hours reviving. Eileen, from next-door, loved to go to the gratifying tree too. This was where we discussed our lives and found the humor in our challenges. The tree was a big maple just around the corner from our houses. High up in the tree was a fork in the branches that, us, the kids called "The Kings Throne". Up in that tree I did not have a care in the world and could watch the entire neighborhood. I sat in the throne and swung from one limb to another. I felt like I was Boy from the Tarzan movies. I'd had a serious crush on Boy ever since the first episode aired. One time I missed the branch I was swinging to and crashed to the ground, landing flat on my back and knocking the wind out of me. Eileen jumped down to see if I was OK. I was as soon as I could catch my breath. The tree was still my safe place, where my thoughts about my father disappeared and I felt free and primal.

I came up with a master plan, inspired by the movie "The Swiss Family Robinson". There was no good reason why I could not live in the forest and make a tree house. I gathered up supplies and put them in an old Marine Corps canvas bag. I kept the bag hidden in my closet and every week I would add another item to it. I gathered up things like rope, Band-Aids, flashlights and batteries, food, and utensils. I kept my plan a complete secret until I decided that a girl from church, Elsie, would be a perfect partner for this lifestyle. I told Elsie about my plan to run away and live in a tree house and about my supplies. She loved the idea and we agreed to keep the secret and continue to stash supplies. We were both serious about making a life in the forest and agreed to make our escape date soon.

Every once in a while my dad did something nice for me. I wanted a new bike for my birthday with all of my heart. We only had one bike and it was my sister's. For this birthday my dad took me out to get a new bike and I was thankful beyond belief. I had wheels of my own; a burnt orange, men's 3 speed. I rode my bike everywhere, including swim practice. I loved the expanded freedom to explore the neighborhood!

Speaking of exploring, I decided that I would catch the school bus one block up the hill from where I normally caught it. I did not want to wait for the bus with my brothers anymore and thought there was more action at the other bus stop. I was standing at the bus stop when the kids showed up one by one. There were about seven of us when one boy jumped tough at me saying, "What are you doing up here? Go back to your own bus stop".

I responded in a mean tone and bad-assed manner, "I can get the bus wherever I want and I don't see your name written on this bus stop." He was older and bigger than me, plus he had gone to King School for a year longer than I did. He walked over to me, did not say a word, and punched me in the mouth. I was shocked! Silently humiliated and holding my hand over my fat lip, I got on the bus to school. I was put in my place, alright, and never mentioned it to anyone. Wow, my big mouth could get me in trouble but I acted invincible anyway. I continued to catch the bus up at that stop and became friends with the kids there, fat lip forgotten. What a rude way to learn that I should think twice before mouthing off to someone, especially someone bigger than me. Someone might think that I would have learned this lesson pretty well, but not a chance. I thought I was tougher than the truth, had a loud mouth, and was finished with backing down from anyone.

Having had about enough of both my father and the school telling me what to do, I was ready to leave my home for good. Now that I had a bicycle and felt free, I thought it was time to make the tree house plan a reality. Elsie and I made our meeting arrangement for noon that coming Saturday. The closer it got to Saturday the happier I was, anticipating a free life in the forest.

Saturday arrived and I carefully began to shuffle my supplies into the garage. I had the duffle bag, sleeping bag, and my survival tools.

The weather turned nasty, with a sleet mixed rain and a severe drop in temperature. Knowing that I was about to become a forest girl, I did not care about the weather. I just wanted to sit beside my own campfire. Plus, I had spent months getting ready for this day and was not going to let anything stop me. I rode my bike to our meeting place, about four miles away and near Elsie's house. I waited for two hours in the sleety rain and she did not show up. By this time, I was wet, cold and very hungry, so I rode back home. Elsie probably looked out the window from her warm home and thought I must be out of my mind. I stashed my stuff in the garage and melded back into the family living room. Nobody said anything about me being gone for so long, they must have thought that I was at a neighbor kid's house. Somehow, that dinner tasted especially good and my appreciation for our furnace was enormous. Ever since that day, I gave up my plan to live in a tree house.

Elsie was a big adventurer and we had a blast together. I slept at her house often where there were beautiful streams to play in. We ventured out along a stream that led us to a big field. Far away, on the other side of the field was an abandoned barn and grain silo that we played in. The silo was attached to the old barn and the whole place was so rotted that it could have fallen down at any moment. We climbed up the inside of the silo and enjoyed the sound of scaring the pigeons into flight. The silo had tremendous echo power and the pigeons' flight sounded like a jet plane was in there with us. We brought our lunches and spent entire days there.

The last time we went to the silo a car drove up, without a doubt being driven by a maniac. The driver floored the gas pedal and spun the car in circles. We heard lunatic laughter from at least two men. The men pulled up, got out of the car, and came into the barn. At some point the men realized that they were not alone and began to search for us. Elsie and I were up in the silo and thought we should sneak to lower ground. As we descended the silo and crept into the barn area the floorboards creaked and gave us away. We heard the men coming to the part of the barn where we were. As soon as we knew that the men were after us, we took off running like gazelles. Luckily, we knew the barn like the back of our hands and had a fast escape route. We were half way across the field by the time they spotted us and we kept running into the familiar wooded area to safety. The magic of going there to play wore off after that close call.

Who knows what those men would have done to us?

Linda, my "tomboy" friend from school invited me to spend the weekend at her house and I was happy about it. We had so much more to do at her house than at mine. The big park next to her home was a kid's dream, with perfectly manicured green fields and hillsides. Linda, her dog, and I spent whole days in the park. We talked about all sorts of things while climbing the trees and playing at the pond. Linda and I were very best friends and spent as much time together as we could. Being tomboys together was fun, but sometimes being mistaken for boys was a bummer. One early morning we were playing in the park and walking around the lake, it was chilly and the fog was thick. Three boys walked past us and they seemed fine, but for some reason I thought they were going to be trouble. They were only a year or two older than us and did not do anything alarming as they passed, but they still set me on edge. We could tell by their glances that they thought we were boys and not girls.

Linda, her dog, and I began our walk down the tree-studded hillside towards Linda's house and forgot all about the boys. Seemingly out of nowhere, the boys appeared and started to push us around and hit us. Linda's dog ran down the hill to her house as soon as the boys became hostile-- some watch dog. We fought them off, me getting another fat lip. Linda grabbed onto the finger of one boy as he swung a punch at her. She pulled his finger back as far as she could and we heard a pop. The boy started screaming and the other boys went over to look at his finger. We took off running towards the house at full speed. Aside from my fat lip which did not hurt all that much, we got away well off; nothing like being outnumbered and outsized by unfair, dirty fighters. A few days later, Linda saw the boy whose finger she damaged with a large bandage on his hand and assumed that she broke it.

Linda and I had only one other altercation where we had to defend ourselves, but this time the boys knew we were girls. It took place on the playground at school during recess. It was a rainy, foggy day and the playground was muddy. There were only a few kids outside because of the weather. Linda and I were playing on the merry go round when two older boys approached us. The boys grabbed onto us and we began fighting for our lives. They were big black boys and trying to rape us. They tried to pull us to the ground and Linda was able to kick one of them in the balls. The one trying to rape me turned to look at his screaming friend and I sent him flying backwards in the mud. We had a split second to free ourselves and run as fast as we could into the school. That was a scary and really close call, but we made it out with only minor scrapes and bruises. Our playground could be a dangerous place and some of what I witnessed out there blew my mind: dog fight betting, beatings and a stabbing. There was never an uneventful day at this elementary school.

The classroom was quiet one afternoon as us kids were working on our assignment. Suddenly we heard loud noises from outside. All of us, including the teachers, went to the window to see what was happening. We witnessed an argument going on across the street beginning in the house and spilled out onto the sidewalk. A mean, big, black lady was beating up a medium-sized black man with a crutch. The swear words rang out one after another. We gasped, oohhhed, and awwwwed at the window. We happened to look out the window to our right and saw more action, two boys with dogs for fighting and people betting on them. The dog-fight and yelling began and the teacher abruptly made us go back to our seats. Not one student seemed too alarmed, we were used to it.

Life was getting more exciting in my neighborhood and I was exposed to new people, rock music, and hip styles of dress. The city was home to a big university with full-blown Hippy, Anti-War, Pro-Gay, and Underground scenes. I started to spend some time with a group of Hippy teenagers who were much older than me. I introduced myself as George and a few of them really did believe that I was a boy. They turned me onto music I never heard before, like, David Bowie, Beatles, The Kinks and lots of Funky stuff. I was practicing the drums every day and so happy with the changes I was hearing in my music. My drumming both was improving and growing in a new and thrilling direction. I talked my mom into buying me a pair of bell-bottom jeans and thought I was the coolest. I added army shirts and hiking boots to my "Look" and it became rare for strangers to think that I was a nine year old girl.

On this rare occasion my parents took us downtown to a music show and to support the Women's Rights Campaign. "Fanny" was the band that played and they were great. The best part if seeing them was that they had a woman drummer. I could not believe my eyes. I had never seen a woman drummer before and she rocked-out! The presence of NOW, the National Organization for Woman, at the rally sparked my interest, but I was too young to fully realize how important this rally was. Why the Women's Rights Movement was new and even necessary was something I could not understand. I know that I would not have adjusted well in the olden days with my attitude about rules and gender roles. The "people watching" was an amazing part of the rally for me, seeing long-haired men, tie-dyed dresses on little old ladies, and beatnik types throughout the venue.

My father was a liberal, caring, progressive man to everyone except his family. He was very involved with the Human Rights issues of the era. The church congregation was also quite liberal, racially mixed, and heavily involved in activism, especially Racial Equality. From time to time our church choir was accompanied by an acoustic guitar player which sure was refreshing. The songs for Freedom rang loudly through our church, with my mom singing her heart out.

I could not help but notice that my Hippy friends enjoyed smoking pot. The more I hung out with them, the more I wanted to smoke with them. I finally got up the nerve and asked one man to pass me the joint. Well, I got a lecture about how I was much too young to be smoking pot and that they were not going to let me until I was at least thirteen years old. The difference between nine years old and thirteen was the same as eternity for me. I figured I would have to do what they said and did not pester anyone about it. I was so glad that they would let me tag around with them, like a little mascot, that I was willing to follow their rules. I overheard their conversations on many topics that I found interesting. I was privy to their "Woodstock" preparations and to their stories of "Woodstock" after they returned. I overheard them talking about the effects that the war draft was having on them, their families and friends, and about their romantic encounters.

There was one porch, or another within a few blocks that they would sit on and talk. I sat with them and listened carefully, sometimes while hula-hooping. Once in a while, I was able to walk around the neighborhood, go to the park or down to the University with the Hippies. I was energized and happy with these people. I was learning new things all of the time and the music set my mind wondering about the world and my future. Led Zeppelin's "Stairway to Heaven" was a life changer for me and resonated with my rich spirit-world connection. I had a soft loving layer, topped by my rebellious layer, all frosted with a complete disregard for authority of any type. The music spoke my thoughts and moved my core.

As far as my romantic life was going, I had a crush on the cutest boy in class, Dean. He was tall, athletic, and funny. We joked around a lot in class and he had a crush on me too, not minding that I was white. Our playful romantic friendship was fantastic but stayed in the classroom. That was as far as that went and was still fun to have a boyfriend. I would rather play football with the boys than anything else at nine years old. I was witnessing couples kissing and hearing stories from my older friends about sex but I did not want any part of it.

My life was entertaining in many ways; for example, being a boy in my own mind. Almost always the sales clerks in stores would call me sonny or some other boy term. Since I was hanging out with the Hippies I started to wear my hair a little longer and, evidently, looked like a cute hippy boy. I was the youngest hippy type that I knew, except for Nathan at school. The girls thought I was the cutest boy they had ever seen. I could not stand it when the girls tried to get near me though. One girl even tried to kiss me, thinking I was a boy.

Down in the basement and just outside of the band room, I was attacked, by a girl who was trying to rape me. This was a tough-ass, black girl and she wanted me badly, thinking I was a boy. I told her that I was a girl but she did not believe me. I was starting to pull my pants down to prove it to her, when I was saved by the band teacher arriving and he scared her away.

There were other times when I would tell kids that I was a girl and they would not believe me. Out on the playground one day, I was the victim of mistaken identity and almost had a bad beating because of it. I was at the playground during recess and minding my own business when I was attacked. An older black boy, one of the toughest in the school, came over to me and grabbed me by my shirt. He said, "Marty, I am going to kick your ass so bad." I told him that I was not Marty but he did not believe me. He had three other boys with him and I was scared to death. I was punched a couple of times and a giant crowd grew around us to watch. I kept screaming, 'I am not Marty!' Thank-goodness some of the on-lookers saw Marty somewhere else on the playground. My assailant let me go and just walked away. I was extra upset because Marty is the same kid who gave me the fat lip at the bus stop. I found it hard to believe that I took some punches for that jerk. The jerk also happened to be the ex-principal's son, making him a common target for violence.

Then I joined the Brownies, where everyone was humored by my being a tomboy. I didn't have to wear their stupid dress. Instead, I wore my patch-adorned sash proudly over a t-shirt or my favorite blue work shirts. Being a Brownie gave me a chance to feel how nice it is to make something for someone else and I discovered cooking. Bisquick biscuits wrapped around hotdogs to make "pigs-in-a-blanket" became my signature dish. What a nice change, there were no weird life experiences for me in the Brownies, just creativity and giving.

School had some good times, too. Our class took some pretty cool field trips. Once, we went to a pet store and looked at all the animals. Linda and I managed to talk our teacher into buying the classroom a mouse. We promised to care for it and keep it on our table. The mouse we picked out had black and white splotches all over it, resembling a smashed Oreo cookie, so we named it him Oreo. Linda and I loved Oreo and were very protective of him. There were some kids in the class who did not like Linda or me, or the fact that we had a pet mouse.

I truly loved my rodents. I had two white mice, two hamsters, and now two new brown mice living in cages in my bedroom. On top of that, there was a cage in the dining room with the family's two gerbils, also a fresh water fish aquarium and a dish with our painted turtles. The family cat was a fluffy blue Persian and reigned indoors, but never bothered any of the rodents or fish.

One day my mom took us kids with her to the farmers market and we loved it! The best part was the animals, most of all the baby bunnies and tiny chicks. I talked my mom into buying me two bunny rabbits. There was a small one that I named Gargantua and a big one that I named Tiny Tim. My dad built me a rabbit hutch. He was a talented carpenter when he applied himself. At the same time, my dad made my mom promise not to take us kids to the market with her anymore. However his demands did not last long. We all enjoyed playing with the rabbits.

Jack, Eileen, two others, and I had a little gang and fought with a group of boys from the next block over. This group of boys is the same group that I threw the brick at a couple of years before. On this day I was being extra rotten to one boy and we made an arrangement for us to meet for a fistfight. The fight took place in the street just a few doors down from our house. Tad was bigger and older than I was but I was fearless and thought I could win. We started fighting, punching and kicking, throwing each other to ground, and rolling around while continuing our punches. He was getting the better of me . . . and badly. I was getting my butt kicked royally. At least ten kids were standing by watching me lose and cheering me on anyway. Finally, a very large, manly girl from across the street came out of her house and broke it up by pulling me to safety. The embarrassment took a few days to wear off but I learned that I was not as tough as I thought.

I learned to save fighting for defense and not pick on kids, especially bigger than me; a humiliating lesson to learn with all the neighborhood watching.

Not only was I less tough than I thought but I was a bigger attraction for hatred than I knew about. I learned this one day when was playing with Oreo in class and cleaning his cage. The teacher was giving us a lesson and I was in a wonderful mood. When the lesson was finished us students were shuffling around. I placed Oreo back down into his aquarium just as a baseball flew into side of it. The baseball shattered the aquarium and sent glass flying up everywhere, including into my face. Denise hated me, and anything that gave me joy, meaning Oreo. I do not know what was up with her that day, but she snapped and threw that baseball. I brushed the glass off my face and cleaned things up. I was pissed off and busy figuring what to do with Oreo now that his home was smashed.

Denise was sent to the principal's office and then the lunch bell rang.

Linda and I were walking down the stairwell to go outside when I had an itch in my eye. I automatically rubbed my eye and knew something was in it. I went to the school nurse and told her about the glass flying into my face and feeling something in my eye. The nurse thought I should be taken to the hospital to have it thoroughly checked. My eye kept itching and my automatic reaction was to rub it. The nurse told me not to touch my eyes, to sit on my hands if I needed to or she would handcuff me. My mother greeted me at the hospital. I was so glad to see her there. A doctor put dye in my eyes to make any glass show up. He shined lights, lifted my eyelids and found a scratch on one eyeball. He also cleared glass shards from my eyelashes.

The dye he used was dark red, blood-colored in fact, and some dye dribbled down my face. Some of this dye was on the collar of my shirt and along with the streaks down my face it made me look like I had been through a war. The concerned look on the faces of the kids and my siblings when I got out of the car was a surprise. I laughed and told them it was dye on me and not blood. I had no idea that anyone on the block cared about me and it felt good. That was a crazy class, what else can I say?

That day was disturbing enough, but then I had another bad day involving my pride. My favorite hat was a green fishing hat with white polka dots and I often wore it to school. I was sitting at my desk one day when Lucy tried to steal it away from me. Lucy was one of the toughest black girls in the school and I thought we got along fairly well. We'd had a few conversations before and I did not fear her. Somehow my hat became her focus and she pulled it away from me. I was able to snatch it out of her grip and the fighting broke out. I pulled the hat to my chest and huddled over it, keeping Lucy from getting to it. She threatened me, punched me a few times, and called me every swear name in the book. There was no way that I was going to give her my hat. I was not going to let any bully take anything from me, ever. She swore that she was going to end up with the hat and beat my butt. The teacher returned to the classroom and we both pretended nothing happened. Lucy never did get my hat and that was the last day that I wore it to class. I got the hint.

What an intense time it was for me this year, realizing that life is not as fun-filled as I hoped for. During one week tragedy hit two students in our class. One boy missed school for two days and the teacher told us that his mother died right in front of him and the family, choking to death at the dining room table. The other boy was paralyzed when a kid pulled his chair out from under him when he went to sit down, landing just the wrong way on his tailbone. We thought this was a harmless prank that we all pulled, not after that accident. He would never be returning to school. I felt sad to see my fellow students suffer and it made me stop and reflect on how much I loved my mom. For the first time, I thought about how horrible it would be if anything were to ever happen to her, and quickly blocked out the tragic thought.

I was old enough now to leave the Brownies and become a Girl Scout, like every other girl of age in the neighborhood. The only good thing about being in the Girl Scouts was our annual camping trip. Every summer our Girl Scout troop met with others at a Scout Reserve in the Adirondacks. I had a great time at the camp even though it was strange being with the Girl Scouts and hearing the types of interests they had. I had no patience for "Teen Magazine", crushes on Donny Osmond, or fashion. I was bored with the girls during the day; the spooky stories at night held me riveted. The hikes were the main reason I went so happily to camp, not the other girl scouts. The camp lasted for a three-day weekend, which was just the right time duration to spend with them.

Soon I reached the age that I was allowed to sleep in the cabin with the big girls. The Girl Scout Leaders slept in the next cabin over with the younger girls. Our topics of conversation were boys, crushes, and sex. One evening we heard a knock on the cabin door and opened it to find two boy scouts. Their troop had passed our troop while hiking that day and some waves and winks went back and forward between some of them, but not me. I had no desire to explore sex yet. The boys were entertaining and we loved the attention from our visitors. The two oldest girls talked the boys into shaving their legs in exchange for a kiss. Silly boys; they thought they would get to make-out, or even more, when only a kiss was promised. Each boy received a little peck on the cheek for shaving their legs. They were so mad at us, especially as we laughed at them hysterically. The loud noise from our cabin was sure to get them caught so they ran off into the night. I saw that girls can be just as mean and rotten as boys; no doubt about that.

✴

On this day, it was pouring rain outside but a bunch of us went out on the playground at recess time anyway. We started a soccer game that turned into a mud bowl so we were walking messes when we came back in. Our teachers stopped us in the hallway and had us line up while they called our parents to bring us clean clothes. The girls were lined up on one side of the hallway and the boys on the other side.

While we were standing there the boys began to say mean things about us, laugh, and point. There was one boy, Vance, leading them all on. I went over to him and flipped him onto the floor, slamming the wind out of him, then walked back to my place in line. All the kids were laughing at Vance who became enraged. Vance ran over to me and slammed me onto my back but I did not get up this time. It was strange because I could hear what was going on, but I could not see or talk. I was aware that all the kids were called into their classrooms and that an ambulance was on its way. While I lay on the floor the bell rang to end the school day. The kids were not allowed to leave by way of this hallway and the surrounding classrooms emptied under supervision. The ambulance drivers loaded me onto a stretcher and down the stairs we went. I had a flash of sight and saw my little brother in the back window of the school bus with worry written on his face. By the time I was in the hospital I started to regain consciousness. I do not know if they gave me something or not. When I woke up my mom was at my side and speaking with the doctors.

The x-rays showed that I did not break anything, but I tore the muscles in my lumbar spine. I was in excruciating pain and could not walk well. I was taken home and my mom rigged up traction for me and put some plywood under the cushions on the couch for extra support. I was placed on the couch with pillows put in various places under my back. I took some anti-inflammatories and laid flat for at least 3 weeks. I was so bored that I could not wait to heal up and get back to school. Mom made me lime daiquiris for the pain a few times and they worked like a charm. I know that there were some conversations between Vance's dad and mine about what happened. Vance's dad is also a Priest, but of a different denomination than mine. I am not sure what was said, but Vance's family moved away before I was back to school. My back injury gave me a permanent excuse to skip gym class for the rest of my school years. Later on I was thankful for the excuse and used it often. After awhile I healed up and got back to doing everything I wanted to.

Later in the year, towards the end of the school recess period one day, I decided to sneak off school grounds with Linda. We went across the street to a corner store and bought some candy. As soon as we came back onto the school property, I was attacked. The vicious pack of girls from my fourth grade class finally got me. I can't say it was exactly a fight that ensued, since it was fifteen against me. I did the only thing I could do, curl up in a ball on the ground and try to protect myself. They took turns pulling my hair, hitting me, and kicking me. It was the school principal who saved me. He came running outside, scared the girls off me, and pulled me up to my feet. The strangest thing about this fight is that the punches and kicks hurt less than they should have. I thought, 'my anger combined with the fear must act like an anesthetic'.

CHAPTER 6
IN MY FLOW

Drumming gave me one of the greatest joys in my life and I was becoming quite proficient with those sticks. The day that my sticking turned into a buzz roll I knew, I Got It! Being able to make so much music with my hands was exhilarating at the least: powerful, loud, primal, and original. When I played the drums my blood ran hot, like lighting and fanning the fire within; there was nothing else like it.

After seeing the, all female band, "Fanny", I knew that I could be a woman drummer so I joined the All City Junior Orchestra. My mom drove me to practice on Saturdays and I loved it! Before long I realized that the orchestra conductor was the father of a boy that I fought with in school. A year earlier, this boy, Greg, was holding the mouse, Oreo. Greg started to play too rough with Oreo, pulling his tail. He was watching my face while he did it to deliberately provoke me. I ran over and took Oreo from him and put the mouse back, safely into his new aquarium. I walked back to Greg and pushed him because he was purposely hurting Oreo to rile me. I hit him a number of times and threatened to pound him if he touched Oreo again.

Greg was also in the Junior Orchestra and must have told his dad about me because he relentlessly ridiculed me for nothing. Every week, for two months, he was hostile toward me and I ended up quitting the Orchestra. I loved the orchestra but the constant harassment was too frustrating and sad to cope with.

✦

A legendary drummer was going to perform at the University and I really wanted to hear him play. I asked my father if he would take me to the show and his reply was, NO. I pleaded with him and asked why and he said, "Because I am your father and that is that". I screamed at him, "You need a better answer than that!" Then he said that they already had dinner plans with friends. Furiously I stormed out of the house. I was heading down to the campus to see the show anyway, thinking that I would sneak in. The walk there was a bit dangerous, but I figured that I could make it OK. Two blocks away from home I ran into one of my friends from my hippy pals, Joyce. I told her where I was going and about the argument that I had with my father. She suggested that I go home and after they go out to dinner, to come back and meet up with her. She said that maybe it was time for me to try smoking pot after all. I wanted to!

I returned home and plunked myself down in a living room chair and tried to look a little mad. I was almost too well behaved and thought my dad might get suspicious that I had something planned. As soon as my parents left, I ran up the street for my pot smoking adventure. I was thrilled that Joyce gathered up a few friends and some other kids from the neighborhood. They were wondering where we should go to smoke. I offered my clubhouse as a suggestion and they thought that was a great idea. I felt honored to have the big kids coming to my clubhouse. Perfectly situated behind our garage, some chairs and had privacy with bushes grown in on the sides. We gathered around in a circle and passed around a pipe. This was a special night; I finally smoked pot!

A buddy of mine coached me on holding in my puffs, but I didn't feel much different. Suddenly we were all startled, by somebody with a bright searchlight creeping around in the yard behind us. Then the man shined the searchlight on us. We panicked and took off running in different directions, never to meet up again that night. I ran into my house and devoured a bag of chocolate chip cookies. I did not feel stoned, but I sure did have a case of the munchies. My first time smoking pot and I was scared about being caught, plus, I didn't even get high like I anticipated. I waited all those years to smoke and thought it would have been more enjoyable, oh well.

This was a life-changing day and would help shape the rest of my life. For an example, I decided not to listen to my father as long as he would not explain himself and be nice about it. My father would put down the iron fist and yell, "I am your father, that's why!" I needed more reason than that if he was going to keep me cooped up inside. If he had handled the drummer event in any other manner I may not have started smoking pot at ten years old. Just like a cliché may read, I began listening to more music and finding deeper meaning in it for me. I developed a strong belief system and my own rules to live by. I had an innate belief that I have the right to Be Me and planned on living on that premise.

The first time I got stoned was an experience, alright! I was riding the bus home from school and saw a few of my older friends in the park, so I hoped off the bus and joined them. It was a beautiful day and we sat on the lush green lawn under an enormous elm tree. The four of us passed around one joint and then another, with the giggles beginning. This time I really felt the pot and could not stop laughing. We lay on our backs watching the puffy white clouds float by and change shape. My friends talked about an upcoming party and they invited me. They were marvelous and I was overjoyed to be included. I was happy and stoned for my first time! Now I knew what everyone was talking about. I became concerned about going home for dinner, wondering if my parents could see that I was stoned. I worried about my eyes being bloodshot and smelling like pot. I was told not to worry and that they could not tell if I was stoned. It was just paranoia.

The walk home was like none other. I noticed thrills in things that escaped my attention before: the gentle breeze moving the leaves to dance and the designs of acorns made where they fell. I felt relaxed because I actually believed that my parents couldn't tell when I was stoned and continued to believe this for about the next two years. I think that my parents didn't pick up on the pot smoking because they never would suspect it from their ten year old daughter. Being stoned at home went smoothly, even when I gobbled up two enormous portions of dinner. I had the biggest appetite of anyone in the family anyway.

My Hippy friends ages varied from mid-teens to mid-twenties and they took special care in advising me about life. They told me to never do heroin no matter what anyone said. I took this advice to heart and never forgot it. I was learning that there were good drugs and bad drugs, just like there were good people and bad people in the "Party Scene". I was told they would hit me if they ever saw me smoking cigarettes, too. I did end up smoking cigarettes later on, always watching over my shoulder to make sure they didn't catch me.

✸

My father said No to anything and everything I wanted to do, to the point of being unreasonable. One afternoon I asked him if I could walk with Eileen to the store and he said, "No." My homework was finished and I could see no reason why not. He was consistently a jerk towards me and also yelled at the whole family. If any of us kids talked about something we were planning on doing, or our personal beliefs, without fail, my father would say something negative. His favorite thing to say to us was, "You have rocks in your head." Dad was a drag and I was becoming increasingly defiant of him. I wished that he would ignore me and simply stay out of my way.

The family was eating dinner and the general feeling seemed normal at the table. I'd had a ruff day at school, was angry that I was picked on and tired. My father looked at me and asked, "Where are your glasses?" I mumbled, under my breath, "Fuck You". I guess I mumbled it louder than I thought, because the whole family heard it. I was as surprised as everyone else that it popped out of my mouth. My father shouted, "What did you say?" I replied in a bratty tone, "You heard me". Before I even knew what was happening, I was being held by the back of my pants, whisked to the stairway and thrown up to the landing. My father was yelling at the top of his lungs, "Get into your room and do not come out for the rest of the night!"

The speed with which my father reacted and for me to be at the stairway landing was astonishing. I went into my room and began giggling as quiet as I could, not to be heard. If I got caught laughing about the whole episode then my father would have doubled his fury. He was bent out of shape because I was prescribed glasses and refused to wear them. Refusing to wear my glasses was the best thing I could have done for my eyes, because they corrected themselves over the next two years.

This Christmas was a dream come true for me. For the past year I had begged my parents to buy me a snare drum. I really wanted a drum set but that wasn't going over well with my parents. Granted, it is true that buying your kid a drum set could be a huge mistake for any peace and quiet in the house again. I jumped up and down happily when I saw the snare drum. The drum had a bracket coming off the stand where a cymbal attached so I could rock-out now. I played and played! Getting my drum for Christmas meant more to me than anything because I felt my parents really knew me and I was loved after all!

Eileen was interested in my drum playing and wanted to learn too. I taught her some basics and it was fun to have a friend who also liked to play the drums. We spent many afternoons in my bedroom practicing drum rolls and rudiments.

As close as Eileen and I were, I knew to keep my pot smoking a secret from her. I did not even tell Linda about it. I did not trust Eileen 100% and thought that Linda might think that it was bad. The fact that we were so young meant that we had not been exposed to drug or sex education yet. The schools educated us about the horrors of using drugs and having sex in the 9th grade which was a bit too late for some of us. A ten year old girl in my class, Annie, left school to have her baby. The news of this left the classroom frozen, not a peep out of anyone, just blank looks. Oddly enough, my mother was the nurse who delivered the child mother's baby.

Getting bolder…This New Year's Eve my parents were out celebrating at their friend's house. My Hippy buddies were throwing a big party at a home, nearby. I was left at home with my siblings but figured that I could sneak out to the party. I said my good-nights and went to my bedroom. I rolled up some clothes and stuffed them under my bedding to resemble my sleeping body then quietly snuck out of the house. I trudged through the blizzard conditions to the house, where I was warmly greeted. The party was happening! There must have been about thirty people, lots of food, joints and bongs going around, plus some extra wild punch.

I was having fun and the music transported me into a dream world. I drank two glasses of punch before a friend came running up to me and took the cup out of my hand. He apologized and told me that there was mescaline in the punch. I told him that I'd already had two glasses and felt simply wonderful. He told me not to drink anymore and handed me a soda instead. I was stoned on pot and hashish, but only the mescaline could explain my other sensations. My body felt like it was made out of rubber and I glided instead of walked. Plus, I seemed to enter into the music and we all moved with brightly colored swirls. I hadn't intended to try mescaline and having to be home before my parents did was not the occasion I would have chosen had I wanted to try it.

At the fantastic New Year's Party I felt accepted by the hip group and I was radiating joy. My older brother saw me return later that night and asked what was wrong with me, as I fell against the wall trying to get my snowmobile boots off. I told him I was just very tired and hurried to my bedroom. I beat my parents back home by a half hour and my brother never squealed on me; Thank-goodness.

My first time snow skiing was a ride alright. I borrowed a pair of skis from Jack's sister and went skiing with the Girl Scouts. I was excited about this new upcoming adventure, but felt some apprehensions too. After we arrived at the ski resort, the seven of us stood outside of the lodge with our skis ready and waiting for our instructor to arrive. The instructor that showed up informed us that our assigned instructor was sick and that she would be taking over for her. None of us thought much about the change of instructors until our first lesson began.

I am not sure how many of us ever skied before, but the group seemed afraid and unskilled. We put on our skis and rode a rope tow to the top of the hill. The rope tow was a fiasco in itself with girls falling down and tripping the people coming up behind them, making for Girl Scout pile-ups. We all eventually made it to the top and lined up along the edge of the slope. Our instructor said, 'OK, meet you at the bottom,' and she skied off down the hill. We looked at each other and voiced our thoughts, 'no way', 'what is she thinking?' and 'I am scared' sums them up. I sat down on the backs of my skis to think this situation over and started to slip. Realizing that I was heading down the hill and there was no way out of it, I yelled! I went flying down the hill, but was never shown how to stop so I made myself wipe out to keep from skiing right into the lodge. Soon, one by one, the girls skied down the hill: screaming, crying and falling all over the slope. After we all regrouped, the instructor hurried over and was overflowing with apologies. She was not told that this was our first class and left us, never taught how to stop, slow down or turn. We were like loose missiles released from the heights and out of control. It is a miracle that nobody was injured. I am glad that I had the adventure, but knew it would take many lessons to make a skier out of me.

My family did not spend money on certain things, like me being able to have a drum set teacher, so I knew ski lessons were out of the question. I did extra chores around the house to earn the $10.00 for the ski trip with the scouts. My parents believed that they should spend money on their children evenly. I am not sure where they got this belief from, since they were both only children. My siblings did not want to play music, bike, ski, or do anything else that cost money. But, if my parents were not paying for lessons for my siblings, then I had to figure out a way to pay for them myself. There is no denying that I was taught the value of money and that I found creative ways of making it. I had money from shoveling snow and raking leaves for neighbors and from cleaning projects for my mom. My sister became a baby-sitter, but I do not remember my brothers having any need or desire to make money, at least not yet.

In Girl Scouts there was tension building up between the troop leader and me. I refused to wear the ugly green dress part of the uniform, wearing only the sash like I did when I was a Brownie. Each week I used one of two excuses to get out of wearing it, either I forgot it was Girl Scout Day or my uniform was in the laundry. The Leader got frustrated with me but did not know what to do about it.

Spring in the Girl Scouts was our famous cookie sale, going door-to-door in our neighborhood selling cookies. I teamed up with a girl who had a wagon which we filled with boxes of cookies and headed out. House after house we sold cookies but I did not like it one bit. The weather was miserable with snow, wind, and cold sleet. There was no way that I was going to spend another Saturday freezing my butt off to sell cookies. Thank-goodness my mom unloaded some cookies at the hospital and many parishioners from church bought boxes too. Between the pressure to wear a stupid dress and the blizzard-cookie sale, I quit the Girl Scouts. My mom was surprised that I'd stayed a member as long as I did, and was understanding.

CHAPTER 7
NAVIGATING

I wanted to tell Linda about me smoking pot but wasn't sure how she would react, it being illegal. We were best friends and I told her everything, except about this. Finally, I got up the nerve one afternoon while we were in the park by her home. Linda was surprised but she told me that she had been thinking of trying it herself someday. I told her that I would see about getting some pot so we could smoke it together on her upcoming birthday. Her birthday was just two weeks away and she thought this was a great plan.

I arranged to get two joints from one of my older friends. This was the first time that anyone allowed me to have pot of my own and they reminded me how horrible the police were; not to mention what my parents would do to me if I got caught. I reassured my friend that I would be careful and not to worry.

I was spending the weekend at Linda's house for her birthday celebration. We told her parents that we would be spending the day in the park and took off. We walked up the hill to our secret place, nested in the center of densely growing trees, which offered us privacy. I lit up a joint and passed it to Linda, we smoked it and then the other joint. I wanted to smoke both joints to give her the chance to feel it because it took me a few times of smoking before I felt pleasantly high. Linda reacted to the pot differently from me and she got stoned her first time. We laughed and joked, rolled around and danced. Being stoned together was so much fun.

We walked about a mile and over a steep hill to a shopping center. Neither of us had any money, but we did have cravings for chocolate. I talked Linda into shoplifting a candy bar with me. We pocketed the bars and calmly exited the store. We were walking through the parking lot when we heard a man calling to us, "Hey, wait up!" I turned around and saw this man who looked like a long-haired hippy, so I thought he was cool. What a big mistake of assumption. We should have run as fast as we could. We let the man come too close and he grabbed us, saying that he saw us shoplifting. We denied it. He escorted Linda and me back into the store and upstairs to his office. He phoned for a State Trooper to come and deal with us, and he promptly showed up. The State Trooper was a big man and taller than life in his uniform.

The undercover cop told us to empty our pockets out and put everything onto the desktop. I thought that if I was sweet and handed over the candy bar with a promise never to steal again that we would just get a warning lecture. I was so wrong. I emptied out my pockets, including the small metal box that I had the joints in. I did not think that pulling the box out was a problem because it was empty. The undercover cop examined the box more carefully than I figured on and he saw a little pot dust and one tiny grain of pot. He stood up, showed the trooper, and immediately separated Linda and I. The Trooper and undercover cop started to interrogate me. The situation did not seem as horrible as it actually was. The cop held the metal box up to my face and asked me what this is. I jumped up and blew in the box, saying, "nothing now" and giggled. In the blink of an eye both the Trooper and the Cop grabbed me and firmly sat me back down into the chair. This was when I realized that these guys were not playing around and that I was in real trouble.

The undercover cop telephoned Linda's and my parents, who were already on their way. Since Linda did not have the pot she was released to her parents on the shoplifting charge. The officers wanted to know where a little kid was getting pot and were relentless in questioning me. They were clearly pissed-off by my complete lack of respect for their authority. I lied for hours; story after story, and was eventually released to my parent's custody, awaiting my hearing date in court.

My father was furious with me and in absolute shock at my behavior. I not only had pot and was shoplifting, but I also had cigarettes. My parents had no clue about their sweet little angel until that day which was when everything in my life changed. My father got down on his hands and knees to inspect my bedroom floor, looking for even one grain of pot. My bedroom was searched as thoroughly as possible. I was punished with not being able to leave our yard, "grounded", for a month and lost all my phone privileges. I was looking forward to seeing Linda at school to hear what happened to her. She dropped a bomb on me. She was no longer allowed to

speak with me and she ended our friendship right there. I was
heartbroken from tragically loosing my friend by my stupidity.

Court day was one of the worst days in my life. Linda's family
retained a lawyer and they sat three rows ahead of us in the waiting
area. I could not see their faces and I felt horrible. I did not feel
horrible for myself, but for the pain I had caused Linda and her
family. We both got a stern warning from the Judge and were
released back to our families. I felt like a lonely idiot.

My brush with the law also put a damper on the older hippy kids
trusting me and I was not invited to their parties. I hung out with
them in the neighborhood but I felt a weird tension between us.
Tension because I acted recklessly and they also thought so. I lost
my best friend and felt distant from my older friends. This left me
learning important lessons of life the harsh way and with plenty of
time to think about it. My father glared at me with a bad vibe and
showed his disgust for me. Luckily I didn't care what he thought. I
retreated to my bedroom and played my drums. At least I still had
the heart-healing drums in my life.

This time period, now turning eleven years old, marked a
significant change in how I was treated by other girls. They were
already critical of my being a tomboy, but now I also, smoked pot.
Added to these was that I listened to music they thought of as wild
noise and rebellious. I looked like a little hippy boy and walked with
some attitude in my step. I had nothing in common with the girls my
own age anymore, except for Eileen next-door. This summer I
talked Eileen into trying pot and she liked it and we had a great time
doing it. We went into a wooded lot near the corner store and
smoked from my pipe. Eileen liked the music I was playing and she
was always pleasant to be around. She didn't have many ideas of
how to entertain us but was game for anything. Thankfully this year
passed by, with it's humiliating and painful lessons.

I was glad to be entering Junior High School and finished with Dr.
Martin Luther King Jr. School. Even with all the things that
happened to me, I was still grateful for the experiences I had by
going down to the Southside for elementary school. I would have
been ignorant about what types of people exist if I was not exposed

to so much at King School.

Martin Luther King Jr. School was a pilot school, a school where the state tried out different styles and theories of teaching. At King I was able to learn at my own pace and liked my studies and my teachers very much. Having a teacher that I felt liked and understood me was more important for my learning than I imagined. Being a kid, I rarely thought about the important role my teachers held in my life. King School taught the elementary courses and the street smarts were the added gift.

The summer between Elementary and Junior High was fun and I made some new friends down the block. A new family moved in, with a daughter and a son around my age.. I liked these kids a lot especially the boy, David. I instantly turned my secret crush from our blonde paperboy to gorgeous David. I would accompany him to his lawn mowing jobs and just watch him push the mower, bare backed and sweating. He was a year older than me and viewed me as purely a tomboy and buddy. He invited me into a bicycle gang with two other boys. Thrilled just to be with him, I accepted. One of the other boys was Jack, from up the street. The club was a chopper bicycle gang. We made "choppers" out of our bikes by adding another set of forks onto the front, raising them up. Our bikes were cool and we fine-tuned them for hours on end, laughing all the while. We felt free on our rides and knew we were a neighborhood spectacle; hooting and hollering!

The four of us were masters at stealing tools from the local hardware store. We would enter the store already knowing exactly what we were after. One of us would distract the owner with a question then another one of us would toss the tool to yet another gang member. The person with the tool would exit and the owner never knew what happened. After four trips to the hardware store, we had an extensive collection of tools. The summer activities with our families picked up and our chopper gang dissolved, leaving the stolen tools to rust where we hid them by burying them.

Church camp held more pizzazz for me now that I could hang out with the pot smoking counselors some of the time. I was included in a couple of gatherings with these older teens, some in their twenties.

Sometimes a joint would go around, but not too often; after-all, it was church camp. It was obvious that sex was on their minds more than a joint now and again. I was left out of the sexual goings-on and that suited me fine. I was not ready for any sexual encounter. Frankly, the idea of intercourse grossed me out and I was not sure if I would ever do it.

I did have a crush that summer on a cute blonde drummer, Mike, who worked at the camp. Mike let me tag along with him while he did his work and he let me ride on his shoulders. He was a fascinating man and he seemed to think that I was a funny kid. Of course my crush went nowhere with Mike, if he even knew about it. No surprise, since he was ten years older than me and model material.

Canoeing was a highlight of this camp and everyone partook in it. About an hour canoe paddle across the lake was a small island we used for "camp-outs." Island Camp-Outs were amusing to the point of tearful belly laughs. At night, we gathered around the campfire and the older counselors told spooky stories. A few memorable summers ago, a counselor walked off into the woods on the island during a story and, thinking he was just going to pee, nobody noticed and we forgot he was out there.

Another counselor was telling the story of a murdering ghost who killed kids and still lived on the island. I was white with fear and being comforted by my big sister who was sitting next to me. The counselor who was hiding in the woods began to growl and shake tree branches which sent us kids into a panic. I leapt onto my sister's lap and peed in my pants. Even to this day, my sister still reminds me about what a wimp I was that night, especially when I was prancing around like a tough guy.

The Island was the destination for the counselors to go and party between the different groups of campers arriving. I went to the Island with the older teenagers once and had so much fun listening to them carry-on. We smoked pot, drank beer, and laughed our butts off. The older teenagers coupled-up and I could guess what was going on in their sleeping bags. I began to look forward to having a boyfriend of my own someday.

The camp hosted juvenile delinquents for one week each summer. That week was always exciting for me because the kids were street wise and wild. I made friends with one girl and showed her my secret spots along the shoreline of the lake. The girl ran-away one night and a search began for her. I knew that she would have gone to my favorite secret place, so I went there and called out her name. I found her sitting in my special place and convinced her to return for super. We walked back to the main lodge together and the counselors were so relieved to see her that she did not get into too much trouble. A closer watch was kept on her from then on though.

Going on the treasure hunts at camp was always a blast and not easy either. We paired up with someone and were given a list of treasures to find. The winner was awarded a prize and credit at the camp store. On the eve of the treasure hunt, word came down from the forest that one of the juvenile delinquent boys had raped one of the girls. The boy was subdued by the male counselors and handed over to the police. My mom drove the girl to the nearest hospital to be checked out. Here I was, in a place that looked like paradise, but was isolated and we were all vulnerable. The whole camp was in shock that a rape happened right under our noses.

The days between the scheduled camp programs left us staff brats on our own. My Mom would take us into town for our traditional stops. We always went to the arts and crafts store; it was huge and had everything we could wish for. My mom taught me beading on a loom and boondoggling (lanyard weaving). I learned to make beaded circular necklaces too. Beading was a common pastime for my mom and sister. Boondoggling came and went . . . with key chains for All!

Every summer my mom piled us into the car and drove out to the county dump to watch the bears. Sometimes a few other families followed. We were not the only bear watchers there; many of the local folks went, too. The big pile of garbage was a favorite place for the bears to come and gorge themselves. The bears looked cute as they rolled around on the garbage pile, but were dangerous. We went at night so the cars would line up and shine their headlights on the garbage heap. I have no idea where my mom got this idea but it was thrilling. Sometime the bears walked up to the sides of cars so we kept the windows rolled up tight. One night, a stupid drunk man got out of his car and was taunting the bears, yelling and getting too close to them for comfort. A bear charged at him and the sound of us simultaneously gasping was loud. Someone ran out and dragged the man into their car before it was too late. Talk about a Sunday Night Show, WOW!

Family Week at camp began and there were some families that came each year for as long as I could remember. Summer Camp was the only time we saw many of our friends and had a great time. The Coppers were a family that came there every summer, and a part of my dads' congregation, so we saw them often. For a year or so their daughter and I were good friends, playing mostly at church.

One afternoon it seemed like everyone at camp was at the swimming area. I was walking along the long dock when the Coppers' youngest boy fell off the dock into the lake. He was only about two years old and could not swim yet. I saw him fall in and, without thinking, I dove in to rescue him. I plucked him out of the lake and set him on the dock. It felt good to be a hero for a day, witness my parents being proud of me and his parents expressed their deepest thanks to me. However wonderful the event was, jumping in the lake for the toddler was more like a reflex than a heroic act.

✵

There was a strange feeling brewing inside of me and I couldn't ignore it. I felt separate from the interactions around me and somehow different from everyone else. I was a misfit of sorts: too weird for the neighborhood girls, not boy enough for the boys, and growing into a rebellious teenager. My personal style and interests were different from my schoolmates and I became alienated by the majority of kids.

I began to stay alone more and listen to music. David Bowie's "Ziggy Stardust" and "The Rolling Stones" had a big influence on me. I loved music and being out in nature most of all. I felt that it was "Me" against the world of rules, except while I was dancing. I decided that I would be true to myself no matter what anyone thinks about it. The more I listened to music the more my rebellious streak formed, magnifying the chip on my shoulder against authority. When I was being picked on or harassed by anyone, I lashed out violently. I reacted drastically when provoked, fast, furious and inflicting as much pain as possible on whomever.

✵

Our family took a car trip to the D.C. area to visit one of my parents' old friends. They had moved away years before and I barely remembered them. He was a friend of my dad's from the Human Rights Movement and from working together with the police force on stake-outs. This man was in D.C. working with the FBI and his family was an unexpected joy for me. They had two daughters, one of whom was my age and we became immediate friends. Her older sister had a handsome son my age and they also lived at the home. The daughters and grandson were "stoners" and we daily snuck off and smoked pot in a nearby cornfield. The four of us spent most of our time shooting pool in their game room, laughing the whole time. The younger daughter and I vowed to visit one another during the year. The vacation was a blast for me and I cherished my new friend.

A few months later, our parents made the arrangement for me to take a Greyhound bus down to visit my new friend. I was excited about taking the bus alone and how grown-up I was feeling. It was arranged so that I could accompany my friend to a day of school. It was cool seeing her at school. It was very different from my school, being private and attended by only rich, white kids. I felt like I was in a dream. I brought an ounce of pot with me but we had to be careful in packaging it. It could easily smell up her whole house. We kept it in double baggies and stuffed between her mattress and box spring.

My friend was in her bedroom doing her homework while I shot pool with her cute nephew downstairs in the game room. The nephew's bedroom was through a doorway off of the game room. One thing led to another and we found ourselves on his bed. We were fully clothed and goofing around, making animal sounds. We kissed a few times but were more interested in being friends than having sex. We were cracking each other up by making animal sounds of all kinds: tigers, birds, pigs, etc. Unexpectedly his grandmother opened his bedroom door and found us on the bed. She totally flipped out. She had been looking for me to punish me as it was. Of all the unlucky things to happen she had changed the sheets on my friend's bed and found our pot stash. She was coming to ask me if I had brought it with me, only to find me in bed with her grandson. We explained what we were doing and reminded her that we did have our clothes on. It didn't matter. She was pissed and called my father immediately. I was on the next bus home, never allowed to return. I was sad that I would never be able to see my new friend again. I stared out the bus window, thinking about how much trouble I was going to be in when I got home. My parents were so mad and embarrassed by my behavior. My behavior was supposed to be a family secret. My parents shared their frustrations about me to only one family, not that one.

✷

I started delivering newspapers in the mornings, which was filled with exciting times. Collecting Day was when I could see the home occupants face to face and met many diverse people. My tips were the best part! I put the miles on and was in top physical shape. There was a magical feeling in the air, being the only person walking around the neighborhood that early in the morning. I was out delivering the newspapers before the sun was up and watching it rising was beautiful. The newspaper route gave me enough money to finance my pot smoking.

✷

I did not hang out with my brothers very much. They loved to read and play board games with their friends and I had no interest in that. They would not have wanted me around anyway. My sister and I got along just fine . . . as long as I did not get caught wearing her clothes. Mom was Sunshine. She had many crafty projects for us to dive into, and dive we did. We made tie-dye shirts, colored sand art, macramé plant hangers, candles, clay angel bells, and our favorite-making terrariums. Dad never participated with us; he just read and watched television in the living room. My family accepted me for whom I was and playfully picked on me, like siblings do. Thankfully my mom supported my belief of my "need" for a pair of Converse All-star sneakers; they were the "in" thing. You were not cool unless you had a pair of what became known as "Chucks". My "Look" was forming in time for junior high.

When school started David, heart throb from down the street, did not hang out with me, just gave me an acknowledging nod and said, "Hello" while walking by. My crush on David evaporated but I ended up hanging out with his sister at school. David's older sister and her hip friends were an inspiration for me, especially how enthusiastic they were about their futures. Often I spent my afternoons down at their house listening to music and smoking pot while their parents were still at work. These girls, four in the core group, did almost everything together and were friends with the hottest boys in the junior high school. I was in awe of how they flirted with confidence and handled the attention with ease and laughter. This group of girls taught me some basics about interacting with boys and being a tomboy with teenager hormones.

Even hanging around with the older teenagers did not over-ride the drawback that the kids I was closest to were all going to a different school. I begged my father to send me to the other school which was within walking distance of our house. My father was only half paying attention to me until I told him I wanted to change schools because I was interested in Spanish which was not offered at my school. My dad was an intellectual and wanted us kids to know a second language. My siblings were studying French but I had given it up after a year, in the fourth-grade. I knew that an interest in language might get him to try harder and transfer me. I was right and he started looking into it. Of course I could have cared less about Spanish or any other language but it was the only thing that I thought might get me into that school.

The transfer away from the school I was attending school was definitely encouraged by the school Principal for a few reasons. To begin with, when school started I became reacquainted with the kids from my first elementary school. They were still boring. Being surrounded by these kids was OK but it was clear we lived on different planets, so to speak. When they saw that I was still a tomboy and, now, a pot smoker as well, they treated me even more like an outcast. The last thing I wanted was to be friends with them anyway.

One day I was minding my own business walking down the hallway in school when a girl yelled an insult at me. Without warning I grabbed her and smashed her head into a metal locker, denting the locker. The incident was quick and furious. I proceeded walking down the hallway as if nothing happened except for muttering a few swear words. I was whisked into the principal's office where I showed no remorse for my behavior, instead telling him how she had taunted me. The principal called my parents and made it sound like the incident was totally my fault. I had no patience for being picked on and going to King School had toughened me up. Of course I reacted violently; I was tired of the judgmental crap and listening to years of put-downs.

Then, some of the teachers at the school knew that I was smoking cigarettes in the girl's bathroom, but never caught me in the act. This junior high school was getting to know me and was not pleased with my lack of respect for authority. The school was big, made of brick and looked like the jail it felt like. I wanted out of there and soon the principal also started thinking this was a good idea. My behavior put most of the kids on alert around me and my reputation gained me some respect with the tougher kids at school. I had one friend at the school, Eileen. Eileen was older than me so we had different classes, but we would often walk to and from school together.

I hung out on the street corner with some older girls, one of them was David's sister. We smoked cigarettes together and thought we were being cool. There was one girl who I was a little envious of because Phil had a crush on her. I thought Phil was the cutest boy that ever lived. Plus, Phil new some of the older hippy kids I had been spending time with. I don't think he knew I existed, standing among the foxy young woman. I was a tomboy to the core and adored my overalls and flannel shirts. It's no wonder why most guys weren't interested me. I had some fun times on this corner and it was a perfect vantage point for watching everyone entering the school.

The principal of this school was a mean man and relentlessly picked on a boy in my first period class. The boy sucked his thumb, so what? The principal would come on the loud speaker every morning and addressed the school. He would often end the daily announcements with, "Stewart, get your thumb out of your mouth." This boy was suffering from public humiliation worse than I had gone through at my first elementary school. I hurt for him. Stewart was short, from a poor family, and didn't need cruelty from the principal.

At last, the news arrived and I was being transferred to the school where most of my King School friends went. I was so happy; good-bye and good riddance to my other junior high school and the whole bad scene. I loved my new school! It was light and cheery, so different than the jail-looking dark school I left. How anyone expects kids to learn in a dreary place that feels and looks like a jail was incomprehensible for me.

This is when I met my new friend, Will. I took on an additional morning newspaper delivery route and bumped into Will one morning. Will lived just one block up the street and also played the drums. He had a full drum set and his father took him to lessons every week. Will was attending my new school and we walked there together. It took no time at all before we became inseparable friends. He treated me like a best guy friend and was in love with a girl down the hill. Having zero sexual energy in our friendship was uncomplicated, pure and relaxing.

Will introduced me to his friends and before long I made some close friends among them. Sarah and Lea were a pair, giggly teens, and Will was in love with Lea. The four of us met every morning and walked to school together. I met great friends by knowing Will and I fit in with this group perfectly; what a happy surprise.

I joined the school band. Will and some other new friends were also members. We played in the drum section together, Will was on the snare and I played the bass, or tympani drums. The tympani drew me in and still are my favorite drums, aside from Taiko drums; the louder and more deeply primal, the better for me. Having "Hall Passes" was a huge perk to being in the band since our teachers didn't know when our practices were actually held. The hall passes gave us the freedom to sneak outside and smoke pot. Sarah and Lea took drums lessons for the better half of the year before their interest faded. It was fun having all of us taking drums and using the fabulous hallway passes together.

The school band was full of new experiences and my drumming was improving every week. There was an occasion when one of us came into possession of the key to the school auditorium. Will and our usual suspects would fire up joints behind the stage curtain and climb up onto the catwalk. Climbing on the catwalk over the stage, way up there on the beams in the dark, gave me the creeps. The catwalk was a favorite adventure for those guys, but after the first time I never went back up there.

Our band put on a performance that was very well attended, including by my family and neighbors. I suffered from my first case of full blown stage fright with the butterflies in my stomach feeling like a tornado of fear. There is no question that I was as white as a ghost. It is a miracle that I did not pee my pants or break out in hives. I just stood there with the other band members waiting to go out onto the stage and take our places. I kept telling myself to just relax and breathe, praying I didn't faint. Stage fright caught me off guard and it took until midway through the show to begin to lift. I was so glad to get that performance over with. I thought I would have enjoyed it more.

I felt lucky to be with the kids I knew from King School and the many new friends I made. Will and his friends were two grades ahead of me, so that meant that I would only have their company at school for this one year. They would go off to high school, leaving me behind.

My new friends and this junior high school gave me enthusiasm for each day. I had interactions and laughs with many social groups at school and in the neighborhood, but really did not fully belong to any of them. Will's friends were my main gang, but I drifted from people to people and enjoyed it. I was welcomed with opened arms by many cliques, but still felt like an outsider only visiting. I knew all kinds of people, all over the city.

CHAPTER 8
RUNAWAY

My reputation as a "Bad Ass" circulated around school and my neighborhood. Bless my Mom, who thought that I was a perfect angel and it was other kids who got me into trouble. The toughest kids at school liked me and respected me but most of the kids, especially the white kids, were afraid of me. The tough kids and I would joke around absurdly and they let me get away with jiving them heavily. My reputation protected me through Junior High School. There was an interesting group of girls at this school that I did not recognize. They acted like tomboys and were very tight friends from a neighborhood I never went into.

I soon became friends with this new gang of tomboys, particularly Sally. She was rugged and her two best buddies were entertaining. Sally introduced me to many older girls from another side of the city that was also unfamiliar to me. Some of these girls were real "Bad Asses" and quite familiar with the seedy side of life. I went over to Sally's house after school a few times a week and we had assorted adventures in her neighborhood. We spent many afternoons at her best friend's house and loved walking between the two places. The garage at her friend's house was turned into a party pad by her older siblings, with couches and a stereo.

I split my time between Will and those friends, Sally and her friends, and Eileen. Will and those friends were two years older than me and therefore had a little more freedom. The rules in our home were strict. Some were truly unreasonable because my father being a control freak.

On one memorable day after school, Will and the usual group of us were over at Sarah's house. We were having a fantastic time together and the hours got away from me. I had to be home at 5:00 for dinner come hell or high water. When I realized that I was running behind, I called my father to let him know that I would be about fifteen minutes late. He was furious and yelling, "You better get home right now, young lady, you're grounded!" That conversation was a turning point for me; I was not going to put up with my dad's nonsensical crap anymore. I had called to let them know I was running a little late and caught hell for it. He was emotionally explosive beyond belief and he had no reason to be an ogre. I decided to run away from home the instant I had hung up the telephone. I asked Sarah if I could stay at her house that first night and she agreed although not without hesitation. She was worried about her mother finding me. I was quiet as a mouse, hiding up in Sarah's attic bedroom while she ate dinner with her family. Sarah snuck me up a plate of dinner and while I ate, told me about her phone call. While they were eating dinner my father had called Sarah looking for me. Sarah told him that she hadn't seen me since after school. At the time I was not thinking in the slightest about what I was putting my family through. After Sarah described the concern in my dad's voice, I became certain that my mother was angry with my dad for scolding me and she must have worried herself crazy.

Sarah and I were chatting up a storm when her mom called upstairs to her. My father was on the phone again wanting to know if she had any idea where I could be. Again, Sarah lied for me. Sarah was getting worried about how much trouble she would get into if she got caught lying and hiding me out. It did not even cross my mind that I could be getting her in trouble. My only thought was to be away from my father and hopefully forever. We figured out how I would sneak out of the house in the morning and meet up with her a few blocks away. Sally calmed down a bit knowing that our plan was solid and that she would be fine. We visited late into the night, fantasizing about my future. I slept soundly through the night.

I do not know what I was thinking when I figured I could attend school without there being a big drama. I snuck out of the house like we had agreed, met up with Sarah and our buddies, and walked to school as usual. Halfway through the first period, I was told to go to the office. I entered the principals' office to find the school police officer, the principal, and my father sitting there. I was read the riot act!

They filled my head with the screwed up reality about what police can do and about detention centers for locking up kids like me. When they finished threatening me, my father ordered me to come directly home after school or else. He went on to explain that I was not allowed to leave our yard for the next month. Listening to what the authorities and my father could do to me was not as frightening as they hoped it would be. To be honest, I missed being home after just one night without my toothbrush. My family was outraged at me and there was nothing I could say to smooth things out. My mother must have cried herself to sleep, or more likely not slept at all. The last thing I would ever want to do is hurt my sweet mother. At the same time, I vowed to not take my father's crap anymore, plus he became harsher.

During the month I was allowed certain visitors but was forbidden from making any phone calls. Will and Eileen came over to visit frequently which took the edge off being grounded for so long. One afternoon, Will brought a new friend over to meet me. This friend happened to be a super cute teenager and I found myself enchanted by his stories. He was a runaway himself and hitchhiked here from another state. We had a mutual friend in the city and he was staying there. I wanted to hear more about his time on the run and quickly became enamored with him. Meeting a real runaway was fascinating for me and sparked fleeing dreams of my own.

Two days later, Will, two other friends, and I skipped school and went to visit our new, runaway friend. We all went over to the friend's house where he was hiding out. His friend's parents were working so we had the house to ourselves. Someone suggested that we rob a nearby house and steal the liquor. We convinced ourselves that it wasn't exactly a robbery; just taking some liquor was only "medium" bad. We went to the home of a kid that we knew, snuck in the house, and took a few bottles of booze. In and out, lickety-split, and back at the runaway's hiding-out house.

We were all lying around the bedroom, listening to music and enjoying our conversations about life and drinking, when the phone rang. The phone rang for the longest time and we all stared at each other in silence. The phone stopped ringing but the caller called again, letting it ring for as long as allowed. Someone knew we were in the house which gave us the creeps so we left as fast as we could.

Four boys and I, who still looked like a boy, were walking down the street during school hours in a sketchy part of town. We walked just a few blocks towards the school where the runaways' friend was in class. During the school lunch hour, one of us went in the school to give our friend the message to meet up with us. The other three of us waited on the corner across from the school, smoking cigarettes and behaving like drunken teenagers do. Evidently we drew the wrong kind of attention our way.

After leaving the school, we took a short-cut through an alley. When we exited the alley we were met with a screeching police car driving up and cornering us. The police car scared the wits out of us and we scattered. One of us was caught between the car and a cement wall, with only a few extra inches buffer zone. He was grabbed first. Soon after the runaway, Will, and I were caught and put into the police car. I had jumped a fence and could have made my escape, but stopped and gave myself up after the police officer said he would shoot. I knew he could get away with it and was not sure if he would shoot or not. I was stuffed into the backseat of the cop car with the others.

The police took each of us to our homes and told our parents where we were found and what we were doing. It was apparent that we had been drinking alcohol and, obviously, that we should have been at school. I was brought to my home and father, and was I in BIG trouble this time! I was already forbidden to leave the house for the next three weeks and my fathers' only choice was to keep adding weeks onto my punishment. I wasn't going anywhere for a long time. My father notified the school, as did the police officers, and I was suspended for one week.

Just a half hour later, the police showed back up at our front door and asked to speak with me. My father invited them in and we all sat in the living room--a tense scene was an understatement. The runaway had told the police a fake address where nobody was home. He had told them he was from out of state visiting his Aunt who was on her way home. One police officer took the bogus phone number for the aunt to the car to call it in. The other officer let his guard down for just a moment and the runaway dodged into the backyard and was gone. The police wanted to know from me who this kid is and where he lived. I told them that he was not from around here and that I did not know anything about him. At this point my father grabbed me out of the chair and pulled my arm behind me and up towards my head. The pain was excruciating and sent me to the floor on my stomach. My father put his knee into my back and pulled my arm higher, not caring about my screams. The police officers watched as my father tortured me until I told them where the runaway was staying. I was so upset with myself. I should have let him break my arm instead. The police officers left the house immediately and went to our friend's and arrested the runaway.

I cannot believe that my father made a rat out of me. The pain was unbearable and I knew that my father was about to tear my arm from the socket. He was enjoying this display of power over me and he would not have stopped until I was dead or he had the information. I had a price to pay with my friends . . . oh, you bet. The runaway was sent to the juvenile delinquent home for a day or so awaiting his transport back to his state to face something horrible.

Will called and told me that that he was arrested, in big trouble, and very upset. I told him what my father did to me and Will was furious about it. My friends understood what I went through and realized that they would have done the same thing. I was forgiven but never saw the runaway boy again. I doubt he would have forgiven me as long as he lived. I felt like a huge piece of shit, a rat-fink, the lowest disgrace there is. The war with my father was now fueled by my pure rage!

I had an occasion to try a Valium with some friends and I liked the feeling of floating as I walked. I ate a Valium another time with some friends and this was stronger than the last one I tried. I liked the type of high feeling it gave me and this began my experimentation with other pills. My father was an epileptic and had some strong prescription medication around the house. Daily, my father took Phenobarbital and Dilantin to keep him from going into seizures. I looked up the pills in my mother's "Physician's Desk Reference" and decided to try a Phenobarbital. The initial high of the Phenobarbital was strong and suited for laying around in nature with friends. The walk home was challenging and I could not wait to get to my bed and sleep. I handed out the pills to only my closest friends, on three separate mornings--three times a charm, right?

On the way to school one morning, I offered some pills to two friends of mine and we ate them. We went to our classes and tried to focus on our studies without our teachers noticing how high we were. After one class I went to the usual smoking area outside the school's back door. One of my friends who took the pill came running up to me in a panic. The other kid who ate the pill was just

brought out of school in an ambulance and the school authorities
were trying to piece together what happened. My friend and I swore
each other to secrecy and I went to all my classes that day like a good
girl.

As soon as I heard the news about my friend going to the hospital,
I sobered right up. I pretended that I was the straightest good
girl/tomboy you ever saw. Thank goodness my friend was fine and
back at school the next day. He was in trouble with his mom but
never told where he got the pill. I stopped giving away my father's
pills from that day on. I still ate one once in a while, but the buzz
was too tiring to come down from and I moved on to better highs. I
came home from school on Phenobarbital, went to bed, and did not
wake up until I had to deliver the morning newspapers. My parents
were wondering what was the matter with me, so it was a good thing
I stopped before they found out, or something worse happened.

My father noticed his pills were coming up missing at the same
time that a known druggy from the neighborhood got caught in our
house stealing them. This druggy got blamed for all the missing pills.
I had no idea he was stealing them, too.

Taking the Dilantin was too much. These were knockout pills.
To think that my father was taking these medications to maintain
some semblance of normal gave me the willies. I was dealing with a
drugged, time bomb and his controlling obsession was focused on
me. My sister, being the oldest and wild in her own "Preacher's
Daughter" ways, was no picnic for Dad either.

My brothers on the other hand never did anything wrong. The
worst thing my older brother ever did was steal one of my dad's
cigars, light it, take a few puffs, and choked on it. He thought he
would hide the evidence by flushing it down the toilet. The cigar
broke apart and the tobacco floated back up, layering the toilet water.
My father came home, went right to the bathroom, and saw the
obvious. My older brother was busted for the only thing he ever did
wrong. As far as I know, my younger brother was the perfect saint,
period.

At least one afternoon a week was spent with my older hippy
friends. I was living through a truly momentous time in American
history. The Vietnam War and Human Rights protests, along with
the race riots, Libertarian Headquarter bombings, and the Women's
Rights Movement made the USA a volatile yet exciting place. The

"Summer of Love" was going strong, at its peak, and the nation was infected by the buzz, music, sexual expression, and equality; WOW! Freedom of expression and power in numbers were the main themes in every movement . . . and I noticed!

I wanted to do my "own thing" but had the problem of being only thirteen years old. I wanted to be on my own and was becoming increasingly frustrated with my lack of freedom at home. The more I acted out the longer I was not allowed to leave the house, and so I acted out some more. My father's controlling spiral went too far and it became a joke when my punishment added up to the next four years. On my 13th birthday my father asked me what I wanted and I told him, "An apartment". He tried to reason with me but I would have nothing to do with his point of view. He told me that I was too young to live on my own and that made me steaming angry. He reminded me that I needed to be sixteen years old to become an emancipated minor and that I was still under his rule. We were at war and my freedom was vanishing. For some weird reason I lived as an older person in my mind, but facts remained facts; I was young.

I made another break for it. I went home after school, packed a few things for the road, and took off. I had some paper route money saved and headed over to the house of a woman I met with my hippy friends. She and her three apartment mates welcomed me. I slept on the living room couch that ended at the foot of a huge fish aquarium. I spent most of the night watching the fish and wondering about my future. My friend was a lesbian. She lived with a gay male couple, her girlfriend, and now me. I felt happy to be free of my father and living with wonderful people who acted with love and respect towards each other. We ate dinner together. We held hands and gave thanks for our meal and everything that brought it to us. The whole household was caring and the women gave me advice about things like sex and drugs. I was treated like a house daughter/tomboy and was well cared for.

The household was asked to appear on a local television show and be interviewed about their alternative living situation. The Saturday morning of the show arrived and everyone was bustling around, getting ready to go. I was asked if I was ready and was surprised that they thought of me as part of their family. I was included on the panel of our household and answered some questions asked by the host. I told the host about the caring and love in our home. Unfortunately, my parents saw the TV show and were immediately on their way down to the studio. We went home after the show and were enjoying ourselves when my father arrived at the house and demanded to know my whereabouts.

My father saw my bike on the porch and knew that I was there. My friends told him I left after the show and he took my bicycle with him. I escaped out of the apartment window and ran to the other side of the city. I ran fast and used swat team-like hiding techniques. I made it over to Sally's house and she welcomed me in, already knowing I was a runaway. First, we took a long walk around her neighborhood and she filled me in. The police were questioning kids at school about me and my dad kept begging her for information. Sally told me that I had better hide out very well because my father seemed to be everywhere. She snuck me by her mother and sister and upstairs to her bedroom. We had a great time together, playing music, smoking pot, planning our whimsical futures, and laughing.

Sally went to school the next morning as usual and I stayed hiding out in her bedroom. I lay in bed, on the top bunk, and stared out the window for hours. I was listening to thought-provoking rock music and wondering what I should do next in my life on this beautiful day. Sally's brother was asleep in the other room and he had no idea I was there. I had to be very quiet but was getting hungry. I had to wait for Sally to get home before I could come out.

At 1:30, there was a hard knock on the front door and I froze, listening carefully. Sally's brother answered the door. It was two police officers and my father. I got down on the closet floor and tried to become invisible in the back corner. They told Sally's brother that they had a warrant to search the house for me and showed it to him. They found me in a matter of minutes and took me to the police car. I waited in the back seat of the police car while the officers and my father spoke outside. I was released to my fathers' custody but would have to go to court because I was picked up on a PINS warrant. PINS stands for *Person In Need of Supervision*. It turned out that Sally was talking too much at school and a teacher overheard that I was at her house. The teacher called the police and that was that.

Court was worse this time around. This Judge was a different one from the one I went in front of back when I was ten years old. This Judge was mean, loud, and definitely meant what he said. He told me that if I ran away again that I would be put on probation or sent to the juvenile detention home. I felt like I got off easy, but the judge had my attention with the way he yelled. This time my father told me that he was taking me to see a psychiatrist.

I was surprised when my father went through with his threat and notified me of our psychiatrist appointment. My father drove us to the psychiatrist's office and waited for me in the waiting room. The psychiatrist was a middle-aged woman and she seemed nice. She asked me many questions about how I felt, and so on. I was shown back out into the waiting room and my father went in and spoke with her for about ten minutes. He came out and the psychiatrist said to come back next week. My father said, "OK, I will bring her in." She pointed at me and said, "Not her, it is you that I want to see." My father said, "No" and we left. As we drove home, my father was bitching about the psychiatrist and saying that she is crazy and stupid. He asked himself, out loud, "why would she want to see me when the problem is you?" This also is what happened with the next two psychiatrists that he took me to see.

The seating arrangement at our dinner table set me up to be the focus of my dad's attention. He sat at the head of the table and I was at the opposite end directly in the line of his glare. I ate my dinner and tried not to make eye contact with him. The power of his focus on me was so thick you could feel the weight of it in the air. What he said, went, he gave orders like, "Get your elbows off the table"! He made us maintain perfect manners while he put his stocking feet up on the corner of the table pointing towards my mother and lit up a cigarette. He smoked at the table while his family was still eating dinner and put his stinky feet in my mother's face. He was charming as a pant-load and had no respect for his family. I wanted out!

Will, Sally, Sarah and Lea, all asked me to stop running away. Will took some time to explain to me how worried I made my parents and all my friends were being harassed by my father every day that I was gone. My runaways were spontaneous and I didn't consider the impact my actions were having on my friend's lives. My father had all my friends under police surveillance but that was just one of their concerns. They were worried about me. They missed me and I missed them.

Sally's big sister was part of a group of teens who were also friends with some of Will's friends. There was one teen in this group that caught my attention, with her "Bad-Ass" walk. She "pimped", bobbed up and down because of the extra-long stride in her step. Her name was Dina and we became fast friends. Dina lived in a rough part of the city and her household was as different from mine as it gets. Dina's family included

her mom and four siblings. One brother was still a baby. Her father breezed through for a night about every three months. Her mom had her hands full raising these wild kids on welfare and food stamps. The household was predictably insane because the kids disciplined themselves, which meant none whatsoever. Dina and I could smoke and drink booze if we wanted to at her house, come and go as we pleased and nobody cared. Freedom!

Dina was far enough removed from any of my friends that my parents knew about and this made it safe for me to hang out with her. I never spoke about Dina at home to protect her in the future. I was thinking that if I ran away from home again I would need to go farther away. Dina had some good friends that were much older than she was. One of them was her boyfriend of sorts; he was twenty-three years old and a member of a biker gang. Dina's lover also was the manager of a fast food restaurant and she hung around there almost every night. The two love birds would have sex upstairs in the supply area of the restaurant. Dina went to his house for days at a time and returned with exciting stories about it. I wished that I had the freedom she did and a boyfriend to run off with.

With few exceptions, due to me not being allowed to leave the house for the next three years, I only saw Dina at school. Every day, Sally and her friends, Will's friends, Dina, and I met up at the same locations to smoke and plan adventures together. My junior high school year was giving me many ideas and new opportunities.

The school psychologist noticed that I befriended Dina and, knowing more about the trouble she was in than I did, called me in for a meeting one afternoon. Dina and her family were no strangers to the juvenile court system and their mother was constantly trying to keep her kids from being sent to detention homes. The psychologist got right to the point, saying, "Dina is Big Trouble". She told me that this group of kids are very bad news and would certainly take me down with them. She said, "Hang around with other kids!" I thanked her for the warning and left, more intrigued with Dina than ever before. Telling a Rebel, "No" never works out well.

Dina and I became "Blood Sisters" and vowed to do everything together from then on, through good times and bad. We pricked our index fingers with a pin and squeezed the bloody tips together, declaring, "Sisterhood Forever"!

One night I snuck out of the house, walked to Dina's, and found her with a bottle of her favorite whiskey, "Black Velvet". We sat in the living room drinking whiskey, smoking cigarettes, blasting music, and thought we were hip. Dina told me about an old man, a friend who works at an all-night gas station. The gas station was at least five miles away and through some rough areas of the city. Being wild and drunk, we decided to walk to the gas station and visit her friend.

We were walking down a street in the most dangerous part of our journey when Dina brought my attention to a car that was following us. It continued to for another four blocks. Dina quickly looked around for something to use as weapons and picked up two rocks, handing one to me. I picked up another rock; we were armed and ready. My adrenaline was surging as I readied myself for the car to come close by. The driver had seen us pick up the rocks and realized we had noticed him. He was smart and drove off, but I kept one rock. I never felt scared during the encounter, knowing that we would pound that man.

My legs were so tired from the long walk in the middle of the night that I plunked myself down in a chair as soon as we got there. Dina's friend was about sixty-eight and looked older than that. He was jovial and I could see that he loved Dina. He taught me how to pump gas and I worked the pumps for the rest of the night, for only two cars since it was about 3:00 in the morning. Dina's friend was full of outrageous stories from his past. He chain-smoked while he told us story after story. One story was about him being chased by the police, while driving a huge truck full of illegal slot machines. The police set up a barrier on the road that almost insured their death. He ran the truck off a bridge and into a creek below to avoid crashing through the barricade. The police dragged him from the creek, arrested him and took him to jail. He told us other stories from his past, but he spent time in jail for that screw up.

Dina's old man friend was extremely generous with her, like the

father she didn't have. He took her out into the country and taught
her how to drive and he promised to show me too. He let us be as
wild and crazy as we wanted to be. He was gruff around the edges,
not the easiest on the eyes, and getting frail. He made a habit out of
buying clothes for Dina and stopping by her house with his gifts. He
had good taste. He asked us if we wanted to go driving in the
country in the morning when he finished work and Dina and I said,
"Yes". I shouted with joy, thrilled that I was going to be taught how
to drive!

We stopped at their favorite Italian restaurant in the country and
the spaghetti and meatballs lunch was delicious. We took turns
driving on a rural road, with light traffic and nothing to hit. I was
nervous and drove a little jerky while I was getting used to the gas
pedal. My heart was pounding and ten minutes of driving seemed
like much longer. I was a white-knuckled, first time driver while
Dina was experienced and cruised along comfortably. What a
beautiful day in the country we had together.

The afternoon after I had left my house we were dropped off at
Dina's and we noticed two police cars parked in front of a house up
the street. Dina's brother came running down the street and told us
the police were looking for me. The police had not searched their
house yet, so I had to get out the back door and escape through the
backyards.

Before I had a chance to get through the house and out the back,
a policeman came running in and he was close behind me. I flew
into the backyard. The policeman grabbed me and I swung around
and kicked him in his balls. He stopped and bent over for a moment,
but I didn't stay around to look. I dashed off through the yards I
knew so well and disappeared.

I hid out at a construction site inside of some big pieces of debris.
I stayed tucked away inside my cubby hole for at least three hours,
until nightfall. I snuck back over to Dina's house, came in the back
door, and spent the night there. It was a night to make my father
seem not so bad after-all. Late that night we heard Dina's father
come into the house and I saw Dina cringed with fear. I had never
met him and knew it was rare for him to come by. Nobody in the
family ever spoke about him, as if he didn't exist in their lives. Dina
told me to be very quiet so I was. During the night I woke up and
had to pee so I got up to go to the bathroom. I went to open the

door and Dina rolled over in bed and said, "Stop". I told her I was
going to the bathroom and she told me that I couldn't go out there
because her father might hear me. She said it was too dangerous to
go out of the room and handed me a cup to pee in. I have no idea
what her father has done to them but Dina was serious and scared
for me. In the morning her father was gone and nobody mentioned
his visit. Her mom was fine and seemed to have gotten through his
visit OK. Dina's mother was a very kind-hearted woman and, a true
accomplishment, under a lot of stress and looked it.

   That morning, Dina and I were visiting in her bedroom when a
much older, black man came through the bedroom door. The
presence of this man was felt dangerously Bad and he did not knock
on the door either. Dina knew him and told him to leave. He was
drunk and big, dressed like he thought he was "Super Fly" himself.
He even had on glitter shoes. He tried to get in bed with Dina and
pulled on her arm when she tried to get away. I knew that he was
about to rape her, right before my eyes and with other people in the
house. I went into a craze and punched him in his head, telling him
to leave her alone. He threw me down on the floor as if I were a
mosquito. I picked up a book and threw it at his head as hard as I
could. The corner of the hard cover book hit him and hurt him. He
stopped and held his ear for a drunken moment. He staggered and
swore at us, then lost interest and walked out of the house. Dina and
I were relieved to see him go and she told me how this man
terrorizes her. The "open door" policy at her house with no
supervision in a bad neighborhood had frightening consequences,
sometimes.

   Later that afternoon we walked to the restaurant where Dina's
lover worked and we were hanging out. The restaurant had a police
officer posted there for security who Dina knew. We told him some
bullshit story of who I was and carried on with our misbehaving.
The workers at the restaurant were all characters in their own right.
Dina's boyfriend arrived for the night shift and the cocktails began to
flow. We smoked joints out back and jived around with the dudes
who worked there. However, the police were looking for me and
were much better at their job than I thought they were. Two police
cars pulled up to the restaurant and surrounded it. The officers
searched for me and found me hiding upstairs, squeezed between
some boxes.

My father had diverse relationships, and his connections with the police force were interesting. I was brought home and released to my father's custody, again. My father had issued a PINS Warrant on me, so back to juvenile court I went. I was feeling bored by the whole system, annoyed with my father, and not scared by them at all. These days, I had a court appointed lawyer and I noticed my police file was getting thicker. I was yelled at by the Judge and put on probation. I was to see a probation officer once a week for the next six months. The Judge told me that if I ran away or broke the law now it would be a violation of my probation and a serious problem for me. Now, I had a chance to see how much I could get away with before the court really came down on me. Probation wasn't that bad and I actually liked being able to talk to someone about how my week was going. I felt like my probation officer supported and understood me, but some of my stories shocked her. Sometimes she placed her head on her hands with her eyes bugging out when I spoke.

I hated being confined to the house for the next many months, but my father's punishment always backfired. I lost count of how many months of punishment I had to endure, because my father kept adding time on to it. My sister was a festive gal herself and was also forbidden to leave the house for years on end as well. She did not stay away from home like I did except for one night. The previous year she did not come home from school one day and ended up at a party. She was in deep doo-doo for that one. I witnessed the tenacity of which my father searched for her and rallied the police. She came home every night since, unlike me. I was light on my feet and wanted to be out in the world and free to party.

One afternoon, Dina and I were out and about looking for something exciting to do. We'd had a few drinks and decided to go to the friend of her boyfriend's house, at the lake. This was a popular house that the "Bikers" slept and partied in. Dina and I went to the restaurant and discovered that her boyfriend was working at a different location that night. The other location was actually on our way to the lake, an hour outside of the city. The bikers house was across the street from the lakeshore.

Two things about Dina, she was courageous and bold. We called ourselves a taxi to take us near to where her boyfriend was working that night. Dina and I had no money to pay the driver so when it came time to pay the bill we planned on jumping out of the cab and running as fast as we could. The taxi driver was an older man, large, and could have used a shave. As soon as the taxi stopped we ran like lightening. The taxi driver chased us further than we thought he would and almost found me hiding. He was close enough to me that my heart fluttered with fear. He would have beaten the shit out of me and then call the cops. We hid for an extra fifteen minutes after the taxi drove off. Here I was, the farthest I had gone away from home during a runaway.

We started to get hungry and Dina told me about "Dining and Dashing". I couldn't believe that I had never thought of it . . . how perfect. We went into an Italian restaurant and ordered whatever we wished. Dina asked for the check on her way to the bathroom. She was going to climb out of the bathroom window. The waitress brought the check to the table and I thanked her. I waited a few minutes to give Dina a chance to get out, and then I got up fast and stormed out the door. We heard screaming from the restaurant and just kept running as fast as we could. We ducked off the street and into the darkness to rest our beating hearts. We made it to her boyfriend's restaurant at the same time he was finishing up work. We piled into his car and drove out to the lake house. I was so excited to be around older people and meet some real "Bad-Boys". I was a "Preacher's Daughter" and the forbidden lifestyle had magnetism. My life on earth could have been for the sole purpose of defying my father!

At the lake house we met, Lester, who lived there and was a real Biker. The house was paneled with dark wood and the furniture was worn and somewhat trashed. The decorations were hunting memorabilia and patriotic junk. The whole house smelled like stale cigarettes, booze, the wood stove, and body odor. I sat near the window that was cracked for some fresh air. It's a good thing I ran away, because they sure needed a woman's touch around there.

Lester was a gentleman but he did not look like it. He looked like a Biker to the core, greasy long hair, beard and mustache, wore an aged, black, leather vest, some belly, and a flannel shirt and blue jeans. Oh, he had his Biker Boots, too. Lester was sweet to me and talked about some lively things going on his life. Two more Biker

guys stopped over for a little while and drank some whiskey with us.
We drank too much, smoked some weed, and all slept very well. It
took us each a few cups of coffee in the morning to get going, I was
feeling my thirteen years. That afternoon, Dina's boyfriend dropped
us off at her house and we began reminiscing over some of the
hilarious moments of our little jaunt.

Dina's old man, step-dad friend, stopped by the house and
brought her gifts. He brought her a bottle of Black Velvet Whiskey
and some Coca Cola. He did not stay very long, but Dina and I were
happy he came and proceeded to get drunk. After a few cocktails
and getting a good buzz on, we thought we would go down to the
restaurant and see if anyone would give us a joint. We found some
local kids and got stoned with them. A worker at the restaurant gave
us some burgers and fries, just in time for the munchies. Dina told
me that she could go to this guy's house and get us some pot, but
that I had to wait at the restaurant for her. Sounded like a great idea
to me, so there I sat and jived with familiar patrons. I waited until
the restaurant was closing, then she finally telephoned and left a
message for me to go to her house.

Dina lived seven, dangerous blocks away, which didn't seem too
far. I figured I could get there without any trouble and set out into
the dark. I had to walk by a bar that was notorious for violence. I
knew I had to pass by it fast. I walked on the opposite side of the
street and hoped nobody saw me. I was almost to the corner when a
black man came running out of the bar and started to chase me. I
recognized him as the same man that walked into Dina's house and
tried to rape her right in front of me. I ran like never before, cutting
through backyards and circled around and back down the block. I
was no closer to Dina's house than when the chase began. I was
behind the houses and could hear that the man was still after me,
yelling about how he was going to fuck me when he finds me. I ran
around to the front of a house and went up on their big front porch.
The porch was the length of the huge house and had solid rails
surrounding it. I curled up in the far corner and fell asleep. I was
going to hide out on the porch until the bar closed and the
neighborhood got quiet enough for me to run to Dina's, but I passed
out instead.

My eyes opened when I heard a male voice say to someone else,
"Hey, there is a girl sleeping on our porch". I looked at him and

smiled. He said, "Good Morning, would you like a cup of coffee?"

"Gladly", I replied and went inside the house with him. He had three housemates and they were some of the weirdest, most wonderful people I ever met. I spent the day with him, Stan, and we talked about the world, music, and partying. We smoked a fat joint, danced, and laughed the day away. He was a Drag Queen who was also a heterosexual. He had long flowing brown hair and swished his hips side to side when he walked.

The other home occupants were all heterosexual, too. A woman lived there and was the lover of a man, who also dressed like a very sexy woman of the night. This couple had great love for each other. He looked "fine" in his halter-tops and platform shoes. The other housemate was a man who looked like a man. They were all in their late twenties. Everyone in the house was happy to meet me and told me that I was welcome back there anytime. I loved my new, strange friends and meeting them was radically cool for me. I thanked them and we hugged. I told them that I would be back sometime soon.

I walked up to Dina's and told her what happened to me. She had been so worried about me and didn't know what to do. We gave each other a big hug and I told her about my new friends and how glitzy they were. She filled me in on how my father had the police at her house while we were at the lake. I was away for my third day now and I had hoped they gave up on looking for me around Dina's.

I was so wrong about that. The police showed up and trapped me in the house, finding me on the upstairs porch. I was taken into police custody and brought back to my house, again. My father was waiting in the living room and madder than I ever saw him before. He said, "I am not going to touch you, because I will kill you". I was released into his custody while waiting for, yet, another court date. I was still not allowed to answer the phone and grounded until eternity. At this point, if it were legal my father would have chained me in my bedroom. I liked being back at home and was surprised how much I missed it. I liked home but not my father picking on me and keeping me inside forever. My father figured that if he did not let me speak to anyone than I would be unable to make plans to run away. However, the more he clamped down on me, the more determined I became to run away. He was a sociology scholar and, one might think, he could have changed his approach towards me.

Court day was getting more intense by the second and my parents

and lawyer were there. The lawyer was explaining to me how I
violated my probation and that she had no idea what the judge would
do with me this time. The judge yelled at me, threatened me with the
detention home, and finally lengthened my probation by eight
months. Probation was a joke to me so the sentence was a slap on
the wrist as far as I was concerned.

I showed up at school and was excited to see Will and Sally . . . I
had missed them. Will, Sally and my friends at school were glad to
see me, too. I filled them in on where I was and some of the
outrageous things I did. The next few weeks went smoothly as I was
really trying to be good. I came directly home from school, was
pleasant, and did everything that was expected from me. After I
showed an effort to be good my father let Eileen visit me and she did
often. She was attending my first junior high school, so I didn't see
her during the weekdays. Eileen was big-eyed when I told her the
stories of my adventures with the Bikers and about being free.

Besides missing school, always having assignments to catch up on,
and slipping grades, I missed delivering the newspapers. My father
delivered my newspapers whenever I was missing and he hated it.
He did not know what to do with me. My mom and siblings were
always wondering when I would leave the next time. I knew this
because of the way they all looked at me and you could feel it in the
air. They were right; it was only a matter of time and I would flee
again. I was running out of safe places to run where the police would
not think of looking for me. Under punishment for what seemed like
the rest of my life, I felt pushed to leave.

My family welcomed the calm around the house, for a change, but
they knew something was brewing inside of me. Since my father had
maintained my newspaper route while I was gone I still had it and
gladly resumed the morning delivery. Early mornings in the
neighborhood was emotionally nurturing for me and I needed the
money.

I got a new bicycle with money I made from extra chores around
the house, the paper route, and selling ounces of pot to my older
friends. My new bicycle was the best! The bike must have been
stolen because it was too good of a deal, but I didn't ask the guy any
questions. My parents decided to let me out for short bike rides
before dinner. I was free again!

I decided to run away on my bicycle to my new friend's house,

The Glitter Rock, Transgender People. I arrived and was cheerfully ushered in. I told them that I ran away from home and that nobody knew about them. We had a great time together listening to music, smoking pot, cooking dinner together, and talking. I really liked these people and it was mutual. They told me that they were a rock band and I was in heaven! I was taken up to the attic and shown the rehearsal studio, mixing board and the whole setup. There was a drum set too! They were the most fascinating people I had ever met. Their band played glitter rock, like The New York Dolls and David Bowie. I listened to them rehearse and danced ecstatically. Most of my daytime hours were spent alone with the soundman up in the studio listening to music.

At dinner I was asked if I wanted to perform a song with them during their upcoming show. I was overjoyed and immediately began to practice my part. What the band had in mind for me was to sing a backup vocal during one song. My part was to say, in a grizzly voice that droned on as if I were a dying man, and as deep and slowly as I could, "James James Morrison Morrison Weatherbe Jack Du'Pree, don't ever go down to the edge of town, unless you go down with me." So, I droned deeply and said my part and they loved it. I was going to be onstage with a Glitter Rock, Drag Band." My life became adventurous again and my thoughts were far away from family.

Show day came and I was so excited . . . and a little nervous to be truthful. We went to the venue, an old building downtown, and unloaded our gear. We are the opening act for The New York Dolls and I got to meet them backstage. I thought this was the coolest day of my life. The band started playing and the people started dancing. I could see a cloud of pot smoke gather over the crowd as soon as the lights dimmed. I waited at the edge of the stage for my cue to come out and went on. I did it, I said my part and the crowd clapped loudly. I almost blew up with happiness and the show was fantastic. I had to keep a very low profile afterwards, being under the legal drinking age and all. When I was thirteen, I looked more like a nine year old boy and the bouncers were bound to zero in on me.

Speaking of zeroing in, who would have thought that my sister and her friends would be at the show? Of course, it was impossible to miss me. My sister told my father that she had seen me at the show and about the band I was with. My sister knew some of the band's friends so it wasn't too hard for my father to find their house. Early the next morning my father and the police knocked at the front door. My father could see my bicycle leaning up against the wall in their hallway. One of the guys warned me that my father is here and handed me my coat to escape. I ran out the backdoor and hit the yards running. I ran over to Dina's house and hid out.

Dina was at school so I visited with her brother until she got home. I told her what happened and, without a care in the world, we smoked some pot and joked around. In the middle of the night, I woke up to a policeman shining a bright light into my eyes and another officer standing behind him. I was pulled out of the bed, yanked out of the house, and stuffed, yet again, into the backseat of the cop car. There was another police car behind us, as this is the law when transporting a girl.

I was brought home and released to my father, again. I had another PINS warrant out on me so I was beginning to become suspicious of my father and the connections he was using. I knew that it was unusual to keep having me brought home and not to the police station when a PINS warrant was involved. He knew the police chief and several officers because of his work and studies as a criminologist. As a Priest and an activist he knew a lot of influential people. He also knew some powerful men in the underworld, possibly the Mafia.

Why did he have the power to keep bringing me home? He was beginning to scare me with all his talk of psychiatry. Was he going to have me abducted for a lobotomy, or something even worse? I had to wonder things like this from time to time, because he was raging and confused about how to handle me.

This time my day in court was drastically different. The judge ordered me to see the social workers my father would take me to. This was a punishment with a twist from the usual and spooky. My father had more control over this punishment than I liked and he reveled in the power.

I saw yet another social worker and they seemed similar in many ways. Maybe that was because my father chose them and he was militant in his ways, so my therapists looked that way too. I answered her questions about my feelings, plans for my future, and what my problems were. I told her my honest thoughts, for about an hour. The social worker then conversed with my father behind closed doors for another half an hour. They came out of the office, said "Goodbyes" and we left. My father was upset because she wanted another meeting with him, just like the others. My father was bent on me seeing someone for help. He continued his search for the perfect social worker, one who would follow only his viewpoint. I saw my probation officer every week and, miraculously, was still in school, technically.

It felt great to be back at school and seeing my friends, with added enthusiasm to do better. "Better" meant not running away from home. I applied myself to my studies, at least did the assignments, and was feeling happy.

Compared to the things I was doing, the smoking cigarettes at school violations seemed small to me, but not to them. Dina and I were caught smoking in the girls' bathroom by the principal herself. She marched us down to the office as we sang "Smoking in the Girls (originally Boys) Room". She turned pink with anger. She called my father and had him come and pick me up. The principal was at a loss of what to do about my continued disrespect for rules. I was driven home by my father, he yelled at me the whole way.

Just a few days later, I was in the boys' bathroom, smoking cigarettes with two boyfriends. A teacher came in the bathroom and I quickly turned to the urinal and acted as if I was peeing. I got away with it! The teacher didn't question me. I bragged about this to my sister. She said, "You think you're hot shit, but you are just my little sister." I cared what she thought of me more than anyone else and I still don't know why. I wanted to be cool in the eyes of my sister for some reason and I looked up to her. As my sister and I got older, the closer we became and grew to become confidants.

I was creative in figuring out how to spend some time with my friends from school. I was forbidden to leave our yard, so skipping school held a special attraction. I started a little business for myself forging hall passes. The idea came to me one morning, as I was forging my father's signature on an excuse for a day that I skipped. I gathered up pieces of paper from the trashcans in my classrooms and soon had the signatures of all my teachers. I darkened the signature so it would show through a piece of paper and I traced it. I wrote the hall passes for my friends, having the signatures of various teachers. My two dollars for a hall pass scheme was thriving for almost two months before I was caught.

One of my teachers presented me with a hall pass that I wrote saying a student would be staying late after class to finish an exam. He believed it was false and asked the English teacher about it, learning that she had written no such hall pass. I was busted. My father was called and the principal brought his forged signatures to his attention, as well. I was suspended for a week and my father's anger made it unbearable to come out of my bedroom. The week at home was a long one but I made the best of it by drumming and listening to music.

Somehow, I still spent time away from school with my friends. We would gather at school and go off together; a favorite spot being the hillside behind the school. We also went to kids' homes after their parents left for work and smoked pot, drank, and some teens were getting it on; yes, having sex. I was still a tomboy at heart and though I was attracted sexually to some boys, I was far from ready to act on it.

✪

All of my phone calls were screened by my father and I was not allowed to speak with anyone except Will and Eileen. I could only visit with Dina and Sally at school. My father would not let me speak with Sarah or Lea either due to Sarah lying to her parents the very first night I stayed away from home. My father held a grudge against Sarah for the longest time, years in fact.

Maybe I had "Winter Cabin Fever" when I asked Dina if I could run away from home and go stay with the Bikers. She said, "Yes". That afternoon we met at her house and she told me that another friend of hers is coming with us. I wasn't big on the surprise but really had no other choice than to make the best of it. Dina said that her friend had called her just after running away from home for her first time.

Dina's friend was a girly-girl, wearing make-up, high heels, and jewelry. I didn't mind her being with us because her behavior gave me lots to laugh about. I soon realized there was something askew; she was ditzy. In fact, I nicknamed her Ditzy. I did not trust her street smarts, and I sensed that she didn't have our back. She was a newbie runaway and was and not very bright so I worried about her making trouble for us.

At the biker pad, Lester, Dina with her lover, her friend Ditzy, and I sat in the living room, drinking whiskey, joking and smoking bong hits. A gorgeous blonde guy arrived and he got all the attention from me he wanted. Lester and Ditzy hit if off and went into his bedroom to have sex. Dina and her boyfriend went into another bedroom, getting it on and bedding down for the night. This left the gorgeous blonde with me. It was late, so we both went to a bedroom and shared the only other bed. I was still a virgin but did not want him to know. I was pretending to be very wise and experienced, like I had been around the block- so to speak. We were laying naked in bed together and I started to lightly rub his chest. He probably knew right away that I knew nothing about sexual foreplay. We lightly fondled each other and everywhere except the genitals, which was fine with me. I was a bit scared to have sex and thought it was plenty of an experience to be laying with this mature naked hunk.

He was telling me that he really liked me and wanted to take me to the state fair the next summer. Going to the state fair with this gorgeous older man was a thrilling thought. Maybe I would ride there on his motorcycle, hoooo. I was enchanted to hear that he wanted to see me again and fantasized about us being a couple. We fell asleep in each other's arms. I woke up to see that he left; no note with a phone number or any "Goodbye". I was glad that I kept my virginity and didn't lose it to a gorgeous liar. I was starting to learn a thing or two about men.

It was winter on the Great Lakes; frigid cold and blizzard conditions. Lester was out somewhere and us gals were getting hungry. The house was poorly stocked with not much more than a few cans of stew. Thank goodness there was our morning coffee. Bikers were always equipped with coffee, plenty of beer and Whiskey, but where was the food?

I decided to do something that some people might think of as a crazy idea. I took a bowl of stale cereal and headed out into the blizzard. I walked a few houses down the road and went up to one, navigating the steps in the deep snow and knocked on the door. Nobody came, so I rang the bell and waited. Still nobody came to the door. I tried the doorknob and found the house was unlocked. I went in, tiptoeing and as quiet as I could be. I went to the refrigerator and rapidly loaded up a bag of groceries.

I was sneaking out, when I happened to glance to my left.

Prominently displayed over the fireplace was a medal of honor from the police department. My heart skipped a beat -- that's no lie -- and I ran my ass off. I could not believe that I picked a cop's house, out of all the choices on the road, to rob. What an adrenaline-flushing way to grocery shop.

The Gals were happy to see me with the groceries I brought back. We ate a grand omelet breakfast and stayed there, warm and toasty. A blizzard was going on and it was a big one; snow by the feet was falling. We talked about so many things, including that Ditzy lost her virginity the night before with Lester.

She told us about how wild he was and that it hurt at first, but then she started to like it. They had sex three times during the night and she loved the primal side of the whole experience. Listening to her made me glad that I had been keeping my pants on! She said that Lester had arranged to do a "Train" with her that night. Dina was familiar with all the Biker lingo so explained to us what a "Train" meant. Lester was going to share Ditzy with his friends; that they were going to fuck her, one after another. This Gal was nuts and concluded that she was a "Sex Goddess". She was excited that she was going to be sexual with a selection of men. 'Yuck', I thought.

The night came and we were in the house drinking whiskey and smoking weed as usual. Dina's boyfriend was there while the Train friends started arriving. These were some down and dirty Bikers; leather, grease and the stench that goes with lacking a shower. Dina's friend, was in the bedroom and one guy after another went in and did their thing. One man who came for the train pointed at me and asked, "Who is that girl?" Dina's boyfriend told him that I was off-limits. It was nice to know that I was being protected from the older Biker's advances. What a night with Dina, never dull and always amazing. I was having a festive time, dancing and had my freedom!

The next day I came up with a suggestion. Dina told me that the bar down the street was the only place around with booze. The bar was closed in the early morning hours so we decided that we could rob it of their liquor. The next morning we went to the back of the bar and broke in through a window. The three of us took as many bottles as we could and it was plenty. We ran back to the house and hoped nobody saw us. Lester was surprised to see a full bar in his kitchen. It was party time and nobody ever questioned us about the robbery.

I had no worries of the police or my father finding me way out at the lake. Dina's friend was beginning to annoy me with her new penis obsession. Dina and I, however, were tight as ever and we passed our days smoking pot and laughing. One day Dina needed to make a phone call so the three of us walked over to the bar, we previously robbed, to use their pay phone. Dina was in the telephone booth, which was inside the bar and down the hallway near the bathrooms. Ditzy and I waited for her outside the front door.

All of the sudden I heard a loud commotion coming from the bar and ran inside to see. There was Dina sitting flat on her ass on the floor. This brute of a guy had decked her. I snatched up a chair and I threw it at the guy with all my might. He ducked out of the way and the chair went flying, breaking a large picture window. We must have been beacons of trouble in the area because the police were already on their way to see who we were. The police came directly to Ditzy and me and started asking us questions. One officer asked us, "What are you doing here?" The simple question threw Ditzy into a nervous sweat. I told him we just stopped in to use the phone. Dina was being questioned separately by the other officer: "Who are you calling? Where are you from? What are you doing here?" The barrage of questions at Dina threw her off and she couldn't respond in the smoothest way. Ditzy was cowering and acting like a jerk. I was taking in my surroundings, thinking about making a break for it. The police were very serious with us and not letting us go anywhere.

The police knew something illegal was going on. It was school hours and we were, without a doubt, school age. The police officers wanted answers to the specifics and we were in trouble there. Before half an hour was up, the police officers had us in the back seat of their cop car. Just as the police were driving us into the city to be arrested for who knows what, Ditzy opened her big mouth. She was menstruating and asked the police to stop by Lester's so she could get her tampons. Dina and I could not believe what just had happened! From the beginning, I knew I could not count on her, but I'd had no idea she was a complete idiot.

We pulled up at Lester's house in a police car, which catapulted him out of his bed. Dina told the police officers that it was her friend's home so she would go inside and get the tampons. The police officers and Dina went into Lester's house and Ditzy and I were left behind, locked in the police car. I was so enraged at Ditzy for bringing attention to Lester and to my hideout. I took out a lock blade that I carried, but had never used until that day. I placed the blade against Ditzy's thigh and pressed it slowly. I was not the stabbing type; it was a heated experiment for me, in a strange way. I punctured her thigh, barely, but none the less, I punctured her skin. She was screaming at the top of her lungs and she probably thought I was going to cut her throat next.

The police came out with Dina and got back in the car. Ditzy was crying and screaming about me stabbing her. The policemen saw that the wound was so superficial it barely made two drops of blood. The cops couldn't search us until we were at the police station and with a woman cop. The policemen had a bad attitude and could not wait to hand us over to the youth authorities and leave. We arrived at the police station, but they still didn't know our identities.

We were in the elevator together: the police officers, Dina, Ditzy, and me. I was furious with Dina's friend for ratting out our friends. Lester was over twenty-one and could go to prison for any number of things that went on with us. Disgust brewed inside me and I hauled off and punched Ditzy in her face. My arms were instantly restrained by the police officers standing on either side of me. As soon as the elevator door opened, an officer took Ditzy away, and Dina and I were separated. I refused to tell the police officers my name and they got more than impatient with me, downright frustrated actually. My probation officer came walking down the corridor at that moment and saw me. That was that, I was busted.

Like many times before, my father showed up and tried to take me into his custody. The police were getting tired of my father asking for favors on my behalf. I knew that I was being handled differently than other PINS warrant teens, but I also knew that my luck was running out. Dina went to the juvenile detention home and her friend was sent to the detention center in a city seventy miles away. I was released to my father's custody and my court hearing was arranged for the next morning. This time I was gone for over two weeks and I violated my probation. Plus, my junior high school was on the verge of throwing me out.

My whole family was mad at me and I fully deserved the cold treatment. They could get by just fine without me causing this massive upheaval in their lives. My family still cared about me but didn't know what to do. Again, my father repeated confining me to the house which always prove to be a mistake. I always liked being back home at first. But I knew it was just a matter of time before restlessness would bubble up inside of me again. I kept my bedroom spotless and well organized. Relaxing in my bedroom gave me time to think. I knew that I had been gone for the longest time and gone the furthest away this time. I had a feeling that I was in big trouble and might even be locked up. I decided that I didn't care if I got sent to the detention center. Dina was there. Knowing Dina was locked up made me curious about what the detention center might be like. I knew that I was a stone's throw away from getting sent there and that it would take very little to piss the judge off enough to send me.

My parents, lawyer, probation officer, and I were all in court the next morning and everyone wondered how rough it was going to be. I decided that I would show disrespect to the judge and courtroom process so the judge would send me to the detention home. I stood with my weight clearly on one foot, chewed gum, had my stomach sticking out of my shirt and said, "Yeah". I was told, "Your Honor", in a shout from Judge. I rolled my eyes and looked bored. I was yelled at severely about my lack of respect and not acting properly to authority figures. I could care less about authority and it was written on my face, with a big smirk. Smash! The Judge hit his gavel on his desk, shouting, "Detention Ten Days"! My mother started crying and my father looked very concerned as I was escorted from the courtroom by an officer. My parents and lawyer knew that I acted disrespectfully on purpose to be sent to the detention home. Anticipation filled me and I broke out in a cold sweat while I was being driven to the detention center.

I was brought into a hallway with a window counter for being booked in at the detention center. I was told to empty my pockets and put my things in a bowl. The booking officer looked at each item and listed them on a large manila envelope. Two woman guards came through the heavy metal door and escorted me to be disinfected. I did not foresee this, a lice killing chemical bath and shampooed until my hair could have fallen out. I was issued a bathrobe to wear while they washed my clothes in special lice killing soap. I was shown to my cell and locked inside. There was one window set high on the concrete wall with thick wire fencing on the outside of it. There was a twin bed on a heavy metal frame with one blanket, sheets, and a pillow. That was all that was in my room. The light was overhead, obnoxiously bright and in a wire cage. I was told to bang on the door when I need to use the bathroom and a guard would come and take me. The entire place smelled of ammonia with stale air mixed in. I sat on the bed and leaned against the wall, thinking. Wondering when I would get to see Dina, if I would ever see her and did she know that I was there? A guard arrived, unlocked the door and gave me my clothes back, finally. I was told to get dressed and that I was being taken downstairs soon.

I was led down a wide cement staircase to another locked door. The doors were wide, thick and made of metal. The building was built with concrete walls. The tall, dark-haired guard led me into a large room where all the girls were spread out into different corners. They were clearly grouped together in tight cliques. The room itself was bright and sunny, with large windows set up high in the wall and caged.

Dina was surprised to see me but we were overjoyed to be together again. I was the youngest and the skinniest girl there and obviously had a much different upbringing than the rest them. There were books, drawing supplies, playing cards, checkers, a television, a radio, and not much else for entertainment. Dina and I sat down on the couch and caught up on what the judge planned on doing with her. She felt that she was going to be sent to a Girls Reform School called Saint Ann's. What a bummer! I knew this was a place that I would not follow her to.

The toughest girl in there was an older black girl who was well-developed. She had big breasts and butt, and her mannerisms were "street" seasoned. She came up to me with her hands on her hips and looked me up and down. Silence fell on the room as everyone watched to see what she was going to do to me. The tough girl said to me, "Girl, You ain't got no ass, no tits either" and then walked back to where she had been sitting. I did not say a word, just acknowledged what she said as pointing out the truth.

We ate in a large dining room at two very long tables. The boys sat at their table on one side of the room and the girls sat on the other side. We lined up single file in a hallway before being led to our table by the guards. You sat where you ended up in the line and the cliques managed to stay together. I looked around at everyone, but did not stare and tried not to make eye contact with anyone. There were about 25 girls and 30 boys locked up, not counting those in solitary confinement. I was shocked when I learned about solitary confinement and about the three kids in there. The food was not memorable but the tension at the table and in the room was. The dining room was filled with the tension of potential violence and the guards were visibly "on guard".

This was "movie night" and we all, girls, sat ourselves in the big room. What mattered most was that the movie passed the time and we all seemed to be getting along just fine. After the movie, we lined up against the wall to be escorted to our cells. I peeked in the cells on my way to mine where the door was closed and locked behind me. I noticed that some of the cells had a toilet and sink, and housed two girls. There were other double rooms without toilets, but I was thankful to be alone. I didn't know how many more girls they could fit in here, because it looked full. I lay awake for a while and stared at the reflection from the moonlight on the wall. I was thinking about the fact that this was no place to be. This day had been surreal and had seemed to last for fifty hours; ten days was going to feel like a month. I managed to fall asleep just fine; after all, it was a stressful day.

Us, girls spent the day in the big room. We stayed in our areas, turf, and in our groups. Dina and I had plenty of time to visit and we began talking about the kinds of things we heard of that went on in Detention Centers. Dina told me she heard about lesbian rapists attacking the girls. She probably saw a television show depicting this horror or something like that. Dina and I decided that our best protection from being attacked by lesbian rapists was to pretend that we were already a couple. We openly flirted and Dina would pinch my butt, calling me, "Sweetie". We sat arm and arm on the couch and told the girls that we were lovers. The girls gave us glares and left us alone. It was unsettling to not hear what the other girls thought about us, in such close quarters, eerie at best.

During the night, a guard came and got Dina and me up for a meeting. In the office at the end of the hallway, two guards sat us down at a table and asked us questions about being lesbians. Dina and I explained that we were faking being lesbians for our own protection. We went on to tell them that we had heard stories of girls being raped in here. The guards filled us in about the reactions from the other girls and how we had scared them into thinking we could be rapists. The girls were so afraid that we might be rapists that they complained, some in fear and others with disgust. The guards told us that none of the girls in the lock up were lesbians and that we did not have any reason to be afraid. Plus, they reminded us that we are "all" locked up and being closely watched. Dina and I got a big laugh out of our theatrics but felt relieved. The guards wanted us to stop flirting immediately and we were locked back in our rooms. I slept easier, knowing the guards really did care about our safety and were paying attention, alert.

On my fifth day in detention, court was being held and the girls being represented that day, including Dina, were loaded into a van. Dina had no idea what the judge was going to do with her, or if she was going to come back. She was arrested for truancy and violating her probation. Her mother did not put out a PINS warrant on her, like my father did on me. The van returned from court and Dina was not on it. She was in much more trouble than I was because her record was years older and thicker than mine. Dina was sentenced to the Girls Reform School for eighteen months. The Girls School was at least eighty miles away and there was no way that she would be allowed to visit with me even if I could get there. Dina being sent away left me feeling sad and alone; my friend and blood sister was gone. I wondered about what kind of place she was adjusting to and if I would ever see her again?

I had five more days to go until my court date and had to pass the time doing something. A popular activity at the detention home was playing dodge ball. This was one of the rare times when the boys and girls played together and it was more like "Death Ball". I have no clue who it was that thought up the brilliant idea of dodge ball for these angry teenagers and in that pressure cooker environment. These tough teens threw the ball for blood; letting out all their pent up anger by hitting the other kids as hard as possible. I ended up with a few purple welts from the game. The energy unleashed on the court was furious and the players' voices were loud. The sound of the balls hitting the walls and floor made my brain jiggle.

I made a friend at the detention center, Zoe, and she was a year and a half older than me. She was well-developed, in a womanly way. I was a straight up and down, a string bean with tiny breasts. Zoe was funny and energetic, so we hit it off. She was from a small town, about thirty miles away, and this was not her first time at the detention center. She had been placed into a Girls' Home where she caused trouble and ended up back here. She told me that her parents did not know what to do with her and didn't want her back anymore. Hearing this made me pause and reflect on myself for a moment. I could not imagine how horrible it would be if my parents did not want me and fight to keep me. I did love and miss my family; I just did not want to live with my father. I would have been crushed if my family did not want me and I hoped they would always love me.

On visiting day, my parents showed up and brought me cigarettes and some clothes to wear for court. My mother was visibly torn apart inside by seeing me locked up in here. My father was strict, saying, "see what happens if you misbehave!" I was glad they came to visit and also glad when they left. Our visit was intense and I felt beyond awkward.

Zoe and I spent hours coloring pictures while I listened to her talk about her boyfriend and her plans. Zoe knew about street drugs and told me the names of many common drugs and what the effects were like. She laughed loudly and I liked her a lot. We decided to keep in contact and I told her how to find me at my school. Zoe helped my last five days of lock-up go by fast and happily. I was certain that I would be released and was going to miss my new friend.

Finally, it was my tenth day in detention and my turn in court. I was loaded into a van along with nine other inmates and some of them were handcuffed together. At the front of the courtroom waiting area, we were lined up and seated on three benches. There was enough space, between us on the benches, for our lawyers and parents to sit. I was told that I would be let out this time, but not to think it would ever happen again. The Judge was stricter with me this time and slammed my police report down the desk. He yelled, "You see how thick this is getting? This is the last chance you get; the next time will be Hell for you." His words made me tremble a little. I did not want to go back to the detention center, ever. I could not wait for court to be over with and drive away with my parent's. Being back home was a dream come true and my own bedroom never felt better. I suddenly cherished being allowed to use the bathroom when I wanted, not waiting for a guard to unlock the door. Ten days in detention shifted my values in many ways when I witnessed what happened to my friends.

Back on my street, the kids looked at me with curiosity and kept a safe distance from me. Eileen told the kids on our street all about me being locked up. I became a notorious Bad Girl . . . and a legend in my own mind. The weird attention I was getting in the neighborhood and at school didn't bother me at all. I got used to people staring at me and whispering amongst themselves as I passed them in the hallways. I reveled in the attention I got from being known as the "Bad One", unpredictable and dangerous.

The school year was coming to a close and the principal and administration of my school made my father an offer. My principal told my father that I would be passed on to the eighth grade on the condition that they never see me again. So be it; I was transferred back to the junior high school I first attended. My friends, Will, Sarah and many others from that grade moved on to high school, so I really didn't mind the transfer that much. I was thankful to be passed into the 8th grade at all after considering my poor attendance that year.

The clincher was that I had to attend Summer School at the present junior high. Having to go to Summer School was wonderful, as far as I saw it. Having to leave the house for school gave me plenty of opportunities to see some of my friends. School took away the frustration of being confined to the house for the summer. The church camp that our family loved to go to, since I was six months old, was sold and closed down. Our whole family was adjusting to the closer of the church camp and we dearly missed it. Summer School was my entertainment, along with the fun outings to the lake, which my mother took us on.

My first day of Summer School was uplifting because the sexist boy happened to be in my class. His name was Scott and he had medium length blonde hair. He was a pot smoker too. Scott was the younger brother of another friend of mine but I'd never noticed him before. Scott and I visited at school and when I visited his older sister. Not too surprising, I started seeing his sister more often than I had before. Sally was Scott's sister's best friend so we both frequented her house.

Scott had a girlfriend, who was close friends' with Sally. She went away to visit relatives for the summer. One afternoon, Scott and I were hanging out in their garage having a grand time. I rode my bicycle over to their house that day and, luckily for me, his sister was out baby-sitting. It was a beautiful summer afternoon, sunny, with a light breeze, and I felt glorious. I was very attracted to Scott and thought it was with him that I would lose my virginity. I just decided that I wanted him for my lover and that was that!

I turned to Scott and said, "I think you should come with me to the woods and play." The expression in my tone and look on my face certainly told him what I had in mind. There was a wooded area across from his house and we walked over there. Scott laid his shirt out on the ground for me to set my bare butt on. We started kissing and caressing each other and I felt different than I thought I would. His kisses made me feel as if I was floating and slightly dizzy. I loved being that close with him and being in the woods was an enchanting setting.

He became so excited and tried to get himself inside of me, but he ejaculated before he got there. Immediately he went soft and my sexual experience was over, literally in the blink of an eye. What a shocker it was for me; finally ready to experience the, long anticipated and forbidden sexual act, only to have it end that way. We had a great time together that afternoon and he was as "hot" for me as I was for him. Scott was handsome, very sweet, and loads of fun to be with. Scott, Nature, Summer, and the perfect circumstances for losing my virginity, but I came away a disappointed virgin instead.

I rode my bicycle home floating with joy about being with Scott. I was miffed about the sexual flub, however. I still thought the way Scott and I related on our first time together was precious. He was also a virgin and was just as shocked as I was that it was over in a nanosecond. For years I had heard that sex was this forbidden, fantastic, cool, and divine experience. I told my sister about my experience with Scott and how frustrated I was about sex. I told her how it had been fun to be with him but that sex was not worthy of the hype. I felt let down. My sister assured me not to worry and that I would certainly like having sex later on in my life. I was a Preachers' Daughter and loved the forbidden, but I thought the sex act would be more of a WOW.

Scott and I began to see each other often and became an official couple. We did some hefty partying and lovemaking. My sister was right! I did develop a liking to sex, indeed. We were having the best summer together and I did excellent with my Summer School classes.

One day Sally told me that Scott was already taken by her friend and that she would be angry when she got back from vacation. Scott's sister also told me how her friend was going to be pissed off at me for stealing her man. I was enjoying each day with Scott and was certain he would stay with me after she returned. I figured that the flack I was going to get was worth being with Scott and I did not care.

One afternoon I had some "whippets", nitric oxide cartridges, which I showed Scott how to use. We hid in my bedroom and took turns with the canister. The buzz was immediately strong and lasting for just a short moment. We each inhaled two of the whippets and proceeded to laugh our butts-off. We went downstairs to make ourselves sandwiches and Scott sat down at the dining room table. Suddenly Scott stopped talking so I turned around to see what was going on. Scott fainted and fell backwards into the wall. I ran over to him and began shaking him. He came back to consciousness after ten seconds or so. My little brother was standing there and asked me, "What is wrong with him?" I answered, "Nothing," and took Scott by the arm, helped him to his feet and I got him to my bedroom as soon as possible. Thank goodness we made it by my brother. Scott rested an hour, drank lots of water, ate a sandwich, and revived himself. The lesson that everyone reacts uniquely from drugs became quite clear after that frightening episode.

Not long afterwards, I informed Scott that my period was late and that I might be pregnant. He freaked out initially, but then he calmed down slightly. I explained that it was not very late and it still might start up. I told him I wanted him to know, but not to worry yet. Of course he worried his guts out. His father would kick his ass. As it happened, my period did start up and our lives were tranquil again, or so I thought. I was not as flipped out as Scott was from the pregnancy scare and did not predict what was coming next. Scott dumped me as soon as his girlfriend got back. He'd had enough of the type of excitement that I brought into his life. He remained a good friend and I was glad that it was him I chose to explore sex with. It turned out that the friction between Scott's girlfriend, our mutual friends and me was not that heavy.

The summer was a great one! Eileen, Will, and I had many party rendezvous and home life was going quite smoothly. Will and I rode our bicycles everywhere after my father lightened up on keeping me captive. My parents were thrilled that I did so well in Summer School so I was given slightly more freedom.

Three friends and I were riding our bicycles around the neighborhood one summer night; trash night it so happened. On a whim, one of us rode up close to the curb and kicked over a trashcan. We all began to kick over trashcans. The loud crashing and laughter could be heard up and down the block. Suddenly, a car came speeding up out of nowhere and drove close to my left side. While I asked myself whether or not this guy was going to hit me, he did. I was knocked off my bike and onto the tree lawn. I jumped up and went running into somebody's side yard. I climbed up high in a pine tree, adrenaline-fueling my agility. I became silent and determined to get away, as I watched the man searching for me down below. He called out, "I am the police and come out now!" My heart was pounding so hard that I thought he could hear it. He finally gave up looking for me after about ten minutes, loaded my bicycle into his car, and drove off. I waited up in the tree for at least another fifteen minutes before climbing down. I wanted to make sure he didn't come sneaking back on foot.

When the car first sped after us, my friends scattered and were nowhere to be found after I climbed out of the tree. I walked home and it was ten o'clock at night by the time I got there. I came into the living room and silently stood there, looking distraught. My father asked me what was wrong and I told him the story . . . with a few twists to the truth. I told him that I was riding my bike and a crazy man came out of nowhere and hit me, that I ran and climbed a tree and hid until he left, but that he had taken my bicycle. My father was shocked and called the police. The police told him that they had my bicycle and we would have to go to the police station to claim it.

We drove to the police station to claim my bike, which was not as easy as I thought it would be. Luckily my father always wore his Clerics -- a black shirt and slacks, with his beaming white collar -- which came in handy at times like this. Priests are treated with more respect than most other people. The policeman that had chased me was there and he told my father that some kids had been knocking over trashcans in the neighborhood and that he believed that I was with them. He told my father that he had yelled out, declaring that he was a policeman, and that I did not stop. I denied knocking over trashcans and told them that I was simply riding home when I got hit

by a car, that I never heard him say he was a cop, and that I thought I
was being hunted down by a lunatic! I don't think that my father or
the cop believed a word I said, but I got away with it and I had my
bike back.

That weekend there was a wonderful party with Wills' group of
friends and some hip high school teens. I was having a great time! I
laughed, drank tequila, and smoked lots of pot. I decided to take a
short walk with Sally and smoke a cigarette, so we set out down the
street. It was a warm summer night and we were having a playful
time of it. We passed by a group of teenagers standing in front of a
house who were in our grade. This group of teens were white, upper
middle class and thought of Sally and myself as scumbags. One girl
yelled something nasty to me, but I was so happy and stoned, I did
not care. Then, this girl said, "how is your whore friend Sally,
anyway?" That was it!

She and her gang took off as fast as they could and I ran after her.
She ran behind her house and I followed her. I caught her and began
punching her in her face and anywhere I could. I went into a craze
that was intensely frightening. I do not think she even tried to fight
back. She was too busy trying to protect her face from me. I was
not stopping and would have probably killed her if her friends had
not pulled me off of her. I walked away, swearing and challenging
anyone to say bad things about my friends. Sally was surprised by
how ferociously I stuck up for her. We walked back to the party and
carried on with our great time as if nothing had happened. The girl I
beat up abruptly transferred schools and got away from us.

I had mixed feelings about starting back at my old junior high
school. I liked having a fresh beginning but I was going to miss my
friends. The new school year was here and off I went, walking with
Eileen who was a ninth grader that year. We stopped at the corner
where we had hung out the previous year. It was a different crowd
there now. The majority of the kids I hung out with had moved up
to the high school. I liked my teachers and especially my English
teacher, Mrs. Williams. Mrs. Williams was a large black woman,
whose smile was sincere and made me feel comfortable. Also
comforting were the splendid autumn days, sunny with a light and

crisp breeze. The trees in Upstate New York during the Fall glowed beautifully with neon colors of varying red, gold, orange, and yellows.

I quickly met some new friends, including Sharon, the younger sister of my sisters' friend. Sharon was raised with liberal parents and her style of dress made that evident. She had bushy, long black hair that packed her aura and wore beads and bangles. She was open-minded and had a boyfriend, Jim. Jim's best friend and I ended up becoming a couple. He had a twinkle in his eye that I could not resist. The four of us hung out together often. I wasn't sexually attracted to him and he didn't pressure me either. Sharon and Jim were sexually active, but I would only go as far as kissing my boyfriend. He did not seem to be frustrated by this and we spent some hilarious times together.

Jim was having a birthday party and we were all there, partying up a storm. We were playing twister and dancing around laughing. My boyfriend jumped up and I grabbed him, pulling him off his feet and swinging him onto the bed. I miscalculated the maneuver and he fell onto the floor beside the bed. He landed on his arm and broke it. Jims' mom and Jim drove him to the hospital and the rest of us went home. I ended the party early and felt so bad about it. I wondered all night about my boyfriend and how he was doing.

My reputation as a "Bad Ass" was well known throughout the school and this accident did not help any. The next day he did not show up for school, so I skipped class and went to his house to see how he was. He was in an arm cast and uncomfortable, but happy that I came by. I was so glad that he still loved me. He knew it was an accident and that I meant to toss him onto the bed. My boyfriend was a little shorter than I was, by a couple of inches. The next day, he showed up at school with his arm in a cast and wearing a sling. Kids asked him what happened and he told them that I broke his arm. The word flew around school, "She broke her boyfriends' arm." I was not thrilled about the way the story twisted as it was repeated and portrayed me as a "Monster Girlfriend."

The four of us were visiting in the attic of my boyfriend's house when Jim started acting like a real prick. At first he was showing off his BB rifle, pointing it out of the window and pretending to be a sniper. He turned the gun on us and said that he could order us to do whatever he wanted. He turned the gun on my boyfriend and told him to give him his pot and money, all while smiling. The situation did not feel threatening, just playful. Jim was as drunk as we were and accidently fired the gun and hit me in my ass. 'Was it an accident' I thought. Pissed off, I leaped over and took the rifle away from Jim, pointed it at him, called him a "Fucker", and pulled the trigger. I hit him in between his middle finger and index finger, straight into the webbing. He yelped with pain and held his hand, while quickly pacing back and forth. We laughed at him and lit another joint. I told him that's what he got for shooting me. I picked the BB out of my ass with the help of my boyfriend and his tweezers.

A few days later, Jim, my boyfriend, and I went to visit Sharon at her baby-sitting job. We coupled up and started making out in opposite ends of the living room. Laughter and play began as Jim was trying to give Sharon a hickey and she started to wrestle with him. We started a hickey fight! Trying to pin each other down and give a hickey broke out into rolling around the floor like happy little kids at play. I ended up with a hickey on my neck, the size of a silver dollar.

We went our separate ways and I returned to my house. My parents and two brothers were sitting in the living room watching TV. I had asked for a weight set for my birthday and was thrilled to get it. My weights were still in the living room because I hadn't taken them up to my bedroom yet. I started to lift my weights and forgot about my hickey. After everything I put my parents through, I did not think a hickey was any big deal or that I needed to bother concealing it from my father. I was wrong about that!

My father noticed the hickey while I was lifting my barbells. He got up from his chair in complete silence, walked over to me, and picked me up in the air by my shirt. He held me as high up as he could and yelled, "What is that on your neck?" I told him I was in an innocent hickey fight. My mother stepped in and told him to put me down, now. He ordered me to go to my room. I gave no resistance and ran up the stairs. I never got in trouble for that, so my mother must have smoothed things out with my dad. Dad was not prepared for raising daughters.

My parents really would have flipped out if they knew what I did with my boyfriend, while they were out at a church meeting. We got very drunk and stoned this night and walked up the hill. At the top of the hill was a busy street that was so steep that cars could not see the other side as they came over the top of it. Just for the thrill of it I asked him to lay down in the middle of the street and kiss me. The kiss was fast and exhilarating knowing that we could be run over at any second. How stupid of us to do this, and I never looked at the hilltop in the same way again. The death-defying kiss took place!

There was one girl that I liked a lot even though she was an off-shoot of the prissy girls group that I had wanted to leave so badly in elementary school. Cindy and I became close friends. She had an adventurous side and was tomboyish cool. She and I went to another side of town that I never hung out in. The group of teenagers Cindy introduced to me were all raised in conservative homes with comparison to myself. There were a few older teens in this neighborhood that I liked very much, including the ultra cute teenage boys. Cindy and I spent most of our time together on this side of town, playing touch football and sneaking off to smoke pot in the woods.

My parents let me sleep over at Cindy's house often and she had Freedom! We told her mom we were going out and wouldn't be home until later, and that was it. We walked the mile to the keg parties in the woods. These teens were the opposite of the teens I hung out with at my old school and had it more together. The older brothers bought them kegs of beer and they owned cars for us to go cruising.

I had a great time with these older teenage boys and the new neighborhood to explore. I had a crush on an older boy, who was a goof ball and had long brown hair. He was always out with us and did not seem to be interested in having girlfriends. One evening, he and I walked down from the top of the hill where the gang was. We walked onto a dead-end street. I was up to no good as usual. We walked by a Cadillac with white wall tires and especially ornate hubcaps. Those hubcaps sparkled under the street light, chrome with a detailed design. I told my friend, "I am going to steal those hub caps." I ducked down at the side of the car while he hid beside me in the dark, waiting. I tried to pry a hubcap off, but was interrupted by a large black man at an open second story window of the house across the street. He pointed a shotgun at me and told me he was going to shoot me if I messed with his car or, if did not run away now! We took off running for our lives out into the night! We ran like there was no tomorrow, which might have been the truth!

Somehow I successfully divided up my time up. I still saw Will on a daily basis, Eileen, Sharon and my boyfriend, and Cindy and that group of friends. I was a busy social butterfly. I told my parents that I was studying with someone or going to the movies when I was really out partying with my friends. As I mentioned earlier, my father has a background in, both, criminology and sociology, so his interrogations of me were thorough and a pain in my ass. He would call the movie theater and asked about the films I told him I was seeing. One night, during one of my father's interrogations, I botched my story and got caught lying, but he divulged his secret. So I began calling the movie theaters for a run down about the film too.

My parents had every reason to worry about me because I was wild and the neighborhood wasn't safe. Rape was common around the University area in which we lived and the ghetto was close by. My parents would have gone bonkers if I told them about the close calls I had. For example, once I was walking up a street near my house and was snatched up and dragged into a garage. The man was someone I knew fairly well and we had some mutual friends, so at first I didn't take him seriously. He pushed me up against the wall and started to undo my jeans. I yelled, "Fuck off! I have herpes and VD so have fun." Apparently, I grossed him out enough that he walked away. Yes, I was livid!

In another rape escape, I was with Eileen and we were walking down a busy street that was notoriously dangerous. This street was close to our homes and we frequented the restaurants there. I was going off, screaming about how angry I was at someone. Eileen was listening to me vent. Suddenly, a tall black man came out of the alley and stood in front of us. He told us to get into the alley. I became incensed and screamed as loud as I could. I called him every curse name you can think of and was jumping around in his face, waving my arms. I said, "Don't even give me your shit, I'm pissed and will kick your ass!" The man ran back into the alley as fast as he could. One thing I learned at school is that black dudes don't mess with crazy!

Dina showed up again and was a whole other type of relationship, blood sisters and bold adventures! I was forbidden from any contact with her. My father had a special dislike of our friendship because he hated her guts. Dina was someone out of my father's control and he didn't know how far she would take me if I ran away again.

On one bizarre day, I was in a mood to party it up and experience some more of the world. Dina came to mind immediately so I rode my bike to her house. At the top of the hill Dina lived on, a man came running out into the street and stopped me on my bicycle. I knew this guy. He was a high ranking gang member. I smoked pot with him before near school and he respected me, or so I thought. He pulled a pistol on me and said, "Get off the bike, now!" I grabbed the pistol away from him and threw as far as I could, saying, "Fuck-off, that's not real." He was shocked and ran away to find his gun, calling me nasty things all the while. What an experience and it meant that I had to ride to Dina's without going that way again.

I asked Dina about taking off on another extravaganza together. Dina said she knew some entertaining people on the other side of town and that I would like them a lot. We took off walking with a bottle of whiskey to keep us over-the-top jovial. We walked along like the world was our giant playground and life was for us to enjoy and wander through freely. We got to her friend's house after dark and he welcomed us in. Dina had known this man for years. I think they grew up together. He was skinny and had tattoos, white, with long hair and dressed in jeans and a T-shirt. We visited and laughed our butts off. He told me that he is a cat burglar, with many powerful clients. He carried himself in a tense, uptight manner, chain smoked cigarettes, and was truly a tough-assed-criminal. He took Dina and I out into the night and taught us some tricks of the trade-- how to run along the top of chain link fences for one.

We went back to the house and decided to go to bed. Dina slept in the living room and I slept with the Cat Burglar. We did not sleep a wink; we lay naked in his bed and talked about life. I asked him to tell me the stories behind the variety of scars he had on his body. There was one scar that looked like a bullet wound. I asked him about that scar; all the while noticing that he was sexy. He explained how he was shot and showed me another bullet scar from a separate occasion. I felt safe and protected here, even though I was lying naked alongside of one of the most dangerous men that I had ever met. He was well-toned and had trigger nerves, reacting to any sounds from outside. This guy was always on edge and had been through many violent times and shootings.

The next morning, there was a bang on the door. I recognized his voice and told the Cat Burglar, "It's my dad." This guy had a

machete over his door jam and took it in his hands. He said he was
going to do this guy in. Suddenly, I felt love and caring for my father
and begged him not to harm him. He agreed and opened the door.
He told my father that he never met me in his life and to go away.
My father left and drove off. I had no idea how my father knew I
was there, and neither did Dina or the Cat Burglar. My father
coming there was so strange and unexpected that someone had to be
following me.

I showed up back at home at dinnertime the next day. I was in
deep trouble, again, and was kept in the house even longer. I stayed
out for the night, came back on my own, and showed some
improvements in my behavior. My father was furious and sat me
down in the living room for a talk, or rather, to yell at me. Thank-
goodness he did not call the police yet. My father routinely sat me
down to tell me what a stupid idiot I was. My siblings received the
exact same encouragement from my father, none!

My father told me that he was notified during the night of my
whereabouts. He said that a police officer had called him to tell him
that a drug bust was called off after they found out that I was in the
house. My father said that he worked closely with the police force
and that he is too shocked for words. He was pacing back and forth
from our living room to our dining room. He asked me if I knew
how serious this was and how many favors he has used up with
influential people he knows. The cat was out of the bag. He did use
the police force for his personal will when it came to me. Finding me
at crime scenes of huge importance to the police was another deal
altogether. I think the bust itself was over heroin and the underworld was involved. I have to admit that I was grateful for not
getting picked up in that mess, but at the same time I could care less
about obeying my father.

I recalled how I felt when I thought this guy was going to harm
my dad. I knew that I had been in deeper trouble than I wanted to
be and that the Cat Burglar was a dangerous, reactionary man.
"There are some people that I do not want to know", this was the
lesson of that week.

Two nights later we were all sitting in the living room as a family,
watching television. There was a knock on the door at 9:00 pm,
which never happened. My mother answered it and there were two
women on the porch, asking to see me. My mother said that I was

unavailable. The woman tried to push her aside, but my mother stood her ground. My mother was a large woman with a giant "mother bear" instinct. My mom told them that if anyone crossed the line, pointing out the door jam, that they would be facing a judge in the morning. The women were mad and cursing me, but did not cross that line. My mother slammed the door but she was not pleased, to say the least. A chill went through me since I had no idea who these women are. This type of hardened woman was something new in my life and I did not know where they came from, or, what they looked like. I was at a disadvantage here.

The next day at school, I was called out of class, and told to report to the principals' office. 'No big deal', I thought. I strolled carefree down the hallway towards the office. There were two women in their mid-twenties standing in front of the office. I came up to them and one of them said my name. My facial expression must have been a dead give-away. They grabbed me and pushed me into the girls' bathroom. One woman pushed me into a stall and bent me backwards over the toilet and against the wall behind it. My chest was opened to her and she looked evil. I was told never to see that guy again or I was dead. I knew that she meant the Cat Burglar. She told me how easy it would be to slit my throat right there and then. The two women let me go and rapidly walked out of the building. Whew, close call; the realization of my real vulnerability was no joy either. These women could get me anytime they wanted to. Meeting the Cat Burglar and spending one night with him has caused more strife and danger than my past two years combined.

I decided the only way to resolve the matter was to have a meeting with the main woman who wanted to kill me. Dina told me what was going on and who these women are. What happened was that the night I spent with the Cat Burglar I was seen by a woman peering through the windows. The best friend of his girlfriend saw us naked in bed together. He did not say anything about his girlfriend or, that I would be dead if anyone found out I was there. Great!

Dina arranged for me to meet with the women on their side of town. I introduced Cindy and Dina that afternoon and Cindy wanted to come to the meeting with us. The three of us walked the few miles to the other side of town, behaving wildly and drinking lots of whiskey. Dina liked her whiskey and we were always willing to drink with her. Oddly enough, I was not worried about the meeting becoming violent. I honestly thought that once we met and I explained what happened that this woman would relax and like me. I wasn't sure about like me, just hoped that she would spare my life.

The three of us arrived at the house and were invited in by a woman. We sat down, and I signaled Dina that she was one of the women who threatened my life. The woman said, "the other woman will be coming soon so relax." I was basically calm and the four of us smoked some pot, drank some whiskey and made small talk. The other woman came into the house. She looked very sure of herself and quite streetwise. These two women were crude and had danger written in their persona. I was meeting with women of another side of life than I lived in. The get-together was a fun party time and the woman did not ask me any questions or threaten me, but if looks could kill I would have been dead. The women knew Cindy and I were from completely different walks of life and that I was a pip-squeak compared to them. I knew they had knives because they already threatened to slit my throat at school.

It got to be dinnertime and I had to be going home. All five of us started walking down the street and I was curious what the women were thinking of doing. As we walked I began to get more and more tense, knowing something was about to happen. I stopped at a motor lodge and used the bathroom. The women were all going to wait at the sidewalk. I walked down the walkway to the door. It was getting dark and thick bushes lined one side of the walkway.

The woman who wanted to kill me walked right up behind me, close; her chest touching my back. In a serious voice she told me that she had thought Cindy was me the whole afternoon. She told me that she didn't like Cindy very much and planned on stabbing her. Dina told her that I was the one who was with the Cat Burglar. She told me, speaking into my neck and tightening her grip on my shoulder, "I like you and will let you go this time; never again". She told me that she was a prostitute for the Mafia and could have me taken out anytime she wanted. She also made the point that if she ever heard that I saw the Cat Burglar again, that I would end up dead and thrown on my parent's doorstep. I got the message loud and clear!

I explained to her what happened that night at the Cat Burglar's and swore that we did not have sex. I told her we were not lovers, had never met before that night, and had not spoken since. I never saw the Cat Burglar or these women again . . .what a case of being in the wrong place at the wrong time. Cindy and I looked very much alike and we bought matching T-shirts and Converse sneakers too. Knowing how close Cindy came to being stabbed for something that I did gave me an emotional jolt.

Cindy and I were hitchhiking down a street near the university and two male college students picked us up. They were hilarious and dressed up in costumes and going an early Halloween Party. Cindy and I were invited to go with them to the party and we went! The party was packed with dressed up college students and the aroma of pot. Our new friends' costumes were well done; one was a Martian and the other was a Surgeon. Cindy and I told the people who asked us, that we are dressed as junior high school teens. We danced, drank, smoked weed, and carried on well into the night. We walked back to Cindy's house and snuck in without being discovered by her mother. We had no problem with falling fast asleep.

I woke up to the strangest sounds: eerie humming, bells, and the clapping of hands. The house went back to early morning silence and then the sounds started up again. When Cindy woke up I asked her about the weird sounds that I heard. She said that a meditation group meets in their attic on Sunday mornings. Her mother, older brother and sister were Buddhists of some sect which explained the chanting and bells. 'What a "different" thing is going on here' I thought. Her mother would sit on the kitchen floor in front of the oven. She would stare at the oven and meditate. I thought she was unusual and did not understand the Buddhist practices at all.

The next Monday I was walking back into the school after smoking a cigarette during lunch hour. I went to open the door when an arm came from behind me and pushed the door closed. I was grabbed, turned around, and slammed up against the door. There was a very mean gang of ninth grade, black girls in front of me. I was scared! I would fight any boys before I would fight a gang of black girls, all bigger and meaner than I was. The black girls fought dirty and loved to scratch up faces and leave scars for life. A girl yelled out, "kick her honky cunt ass now!"

I never did anything to these girls and could not understand why they were so mad at me. A girl said, "Cindy". I said, "I'm not Cindy, she just looks like me". I began to plead for my life. This one girl, obviously the leader, had her mind made up to beat me bloody. Just as the situation worsened for me, a girl saved me by saying, "she is not Cindy." This girl knew who I was and told the other girls. I was told to tell Cindy, "She is dead" and she let me go. I was feeling thankful, a close call alright. They would have shredded me.

Cindy told me that she has a new boyfriend and he is a gorgeous mulatto. Her new boyfriend was one of the best-looking boys in the whole school and he dumped one of the mean girls to be with her. That explained the whole thing and I knew she was going to continue to be endangered for a long time to come. Nuts how she was almost stabbed for being me and I was almost beaten bloody for being her.

Cindy parked cars in a grassy lot next to her home during the university football games. Cindy and a friend of hers did this for a few years and made good money at it. The cars were parked next to Cindy's and behind her friends home. This sounded like a good time and money so I talked them into letting me park cars with them. I told Cindy that the lot was really hers and she should not give her friend as much money as she had been. By the end of the afternoon I had embezzled money and talked Cindy into hiding money from her friend. The friend caught on to what we were doing and got really mad. She told me that I was a lying thief and cheat. I did not care what this girl called me, or who she told about me ripping her off anyway. I stole the money without a second thought. The girl's mom called Cindy's mom and I was banned from parking the cars in the future.

✴

Dina and I decided to go downtown to watch a parade. She was a crazy one, indeed. Her idea was to get on a rooftop overlooking the parade route, fill condoms with water making water balloons out of them, and tossing them off the roof. That was exactly what we did! What a scream it was. The energy of being so defiant was exhilarating and surging through my body. Then, we phoned two of her friends, older men, and she told me they were exciting to hang out with. Dina called both sets of friends and nobody was answering their phones. Night came and we wandered the streets looking in parked cars for change and cigarettes. It was amazing how much change you can find in cars.

Dina had a friend who lived in a hotel downtown but the night watchman would not let us go upstairs. We left the building and guessed our chances of getting past the watchman. We looked at the situation and decided that we would try sneaking in. We got down on the floor and crawled along the wall, under the counter, and then up the staircase, behind the wall. We did it, stealth in action. We were so proud of ourselves. He was not home and we had to sneak back out, deflating our outlaw egos.

It was late and we kept calling her friends, but nobody answered. We decided to spend the night in a parked car, a big Plymouth with plenty of room for us. In the morning she was able to get one of her friends on the phone and we met him for breakfast. He bought us yummy breakfast at a diner and then we went back to his house to shower. After I finished showering only Dina was at the house. Her friend had to go somewhere and would be back later on. We had the place to ourselves. I asked Dina if she thought her friend would mind if I used his toothbrush. Dina said, "I would not use his toothbrush because he eats pussy." I was disgusted and got away from the toothbrushes. We talked about oral sex and I thought it was the grossest thing I ever heard of. I told her there was no way, no how that I was ever going to have oral sex, Yuck! Dina laughed with me and never admitted to partaking in oral sex or not.

It was later that afternoon when Dina went too far with her pranks. We got dropped off at her regular restaurant hangout and were joking around. The security policeman was wandering around the place and watching us. I pretended to be speaking with Dina….mumble . . . mumble. PIG, loud, so he could hear it. The officer came right over to me and picked me up in the air and said, "What did you say?" I told him PIG, Pride Integrity and Guts. He put me down and said that I was lucky that I knew that. He was not in the best mood that afternoon. Normally he would have laughed with us.

Dina did a very dumb thing and reached for his gun. I have no idea if she was really going to grab it or not, plus, it was in the holster. In a second, the policeman had his mace and sprayed her in the eyes. Dina started screaming and I got her into the bathroom where we washed her eyes, repeatedly. They were swollen and sore for a few days and she will never try that stupid stunt again.

CHAPTER 9
ADVENTURES OF A WILD TRIP

I was a very good student when I felt like applying myself to my studies. My favorite classes were English and Woodshop. My English teacher was my favorite and she often told me that I wrote like a machine. When her assignment was to write a story, I cranked out page after page, pen flying.

One afternoon in English class, I noticed a girl peering into the classroom through the window in the door. Since the door window was small I could just see part of her head, but I recognized her anyway. She waved and motioned for me to meet her after class. It was Zoe, my friend from the Juvenile Detention Center. I met her on the corner and we smoked a cigarette between my classes. I was shocked that she showed up in my life again. She was living in a group home for adolescent girls who were all in trouble and either their parents did not want or were not allowed to have them. She lived with five other girls and was going to be enrolled in my school the following week. Zoe and I agreed to meet after school, for a walk around the neighborhood to catch up.

I enjoyed visiting the group home and meeting the other girls living there. Zoe visited my house a few times too. We had long talks about what we could do together and made some plans for our future. We fantasized about the places we would visit and the boyfriends we would have. Zoe still had her boyfriend. He would show up once a month for hot sex and disappear again. Zoe didn't seem bothered by her boyfriend's selective interest in her. Zoe became close friends with a girl in the home, Beth. We liked each other, too. Beth was short and super feisty, always bitching about something.

The two of them skipped school one day to visit their boyfriends and were caught. The school had been advised to call the group home at any sign of trouble so they did. Zoe and Beth were not allowed to leave their group home for two weeks, except to go to school. They were angry about it. The punishment stopped our plans to go to a party that was to be a blowout, grand time; disappointing all of us.

It was Sunday and I was visiting Zoe and Beth at the group home. They weren't accepting their confinement well at all. Beth said, "I have had it, I am going to run away from here." Zoe said she would join her and they should hitchhike to Canada. The weather was still cold and would be worse the farther North they went. I suggested they hitchhike south instead and go to the beaches in Florida. Both girls said, "We do not know how to get to Florida." I told them it was easy, just go South, and that I would take them. That was a life changing fifteen minute conversation. I was clueless about what this plan, or lack thereof, entailed.

I told the girls that I was going to my house to get my paper route money and a few clothes and would be back. I went home and packed a daypack, got my cash and threw the pack out by bedroom window. I told my mother I was going to take a little walk and left. I had $26.00 and a half an ounce of pot to my name.

I met up with Zoe and Beth who were ready to get on the road. They put their things in the recreation room down in the basement, and climbed out the window. The three of us, wild teenagers all, walked down to the highway on-ramp, stuck out our thumbs, and were picked up in less than five minutes. A semi-truck pulled over and we piled into the cab. Zoe and Beth looked like the young women they were while I looked like a ten year old boy. The truck driver was polite to us and asked us very few questions. He bought us a meal and we enjoyed each other's company. We rode with him into Pennsylvania to his destination and hopped out of his truck. The three of were so happy to be free, walking down the side of the highway, thumbs out and ready to get to Florida.

We saw State Troopers driving towards us with their lights flashing and we flipped out. We wasted no time, running up a steep, practically straight up, hill to the top. This escape was physically demanding but we made it. We ran down into the woods on the other side of the hill. The woods were thick as well as out of sight from the highway. I knew that nobody could see us. The Troopers, however, knew we were there somewhere and were interested in us. They drove near on a narrow dirt road in the wooded area so we hid deep in the bushes.

They parked around fifty yards away from us and we were scared they would find us. We kept quiet as mice and waited them out. The policemen stayed parked there for at least three hours. We were going bonkers between needing to pee and wanting a cigarette. For a while we thought that the Troopers would spend the night. It was pitch black by the time they finally left and we made our way back down the hill to the highway. We crossed the highway and walked to a strip of shops, motels, and a diner. The three of us went to the diner and shared an omelet with hash browns and toast. We talked a sleazy motel into giving us a room for $7.00 which we thought it was the Ritz because we were free! My $26.00 was not going to get us very far and the others only had a few dollars between them. We slept great and were on the road early with our coffee in hand. We smoked a fat joint and each ate a "Christmas Tree." The truck driver who gave us a lift, also, gave us the "Christmas Trees", a kind of Speed. Zoe knew about "Christmas Trees", but I never heard of them before.

The day was warm, clear, sunny and fabulous for hitchhiking. We were picked up right away by two big, fat and hairy, hippy-type dudes with their two young sons in a big Buick. The sons were only 5 and 6 years old and were rather mello. We did not ask them any questions and they returned the favor. These men were partying away, joint after joint and drinking beer after beer. We drank and smoked with them until we were all drunk. Beth got sloppy drunk, meaning that "drunk ass" Zoe and I had to help her along. We were let off at an exit in the D.C. area, where we were stopping to visit a friend of mine.

My parent's friends' grandson had the cutest friend, Buster. Buster was a sixteen-year old blonde and we did a little flirting while I visited there two years before. I had not spoken with Buster since my visit so we really didn't know each other well. I wanted to stop anyway just because we were free to do whatever we want. The three of us played silly and walked along the roads feeling as if we owned them. We felt on top of the world and treated every moment like a happy dream full of opportunity.

We made it to Buster's house around 4:00 pm. The neighborhood was upper class and conservative, so we really stuck out. Zoe and Beth waited at the corner of the street, while I went up to the house and rang the doorbell. Busters' dad answered the door and I asked if

Buster was home. His dad said, "He is not home yet and who are you?" I told him I was a friend he met two years ago and just thought I would say, "Hi." I thanked him and left. The three of us headed back to the highway and continued on our way south to the beaches.

We were sobered up by then and walking along the highway at twilight. We started to get hungry, but were well aware of how little money we had left and that we were only in D.C. Beth stated that she would be a prostitute so we could all eat. I replied, "There is no way that I would sell my body, to anyone, for any reason." I told her if that's' what she wanted to do, go ahead, but count me out. At that moment a hot-rod car pulled up for us. We jumped into the back seat of the tricked-out Mustang, with two young guys sitting in the front. These guys were totally thinking with their penises when they picked us up. One of the guys asked us if anyone wanted to give him a "blow job" for twenty dollars. I reached over and pinched Beth, while whispering, "Here is your chance." Beth replied in her regular tone, "No, I will wait until we are poorer." Zoe busted out laughing. The timing of the question was hilariously perfect. The guys looked at us as if we were totally crazy and we were. We rode with them for a few hours down the highway. They were an entertaining treat.

Our next ride was from a businessman driving to Richmond, Virginia. We piled in the back seat and fell asleep. He listened to the radio the whole time and spoke very little. He was generous and bought us dinner. I thought it was amazing that people asked so few questions about us, but I was glad about it too. We were dropped off in Richmond at night with full tummies. We sat on a highway overpass looking out over the city. We figured it would be easy to walk around a bit and find a party. We walked around for about an hour in a neighborhood, mixed with houses and industry. It was a boring walk and it seemed like there was nothing in Richmond of interest to us. It was getting late, but we decided to keep heading south. We walked back to the highway and stuck out our thumbs.

We got picked up by a young white guy in a van. He was obviously a house painter and had lots of equipment in his van, but we made ourselves comfortable. He was driving home from a job and wanted company to help keep him awake. He was boring in a mono-toned way, odd for the "pot head" he was. He gave us each a THC pill, which we ate. Neither of us had ever tried a THC pill before and thought why not. We were thrilled to have the ride in more ways than one and the pills were powerful. He dropped us off a few miles north of Fort Bragg, North Carolina at about 3:00 am. The highway was pitch black without a car in sight. We were acting like clowns and telling spooky stories about giant rats on the highways eating people and laughing. We were carefree as ever and seeing colors and halos from the pills. Finally, a car was coming and we put out our thumbs.

Before the car started to slow down, I knew, with every cell in my body, do not get into the car. The car pulled over and Beth and Zoe started to run up to it. I grabbed Zoe's arm and told her that we cannot get into that car. She swung my arm away and said she was getting in. Beth was already half inside the car and I yelled, "No!" I did not know what to do, I was about to be left alone in the middle of the night, in the middle of nowhere, N.C. Against my instincts, I got into the car with them, just to stay together. I had never heard of intuition before, but I had a strong inner quake from this situation. The car was a big, black Cadillac, with three black men in it. The men looked like they were in their late twenties and barely said a word to each other or to us. I was filled with the creeps and Zoe and Beth were also feeling something was very wrong by this point. The car pulled into a gas station for a fill up and two of the men got out and went inside.

The man in the front seat of the car turned around and said to us, "Get out now; they are going to rape and kill you." I thanked him, and we jumped out of the car as fast as we could. The gas station attendant had a look of horror on his face when he saw us. He screamed to us, "Get inside the station; Now!" while he put his hand on the gun in the holster he was wearing. We ran inside of the office area and were watching the Cadillac out the window. The three black men started arguing when they realized that the one guy let us go. They paid for their gas and sped out.

The gas station manager was a hip kind of redneck, southern man. He was a partyer and his hair was medium length. He was slender and tall. He spoke in a "matter of fact" way, with a soft tone to his voice. His name was Dan and he was a hoot. It was a blessing we met him. We hung out at the gas station listening to his stories while he coached us on what it is like down here in North Carolina. This gas station was located on I95, at a major interchange. He was on the

CB Radio constantly, either talking or listening. The language of the truckers was fascinating and it was interesting listening to the goings-on. Some news came in that there was a car load of white guys who were pulling up next to cars with inter-racial couples inside and blowing their heads off with a sawed off shot gun. This was going on right where we were. What an eye opener! Dan told us why he carried a gun and that the racial tension there was serious.

We were clueless about many things, as I am sure anyone would guess. We thought we were so worldly, tough, and cool and that we knew everything. Zoe, Beth, and I realized what a close call we had, just escaping from a very brutal death. Somehow I became senior advisor of our group because of my intuitive hunch. Beth did not listen and got into the car first, and that was a big part of us almost getting killed. Beth was starting to get on my nerves, because she talked a lot about, what I thought, were stupid topics. I gave her the money to walk over and buy a carton of cigarettes for us because they were cheaper in N.C. Beth came back with her menthol brand cigarettes and not my brand; plus Zoe didn't smoke menthol. I traded the cigarettes in for my brand, but gees, it was my money. Aside from that, everything was going fine between us all.

The sun just came up and Dan finished his shift. He took us out to breakfast and then back to his place. We took showers and were ready to set off south again. We smoked a few joints with him and he gave us some cocaine and pot to take with us. I was designated the "keeper of the drugs" and was saving them for the right time. Dan dropped us off at the on-ramp; the place he knew would give us the best chance of getting picked up. We thanked him and told him that we would stop in if we ever pass through there again. Meeting Dan had me thinking that our best party life was beginning and imagined myself dancing on the beach!

Right away, a businessman pulled over and picked us up. Jackpot! The businessman was innocently sweet and going to Tampa, Florida. The man looked like a thirtyish, straight family man and safe. We felt safe enough to get some sleep and he bought us a meal at a truck stop. He barely spoke and his presence was relaxing. We woke up to him saying that he was home and we had to get out now. We were off the highway and on a rural side road, somewhere around Tampa. He drove off and there we were in the dark, on a dirt road with nothing around. There were telephone poles and, far and few

between, some streetlights. It was around 1:30 in the morning and
we had no idea where we were. We walked down the road and joked
around, totally unaware of the alligators. We figured that we would
come to some town or something, eventually.

The three of us were worry free as ever and excited beyond belief
that we had made it to Florida. The air smelled of the ocean and the
humidity felt thick and sticky. Nobody passed by us for the longest
time. We were in the Boonies for sure. Finally, a pickup truck came
by and slowed down next to us. The driver stuck his head out of the
window and asked us what we were doing out there. We told him
that we just arrived and were looking for a party. The man seemed
like a cool enough guy: cute, around 30 years old, with a cowboy hat.
He invited us to jump in and go back to his place and party. We
squished in the front seat of his truck and he drove to his house,
which ended up being close by.

He played great music and we drank a bottle of apricot brandy
that he had. I busted out the cocaine and the pot that Dan gave us. I
chopped up lines for us and we danced to the music and got wild
together. Zoe and our host went off into his bedroom, and you
could guess what they did. I fell asleep in the living room for a few
hours. When we were all awake and ready to start our day, he told us
he would drop us off wherever we wanted to go. I told him that we
would like coffee and to do our laundry. He stopped by a coffee
house and bought us coffee, then drove us to the Laundromat that
was only a few blocks from the beach. We thanked him a lot and he
drove off. The weather could not have been nicer and we could hear
the ocean!

The clothes were in the wash and we were delighted beyond
words to be in Florida, about to start our new lives on the beach. I
went into the bathroom and as I started to come out, I saw two
policemen speaking with Zoe and Beth. I quickly shut the door again
and waited inside until they left. I came out and asked them what the
police officers wanted. They said that the cops had wanted to know
why we were there because they had never seen us before. Zoe told
the officers that we were in Tampa visiting her Grandmother. Zoe
and Beth said that the policemen were nice and they did not think
anything was wrong.

We agreed that we needed to get out of there as fast as possible.
We were folding up our clothes, and a mere moment away from

leaving, when the policemen returned. This time the police officers saw me. They told us that we needed to come down to the police station and call Zoe's Grandmother. We were busted! Zoe knew of a house she could call where nobody would be home to pick up the phone. She said that it was a friend of hers who would cover for her anyway. We were put into the back of the police car and taken to the station. I was upset; being so close to the ocean but still far from getting there.

We were marched down a hallway, with a long bench and told to sit there. The police officers took Zoe into an office to phone her Grandmother. I was concerned about getting busted for the pipe and pot I was carrying. On the end of the bench was a neatly stacked pile of newspapers. I slowly and carefully placed the pot and pipe in between the newspapers and hoped nobody saw me do it. Ten minutes later, Zoe was brought out and we were told to remain sitting there. We discussed our problem and thought up our strategy. We thought that if they never find out our identities, that eventually, they would let us go. Neither of us were scared of the police, or our offenses, and we knew we would find a way to escape.

Who walks by but the man we were partying with the night before, the one who had sex with Zoe. We were ratted on; he was a cop and an asshole! We were in an uproar that quickly got worse. A policeman came out of the office and said, "Beth, Zoe, and you are being detained." The police still did not know who I was, but it did not take them very long to figure it out. One distinguishing detail that was evident to anyone was that I had braces on my teeth. They had us. As soon as Zoe used an area code, the police called the police department there and busted us. There were warrants out for us and there was an All-States Bulletin issued.

We were taken to the Juvenile Detention Center for Sarasota-Bradenton and were booked in. We had the usual lice bath and were issued the ugliest clothes, plain and simple. We were issued Keds sneakers, which I loathed. This Detention Center was a country club compared to the one we had been in. The boys and girls were kept together in an enormous room. There were big windows that looked out into a park-like setting, with palm trees and a basketball court. I found it unbelievable that we had a pool table. In New York they never would have given us pool sticks and hard balls to kill each other with. The room was surrounded with one-way mirrors so the guards could constantly watch our every move.

The food was great. Southern Cooking appealed to me. I took a liking to grits with maple syrup while on the road, and there were plenty of grits there. One big difference at this detention center was that we had the chores of washing the dishes, food service, scrubbing the place, and doing the laundry. There were fewer teens in there compared to what we were used to. The teens were all white and friendly to us. They thought we were ultra-cool, being runaways from New York.

We had no idea how long we were going to be locked in there and days went by without a word. We never went to court in Florida and were finally told that travel arrangements were being made to fly us back to New York. We enjoyed ourselves there, shooting pool, sun bathing, and dancing outside. I made friends with a cute boy who was in there for stealing and skipping school. We ducked down behind the end of the pool table, thinking that we would be out of sight from the guards, so we could kiss. We were kissing when the guards came and broke us up. Beth pointed us out to the guards with arm motions and by pointing at us. The guards locked me in solitary confinement, which infuriated me.

I had nothing to do in solitary confinement except think. I thought a lot about how I was going to punch Beth in the face as soon as I saw her again. I was also thinking how much this sucked and that maybe a life of crime was not a very good idea. There was nothing worse than being locked up. For an added torture, the floor was stone tile with sea foam green specs in it. To help pass the time I began counting the specs and got up into the thousands. I always welcomed mealtime as I had a big appetite and needed something to do. I thought about what it was going to be like when I walk off the airplane in New York and seeing my parents again. There was no doubt that I was in real trouble this time. Months earlier, my probation officer said that I had run out of second chances a long time ago. Being in my present situation, New York felt like it was far into the future.

48 hours later I was released back into the main room. I had time for my anger towards Beth to stew. I walked directly to her with murder in my eyes and saw the fear on her face. I punched her in her face as hard as I could. Beth went flying backwards, started screaming, and holding her face. Two guards came running, took an

arm each, and hauled me back down the hall to solitary confinement. I felt such satisfaction out of punching her that I did not mind being locked up this time, as much. A day later a Guard let me out, after making me promise that I was not going to go after Beth again. I agreed since I did not want anything more to do with her, ever.

I had dish duty and learned how to use the industrial washer. A big palmetto bug came floating across the dishwater and I screamed. Palmetto bugs are giant cockroaches that can fly and are thoroughly creepy. I freaked out and shook, while loudly refusing to do any more dishes. I was told to get my ass over there and finish the dishes or go back to solitary confinement. The cook went to the sink and took the palmetto bug away for me so I could finish the dishes. This was my first experience of one southern fact, that bugs in the semi-tropics are bigger than in the North.

Sunbathing was the best and I needed the relaxation time. We enjoyed water fights with the hoses. It really was a country club for us. We knew where we were heading and wanting to soak up all the Florida sunshine we could. Ten days later we were being transported to the airport under guard. The police told us that we were going to be met by the police, our lawyers, and my parents in New York. We were also informed that the flight crew knew that we were prisoners in transport and would be keeping a close eye on us. The police in Atlanta, Georgia will be watching the gate to make sure that we did not escape during the stopover. The police waited until we boarded the flight, were belted into our seats, and the doors of the airplane were shut. Beth was seated a few rows behind Zoe and myself. Zoe and I were seated together and I was so glad that we were.

Zoe and I made a plan to escape off the flight in Atlanta and we had about an hour to get emotionally amped. We were going to have to be fast and unstoppable. We decided to get rid of Beth by leaving her behind. She suspected we were up to something because we did not speak with her during the entire flight. The plane pulled into the gate and people began to exit the plan and we mixed into the crowd. The flight attendants were so distracted with their tasks that we walked right by them and off the plane. We walked out of the airport as fast as we could without looking like we are escaping something. We got outside and ran to the main road faster than ever before! "Free", we shouted!

Atlanta is a big city and we knew nothing about it, so we simply picked a direction and followed it. Zoe and I were thrilled to be on our own again and to be starting our new life phase without Beth. It was a warm, sunny, and glorious day to roam!

Zoe and I were walking along a busy boulevard, just taking in the new city and strolling to somewhere. A VW Beetle drove past us and honked the horn. The driver was waving and smiling at us. We waved back at him and just kept walking thinking nothing of it until we saw the VW Beetle parked at a liquor store. We immediately went over to it and hung around the car, waiting for the man to come out of the store.

When we saw him I said, "We saw you drive by. We are new in town and want to party." He invited us to come to his house and party it up with him, so we did. We got into the bug and drove a few miles to a funky trailer park. His name was Rob and he had a small trailer in the park where he lived alone. Rob was an energetic character: medium length brown hair, glasses, and a hairy face. He could be on the record cover of Cream.

It seemed that Rob did not have a girlfriend and worked as a passenger van driver from the airport during the night. Rob was on his way home from work when he picked us up. He lit up a joint and poured us shots of tequila, making us feel right at home. He was a hardcore partyer and we were in for a time of it! He told us that we could stay with him for a few days if we wanted so we took him up on his offer. After all, we had no place to go to.

His trailer had one bedroom and two long bench seats in the living room area. We were very wasted and having a fun time, visiting with our new friend and telling him about escaping from the police. We landed in a curious place and Zoe and I were floating high and playful as ever. Life in Atlanta was starting out supremely in my teenage mind. Party, Party, Party, that's all we thought about and did.

We were seated around the living area with the front door opened to a lovely day. Two teenagers popped their heads in the door and said, "Hi." Rob invited them in and introduced us. The boys were sixteen-year olds and one of them was especially cute, catching my eye. The cute one lived next door with his dad and brother. Oh, did I like my new neighbors. They brought some beer with them and joined in the party. We were having the time of our lives, magical considering that we were in police custody that same morning.

Rob's friend drove up in a pimped out automobile and parked

right in front of the door, on the walkway. A tall black man got out and he was "Bling" all the way. He had on a fine suit and lots of big rings. His shoes were dark green glitter pumps made of plastic. He was very dark-skinned, with a big afro and he looked to be in perfect shape. He glided when he walked and had his strut down. He acted like a king when he entered and sat down at the table. His energy was gigantic and filled the tiny trailer.

I felt the two boys tense up when he arrived. They had obviously met before. Rob treated him like a king and poured him a shot of Tequila. The man pulled out some cocaine and chopped up some lines. He passed the tray around the trailer and we each snorted one. He asked us who we were and we told him we ran away from New York. He looked at us in a way that you knew his brain was churning over some idea for us. His eyes were deep, big and black, with years upon years of bloodshot in them. I felt his power when he looked at me. He did look at me too, as I sat on the other side of the table, to his right. I observed the conversation and laughed a bit, but tried to be invisible to this man.

Rob's "Ruler" friend took out a bag of powder and some syringes, setting them on the table. Rob handed him a spoon and he cooked up some heroin. He filled the syringe and tied his arm with a tourniquet and hit himself up. I was big-eyed watching him and never saw anyone shoot up drugs before. Instantly, his eyes rolled around and he relaxed against the back of the chair, with a huge smile on his face. He sat up after a few minutes and started talking again. Rob wanted some too and the guy was asking for money, plus, the money he was owed.

Rob became frantic and went into his bedroom. We could see that he was searching through pants pockets and all over for any money he might have. Rob gave him some money and he did get a small bag. He hit up in front of us too. Zoe and I watched as Rob got down on his hands and knees, begging and crying for more. He was given a spoon with some heroin in it and he relaxed again. I was watching the pathetic episode carefully and knew that Rob was a heroin addict and this powerful man was the supplier. 'Rob's addiction was strong' I thought to myself. Zoe was observing the scene too but had a different take on it than I did.

I was still enjoying myself, listening to music, smoking joints, drinking tequila, and snorting a few more lines of coke. The King

Man, called Cash, turned his attention towards me and it felt scary. He was cooking up some more heroin and asking me where I had met Rob. He filled the syringe and set it down on the table, then reached inside of his jacket and pulled out a pistol which he put down on the table by the syringe. He looked at me and told me that I could have a shot of heroin . . . if I want one. I replied, "No thank-you." He ordered, "You are going to do a shot." I told him, "No, I am not." I could see horror written on the faces of the two neighbor boys and Rob was standing as far back in the corner as he could get, practically in the cupboards. Zoe sat at the table and didn't appear to be on high alert or think a big problem was coming down.

Cash gave me a mean glare that was supposed to terrify me, but it didn't. I was unwavering and going to hold my ground, no matter what! He said, "Do it, you will like it." I told him again, "No thank you." I crossed my arms and sat back in my chair. He stood up, picked up his gun and walked around the table to my right side and put the gun to the side of my head. He said, "Give me your arm now!" I told him, "Fuck-you! Go ahead and shoot me, because I am not doing it!" That was the last thing anyone expected, including Cash. Cash was so surprised at my bold guts and tough attitude that he decided to spare me. Cash ended up liking me and the atmosphere lightened up in the trailer. It had been tense, to say the least, when he had the gun up against my head. Rob, the boys and Zoe were shocked at my response and power, but more so over Cash deciding to like me.

Cash left and Rob went to work, so Zoe and I could finally visit and assess where we ended up. The boys stayed for a few hours and told us whom Cash was and filled us in about Rob and some of our new neighbors. Cash ran the place by supplying the drugs, prostitutes, and muscle around that neighborhood. Zoe and I had no idea what it was like to live in a trailer park filled with heroin addicts, with a few exceptions, in a poor black area on the edge of Atlanta, Georgia. The boys wished us a good night and left, saying that they would visit tomorrow. We told them how happy we were to have met them and bid them a good night too.

It was a star filled sky, warm and peaceful. Zoe and I sat on the front steps and smoked cigarettes, talking about our situation. We decided it was fun enough there, but that we needed to hook up with more hippy-type people. Zoe had been around the streets longer and

had done harder drugs than I had. Cash did not seem threatening to
Zoe. She even sort of liked him. I, on the other hand, hoped we had
seen the last of him. He was unpredictable, had a gun and I had seen
the way his eyes rolled when he hit himself up.

Rob kept his trailer a little funky and actually it was downright
dirty. After our morning coffee, the first thing we did was clean his
trailer and air it out. We all chain-smoked cigarettes inside the trailer
and it reeked of booze. Another sunny, warm, beautiful day and we
were content playing house in Atlanta. Rob got home from work
with some groceries and was appreciative about the cleaning we did.
We enjoyed lunch together and Rob went to sleep. Zoe and I were
on the front step, visiting, smoking and happy. The two neighbor
boys came over after school and we talked out front for a while. Rob
woke up and invited us all in for a joint, so we went in and began
another afternoon of partying. Rob chopped us a line of coke and
we drank some beers, smoking pot the whole time. We blasted
music, mostly Jimmy Hendrix, and danced. It came time for Rob to
leave for work and we said our evening good-byes.

The cute boy, Tommy, and I started making out on the couch and
soon went to Rob's bedroom. I shut the door and we got naked after
deciding that he would spend the night. His father worked in
another city during the week and was only home on the weekends so
he could stay. We were enjoying having sex and talking about life
until late in the night. We were having a great time together and
knew that Zoe and his friend were to. Tommy and I heard someone
arrive and talking in the living room, but we did not think much of it.
We just figured it was a friend looking for Rob.

The next thing we knew, the bedroom door opened and in came
Cash. Cash was super wasted and brandishing his gun. Cash was the
most feared man in the area so when he ordered Tommy to leave, he
did. Tommy grabbed his clothes and went into the living room. Zoe
and the boys were listening closely and wondering what to do about
the situation.

Cash hopped into the bed, next to me and tried to kiss me. He
was all over me and I started to fight back. He was much bigger than
I was, but he was also more wasted. His eyes were rolling up in his
head and his speech was slurred. For a second he put the gun down
on the floor next to the bed and jumped on top of me, trying to pull
his pants down at the same time. I punched him in his face and neck,

screamed, bit him and threw him onto the floor a couple of times. He kept trying to rape me, telling me he could do whatever he wanted with me. I grabbed his leg and put it through the window. Cash grabbed the gun from the floor and laid back needing to rest. Whatever he was high on kept him from feeling the full pain I was inflicting. All our fighting wore him out, but he still held the gun on me. I told him that I want to leave and he should just forget about it and go to sleep. I had him talked into letting me go, but he said, "You need to leave naked." I jumped at the opportunity and started to grab for the door handle when he pulled me back onto the bed.

We fought some more. I kicked him in his balls and choked him by pulling his head back by his hair but he kept fighting until he was tired again. He smoked a cigarette and kept the gun pointed at me. One of the boys knocked on the door and said they needed to talk to me. He shot the gun at the door and I heard panicked voices from the living area. I could not tell if anyone was hit but nobody left the trailer.

I was finally able to talk him into letting me go, by telling him that Zoe has a crush on him and she wants to make love with him. I told him I was Tommy's girlfriend but Zoe wanted him badly. I explained that I would get dressed and go out and get her. I half-put on my clothes fast and began to open the door, when Cash said, "I have a gun on you and will shoot you if you try anything." I opened the door and there was Zoe and the guys sitting on the couch directly in front of me. I looked at Zoe and with my hand down and in front of me, pointed to the door and signaled on the count of three. I put out one, then two, then three fingers and Zoe and I hit the door running. We heard gunshots and just kept hauling ass as fast as we could.

Tommy's trailer was much larger than Rob's. I dove under it, popped out the other side running like lightning, ran a few trailers away, and jumped into the back seat of a parked car. The car was filled with papers and crap, so I buried myself under it all. I did not know where Zoe ended up and hoped she was OK. I did not think she was shot and had no idea if the boys were.

I hid on the floor of the parked car until sunrise. The weirdest thought came; I realized that I had jumped under a doublewide trailer but my body never touched the ground. I knew then that some other force was at work here, probably a Guardian Angel. Finally I heard

Tommy's voice quietly calling me so I figured it was safe to come out. Boy, were we ever glad to see each other and had a lot to talk about over morning coffee. I told them what happened with Cash, how we fought and talked all night and that he never raped me. I told them what I said about Zoe wanting him so he would let me go. I was on edge wondering when Cash would show up again and what I would do.

We all went over to Tommy's trailer and he introduced us to his older brother. His brother and most of the trailer park heard the commotion and gunshot coming from Rob's all night. His brother was OK with us being around the trailer, we stayed there until Rob came home from work. When Rob returned we went over and told him what Cash did. The trailer was a wreck! I began picking up some of the things that got knocked over from my struggling and fighting. He had a broken window, glass and blood in the bed, and a bullet hole through the front of his trailer. Zoe and I cleaned the place up, all the while cursing Cash. I told Rob that we are going to stay at Tommy's tonight, because I was afraid Cash might come back for me. Rob felt sad for me and apologized over and over for what happened. I'm certain that Rob understood why I might not want to stay there. He said he was going to talk to Cash about what he did and tell him how un-cool and unacceptable that was. However, I knew that Cash was the man with the heroin, so whatever Rob would say, he would never offend him enough to jeopardize his only supply.

Zoe and I went over to Tommy's and visited in the living room while eating our sandwiches and watching television. I was startled by hard knocking at the door. In my gut I knew it was Cash. Cash knew we were inside the trailer but we did not answer the door. He began to pound harder and I thought he was going to break the flimsy door in. I went to the door, kept it closed, and yelled, "I never want to see you again, go away!" He explained that he is there to apologize and feels very bad about what happened. I told him that what he did is unforgivable and leave me alone. He begged for my forgiveness and started crying at the door jam. He said, "I have flowers for you and I feel like shit about what I did." I repeated myself, "No apology is good enough for what you did, fuck off!" He finally got in his car and drove off, leaving the flowers on the doorstep. We were not expecting his reaction and were relieved to know he wasn't going to kill us. Tommy and his brother were afraid of Cash, as were everyone else in the area, all except Zoe and myself.

A week went by and on our walks Zoe and I made some other friends in the trailer park. We met a hippy dude with hair down to his mid-back who was outside washing his van. He lived on the trailer lot across from where our block ended. He was cool and not a junkie -- just joints and wine. Zoe and I visited with him at his place a few times, but he did not want anything to do with Rob. He told us, "Rob is a junkie and has dangerous friends." I told him how I knew that all too well. He wondered what we were doing there and advised us to keep on hitchhiking. He seemed to really care about us and wanted us out of there. We liked him and trusted him but we stayed put anyway. Why we stayed there at all remains a mystery to me.

We also made friends with an older, teen-aged woman who lived across the street. She was a skinny blonde who had no problem dressing up to show off her body. She went heavy on the makeup and carried herself like a horny, young piece of ass. She was feisty and liked to party. The stories she told us about her plans and things like birth control pills raised my eyebrows. I wanted birth control pills but was afraid that a clinic would turn me in to the police. I was not using condoms with Tommy and we did not give much thought to pregnancy. Like a fool, I assumed that I wouldn't be one of those knocked up girls.

This wild young woman liked to do drugs, hang out, and drink beer with us. She was always posing it seemed, so she stood in the doorway with her butt showing to the street. She never talked about it, but she was into heroin if anyone gave it to her. She had recently moved to the trailer park and lives with her older brother, a hot-rod car fanatic. Her brother never came over to visit and was gone most of the time, either working-out at the gym or with his girlfriends. Life in the trailer park was getting more interesting all the time. Cash only came by once and he acted politely and the visit was brief.

Occasionally Zoe and I walked around the neighborhood, up to the corner store, and on to a diner. Cash felt horrible about trying to rape me -- and he should have -- that he put Zoe and me on his account with the diner. He also gave us each fifty dollars. We ate at the diner a few mornings a week. I always ordered the same thing. I lived on cheddar cheese omelets, grits, toast, and strawberry jam. Zoe spent some of her time at Rob's while I was at Tommy's house

being lovey-dovey. Zoe and I were a team and were never away from
each other for more than a few hours at a time. Zoe and I spent the
nights at Tommy's house, and made a point to visit with Rob every
day. Rob loved our company and we made him laugh a lot with our
stories.

Rob got me a job at a hotel and drove me there to meet my new
boss. This woman was a dyed blonde, about fifty years old, heavy,
and had her pistol on the counter. She was a no-bullshit lady and
wasted no time in putting me to work cleaning the rooms. This hotel
was a bit nicer than a dump and was on the strip outside the airport.
I went into my first room to clean and was promptly grossed out.
There were dirty condoms in the sheets and the place stunk of roach
spray and cheap perfume. I quit in my mind, but had to stay there
until Rob returned to pick me up, after his shift. I did the best I
could to pass the time, including ripping off some cartons of
cigarettes. Vending machine robbery and cash box theft from
laundry mats were two of the skills the Cat Burglar taught me,
besides running on top of chain link fences. Rob picked me up and I
told my tough-ass boss, "Thanks, but the job is not right for me" and
we and split.

Two weekends later Tommy's friends from another part of
Atlanta came over and wanted to see Rob. There was Tommy, his
three friends, Rob, Zoe and myself packed into Rob's tiny trailer.
These friends wanted to sell Rob some pot and THC pills. We were
having a great time together. I ate one of the THC pills and smoked
a hit of opium. I did not know then that opium was the same as
heroin. This was a sticky, black paste that had a sweetish smell to it.
Wow, I had a happy high going on. Tommy's friends were going to
go to a concert later that night, in Underground Atlanta. The concert
was ELO, the Electric Light Orchestra, and the "Underground" is
just that. Underground Atlanta was like a small city of nightlife built
under the ground. There was some talk about us joining them and
we hoped that they'd take us along.

Things turned drastically when Cash came over. He could not
know about any drug transactions on his turf. These white boys
from the suburbs were in more danger than they realized. Cash put
out some lines of cocaine for us and cooked up a few syringes full of
heroin. For himself, Cash had one syringe of speed and another of
heroin. He tied off both of his arms with tourniquets. He acted like

he was in a hurry to get drugs pumped into his veins, he must have been needing it badly. We watched as he hit himself up, slowly in one arm, and then the other. He was so high that he began to pull blood back into the syringes and squeeze it back into his veins. He stared at the needles dangling from his arms and kept them hanging there like he was admiring them. Sick. Well, it did not stop there; Zoe asked to be hit up with heroin and I flipped out!

Hearing Zoe say that she wanted to be hit up suddenly made perfect sense to me. Now I knew what her and Rob were doing together on those evenings. I jumped up and yelled, "I will kick your ass if you do it!" Cash got in my face and asked me, "who the fuck do you think you are? She can do whatever she wants to". I did not back down a spec and stood up as tall as I could, puffed up in fact. I told her, "this is going to be It!" The whole trailer went silent and all eyes were on us. Cash jumped back in my face and asked me if I ever did heroin before? I told him I never tried it but know it is bad and that's where I draw a line. He told me, "Shut the fuck up, unless you have tried it and know what you are talking about." I was furious and disgusted looking at Zoe sitting there in want.

The scene was intense, seven of us packed into a tiny trailer and I was going to choke Zoe half to death. I snatched up the straw and snorted a big line of heroin and said, "There, I did it, Now, I will kick her ass if she does it!" I pulled Zoe out of the trailer, kicking and screaming, with Tommy and his friends following. Everyone was giving me a hard time for being so controlling of Zoe and threatening her. I told everyone, "Fucking leave me alone and she is not going to become a junkie when she's with me."

Zoe had spent two afternoons with Cash and had sex with him for money, which is probably when he got her hooked in the first place. I believed that he was preparing her to be a drug-addicted prostitute and I wasn't going to let it happen.

Zoe was angry at me at first but as soon as we were in downtown Atlanta her mood changed. We were back to being tight as ever, with a new city to explore and go wild in. To get downtown we, Tommy and his friends, hopped on a train, onto the outside of it. Hopping the train was exhilarating: running up alongside of the train, grabbing onto the rail, hopping up, and hanging tight. It was fairly easy and Tommy's friends knew the right place to catch it. Atlanta was exciting and we were going to see the Electric Light Orchestra in the

Underground. The heroin I had snorted earlier had already kicked in
and worn off, so we ate a hit of acid – welcome to another world. I
had a glide to my stride, accompanied by a joy giving halo everywhere
I looked, colorful too. I was wearing farmer pants with no shirt on,
still a tomboy at heart. I had no breasts to speak of anyway, ½ a size
A. Nobody ever thought I was a girl.

After a spirit transporting show we went to a party in a nearby
luxury hotel. Some partyers at the concert invited us there for a
hugely festive time. We walked over and found it to be our
glamorous new playground. We wandered in the entrance and
headed towards the elevators, we looked like trouble. I noticed a
closed restaurant and bar off of the lobby blocked only by brass
stands with velvet covered ropes. Zoe and I bypassed them with
ease. We grabbed a few bottles of wine and I put two bottles into my
farmer pants and we walked out smoothly. We got away with it! The
party was happening and they were passing around the biggest joints
I ever laid eyes on. These extra-long rolling papers are wild. The
hotel was filled with church groups for some sort of religious
convention. Our party hosts were with a church group from
Nashville, Tennessee. We partied into the wee hours of the morning
and what fun it was!

Out on the street I found a wooden box and took it to the corner
of a major intersection. This is downtown Atlanta and the streets
were busy, both with pedestrians and traffic. I jumped on top of the
box and started to mimic my father preaching. Nobody even gave
notice. It must be a hard profession to be a "soap box" Preacher.

We all decided to go over to Tommy's friend's house in the
suburbs. We took a train to his stop and saw that he lived in an
upscale area. At his house there was a spacious recreation room
downstairs and everyone congregated there, at first. The guy who
lived there was a gorgeous young man, with flawless olive skin, and
he wanted to visit with me privately. I went into his bedroom and we
laid on the bed, caressing and talking about life. He said that he was
shocked by how smart I am. I am certain that I spoke of freedom
and creativity because that's what my life was all about. He told me
that his friend thought Zoe was nuts. I thought, 'so what' and
ignored what he said. I did have sex with this beautiful olive-skinned
young man. I knew that Tommy assumed that we had sex so when I
returned to his side he was a bit colder towards me. His friends gave

us a ride back to the trailer park and we never saw these friends of Tommy's again. Tommy and I grew distant after that night, with him knowing that I was not faithful whatsoever, yet.

One night at Tommy's, there were some friends of his older brother and they gave us some very strong THC pills. Zoe and I got extremely high and I was spacing into everything, like morphing. We were drinking tequila, doing lines of coke, and smoking a lot of weed too. Tommy's brother had a video for "tripping" people to watch, with whirling colors and flashes of light. I was being drawn into the video and listening to the music when Zoe hit the floor. I freaked out and had to think fast. I yelled, "We must drop her off at the hospital entrance, now!" None of us had a car so the guys quickly debated the options. Tommy and his friend thought that we might be able to borrow the neighbor's new hot-rod. I went over to his trailer with Tommy and walked in the door. We found the owner alone and sleeping on the couch. I said, "Hey, Hey' Hey", and he just made gurgles for a response. I asked him if I could borrow his car to take my friend to the hospital and he groaned. I took groan for "Yes", took his car keys, and ran.

We pulled up to Tommy's trailer and put Zoe into the back seat and took off to the hospital. I was shaking with worry for both Zoe and myself. Tommy was driving. Just a few blocks away the car stopped dead in the street. We were stuck right in front of a notoriously dangerous housing project at night, in a broken down hot-rod, and super high. I was screaming, "Get it going" terrified that Zoe might die at any second. I was pacing around the car and kept screaming. Suddenly, the car burst into flames and we scrambled and pulled Zoe out immediately. Thank goodness we were already outside of the car, except Zoe. We all dragged her onto the lawn. At the same time, we heard police sirens blaring. I could not believe what was happening, hoping I was going to wake up from this nightmare any minute.

Tommy, his friend and I pulled Zoe into a woods, not far away and hid her in some bushes. We ran back to watch discretely what was happening. We saw police cars and fire trucks. The car was a goner and we watched while they loaded it onto a wrecking truck. We knew better than to show our faces and I was terrified over Zoe. We went back to the forest for Zoe and saw that she was looking slightly more alive than earlier. We pulled Zoe back up the wooded slope to the trailer park. We sat Zoe on the front steps of Tommy's trailer and I sat beside her. Tommy and his friend went inside to make us some strong coffee and I hugged Zoe.

I knew that trailers have thin walls, especially when it came to sound, but hearing the conversation in Rob's trailer next door was uncanny. I heard a crucial earful! I knew that something mysterious was happening when I could hear every word. The men inside, burnt car owner for one, were so outraged about the car being stolen and burned that they wanted us dead.

The man who owned the burned car, Rob, and some other guys said that they were going to kill us and since nobody knew shit about us they would get away with it. It's true we were runaways and if someone found us dead at the side of some road, who would really think that it was worth investigating? Dead runaway girls wouldn't surprise many folks.

The guys in the trailer did not know that I heard what they were planning, so I simply walked in, went to the bedroom, grabbed my pack, and stuffed it with our things. It took twenty seconds, tops. I walked out of the trailer and helped Zoe up on her feet. I started to walk away from the trailer with her on my arm and told her what I overheard. I told that we were on our way to the highway and had to get there as fast as possible. We were getting the heck out of the state. I told her that those guys want us dead and this is very serious. I was thinking the murder plot would sober her up faster. We walked a few blocks and our hippy neighbor pulled over to see if we need a ride. We were saved!

Our hippy neighbor was a true Guardian Angel and he understood that we were in bad trouble. He got us drunk on "Annie Green Springs" wine and drove us all the way to the South Carolina state line. We thanked him gigantically, hugged and hopped out of the van. Back on the open road again, knowing we barely made it out of Atlanta with our lives. Zoe was a heroin addict and what a fabulous mess we were in. I could only repeat, "Great, just great!"

Zoe and I were picked up by a country-man driving a pickup truck. He was wearing dusty clothes and had a rifle in his rear window rack. After what we had been through, he did not seem scary at all; but he sure was strange. Zoe sat in the middle and we drove up the highway. The man was probably in his early forties, slender, wearing jeans and a cowboy hat. He had a deep southern accent that I could not get used to.

He began to say the most fucked up things. He said, "So, I know you girls want some beef steak" and put his hand on his crotch. I had no patience for creeps after the night we just went through. He was really the one in danger here. I said," No, we do not." He said, "Oh, yes you do" and put his hand on Zoe's leg. Zoe just froze solid. I grabbed his hand off her and threw it back at him. I firmly told him to just pull over and let us out. He said some more crap about sexual needs, as he pulled over and let us out. "What an asshole", I said to Zoe, who was a bit shaken from it all. I was still picking forest debris out of Zoe's hair, left from her overdosed night in the woods. Off we went, thumbs out, returning north to North Carolina. Zoe and I decided to go back to Fort Bragg and visit Dan.

We were picked up within five minutes and our ride was with a semi-truck driver and his best friend. These two guys were wacky beyond belief. We were piled into the cab of the, slicked-out, semi-truck. It was huge inside, with a loft bed and space behind the seats. These guys and us were laughing and smoking pot, plus they had some reds and booze, too. We were hauling ass down the highway in a torrential downpour having a party.

The driver wanted to get something from his pack and left me to steer the truck. I was as nervous as I could be and tried to pretend I was cool. We could have died at any moment. I had no control over this truck in the rain, just worked to keep the truck going straight. Zoe and I were very wasted and tired, with all the excitement and drugs. We went barreling up the highway and were let out at the intersection on I95 where Dan worked.

We surprised Dan and he was happy to see us! We told him about our adventures and he was glad we were still alive. His best friend, Ron, came by the station and we were introduced. We had a great time visiting and were going to meet back up with Ron the next morning. We went to Dan's place after he finished his work shift, to shower up and change. We could finally wash our clothes! I had stuffed our things into a bag, dirty or not, when making our getaway from Atlanta. The three of us met Ron for breakfast and they went all out for us, steak and eggs, and Bloody Marys. We spent the day with Dan and Ron having fun and driving around Fort Bragg.

The weather was beautiful, sunny and warm with a gentle breeze. Zoe and I spent the night shift with Dan at the gas station and hashed out our plans. I know he was glad that we were rid of Beth and I told him how she turned me in for kissing a boy. I was entertained mostly by listening to the interactions over the CB. Zoe and I were privy to many sleazy things going on out there, on the highway, in the night. There were some prostitutes who had their CB code names and conducting business with the truck drivers. The life of a trucker is another world all their own.

The next day, we went to breakfast and Ron presented Zoe and me with a proposition. We would sell drugs at the Blue Oyster Cult and Foghat Concert in return for being taken great care of. We agreed to sell drugs for them and thought the show would be a rocking time. That same day Dan moved from his trailer into a condominium with us. Ron lived somewhere else but he spent almost all of his time with us. Ron was mysterious and we never saw his home, maybe he had a wife? I had a crush on Ron and Zoe liked Dan a lot.

Ron was very protective of me and showed it. He was much older, a little overweight, Italian-looking, and quiet. I snuggled up next to him, with my clothes on, and we would fall asleep. I slept with my head on his chest and his big arm around my shoulder. We never spoke about anything sexual and nothing sexual ever happened between us. I felt safe and protected, and I was. I did not sleep this well in Georgia, as anyone could guess.

Dan, Ron, Zoe and I cruised around in Ron's Camaro Convertible and they took us through the whole city. The men seemed to be scoping things out, as if looking for something, but they didn't say. The condo was nice, bright, clean and big. Our new friends were completely sane compared to the people we met in Georgia. These two men were real drug dealers and we were officially working for them now. They took us to restaurants often and gave us all the drugs we wanted. They did not have anything to do with heroin, luckily. There was plenty of pot to smoke, cocaine, LSD, booze and they kept us in cigarettes. The weather was splendid and so were our lives!

Zoe and I were anticipating an exciting first day with our new job. They drove us to the huge concert and parked the car out of the way. Zoe and I were given hits of purple windowpane acid to sell. They told us to keep coming back to the car to drop off the money and get more acid if we needed to. Ron and Dan were going to be spending the day in the car, waiting and watching. I wore my farmer jeans and had the acid in my bib pocket. Zoe was standing with me and keeping an eye on what was happening around me. The show was wild, loud and packed with southern, crazy partyers. I went to a place on the ground level in the auditorium that I felt was perfect, and yelled, "Get your acid here!"

A line quickly formed and I was instantly doing a steady stream of business. Finally I told Zoe that we have to go back to the car and drop off the money. We both had our pockets filled to overflowing with bills, plus I needed to pick up more acid. Dan and Ron were thrilled to see us and excited at how well we were doing. They were smiling and praising us as we got out of the car. Back at the show the same thing happened. I yelled out, "Get acid here!" That was all I did and the people in line brought new people into the line. I handed out hits of acid and took dollar bills, soon filling my pockets and Zoe's, again. We went to the car and dropped off the cash, got more acid and returned to the show. Dan and Ron were bubbling over with happiness. We took some time off selling and danced to the music of Blue Oyster Cult. The crowd was colorful and filled with military looking guys. The show was just the change we needed to let loose again and shake off Georgia. What a day at work, I like this job.

Ron and Dan were overjoyed with us, and the mountain of money we made them. The guys had dollar signs in their eyes and fantasized about our bright future together. We were wined and dined to celebrate our success.

The next night, at around 9:00, the guys drove us to an intersection near the army base. "Army Base?" I asked them. Dan told us about Fort Bragg and how big it is. Army men consumed a lot of drugs, every kind that exists. The intersection was hopping, with young people walking around in the streets and piling in and out of the bars and party houses. The night was warm and humid; I had a strange gut feeling. I don't know why but the Army was not my scene and I discovered that I have a uniform phobia. We parked the car and Dan and Ron told us they would be there waiting for us. I was loaded up with acid, Zoe was with me and we went to the party intersection. We roamed around for a bit and then saw our perfect spot to sell.

We went into a party-house, swarming with very drunk and

boisterous people. This was clearly an "Army Place" and it was obvious that Zoe and I were foreigners. We walked to the back of the house to a porch, just off the kitchen, and I told some people I have acid for sale, if they want some. The people got so excited about being able to buy acid that they were pushing and cutting in line to be next. We sold many hits of acid there and decided that to be safe it was time to change our location. We went to the side of a bar, in the darkness, where lots of people were partying. I was selling some hits to two guys when I heard a man yelling and coming towards us. Quickly, I handed the acid to the guys and stuffed the money in my pocket. Zoe and I began to walk fast in the opposite direction of the yelling man.

I knew something was wrong and my heart was racing. The man screamed, "stop them, they are rip-offs, the acid is fake!" The man was close to us and a crowd was gathering fast. He said, "I took the acid hours ago and nothing happened." Then another man said that he was not feeling anything either. The crowd was getting scary and wanted to beat us. We ran like wild fire and jumped into the convertible. We shouted to Ron, "Haul ass!" Ron and Dan saw the mob and floored that gas pedal, squealing out of there.

I was fuming angry with Ron and Dan for not telling us they made us into rip-offs. They endangered us by not telling us that the acid is fake, those assholes! I knew that a lot more people knew who I was than me knowing who they were. I told Dan and Ron that I was no longer selling at the GI intersection. We got away this time, but might not be so lucky in the future. I told them, "Get some real drugs to sell or forget it." Ron and Dan never saw me upset before and were trying to calm me down, promising they would never do that to me again. Zoe was not nearly as verbal as I was, just kept saying, "Yeah."

The next morning, after we ate breakfast at our favorite restaurant, we decided to drive around. We passed by two, hippy guys hitchhiking at the highway on-ramp. Dan and Ron thought it would be fun to pick them up and check them out. We doubled back and picked up the two guys. The guys seemed like a fun duo so we invited them back to our condo for a smoke.

Zoe and I liked these two men a lot and I had my eyes set on one of them. Luckily for our friendship Zoe liked the other one, which seemed common for us. The two guys spent the night with us at the condo and we partied until sun up. Dan went to work his night shift and Ron stayed with us. The next afternoon, Ron and Dan had to go do some errands and the four of us stayed at the condo. We were all smoking pot and laughing about life. It was a beautiful day and I invited the guy that I was gaga for to go for a walk. We walked back into the wooded area of the property and sat on a log in the sunshine. Minutes later, we lay down on the other side of the log and proceeded to have sex. He was so much fun . . . and sexy too! We walked back to the condo and acted as if nothing intimate happened. Zoe and the other guy looked like they had sex; being nervous with their hair tussled. The four of us drank some beers and shared our hitchhiking stories.

Ron and Dan returned and seemed happy to see us. I missed them and wondered what my next job was going to be. Ron took out a baggie of coke, chopped up some lines and the party started. The six of us joked around, high and drunk, again until it was light out. We all went out and ate a hearty breakfast; I was so hungry. Ron and Dan told the hitchhikers that we were dropping them off at the best place to get a ride. That was that, the hitchhikers were dropped off, we said our good-byes, and waved them good luck. Ron and Dan told us that the reason they had picked them up was to rob them. I was shocked that they were going to do such a horrible thing to those guys. They told us that they picked up hitchhikers from time to time, took their money, and let them go. Ron said, "We did not rob them because you liked them and were having fun."

These men were not the sweethearts that I thought they were. My impression of Dan and Ron was souring and I was not as animated as I was before. It was pretty obvious that I was no longer enthralled by our arrangement. I spoke with Zoe about leaving and heard how she felt about it. Zoe was ready to move on, too. She wanted to visit her old boyfriend. Zoe wanted a big change and I knew we had to stay together so I agreed to it. It wasn't like I had big, demanding plans of my own.

The next day we said good-bye to Dan and Ron, explaining to them that we had to go north ... now. We thanked them and they were sad to see us go. They dropped us off at the highway and gave us some money, cigarettes, hash and pot. We waved good-bye and were free with our thumbs out, once again.

Two young men in a festive mood and very wasted picked us up.

The men are paratroopers and on their vacation leave. The two men were members of a sky diving club and were on their way to the clubhouse to party. The conversation between us was light hearted and full of laughter. I thought to myself that these were actually sweet young men; what a change. The men invited Zoe and me to go to the Sky Dive Club with them and have a drink. We didn't have anything else to do, so we went with them. The four of us were drinking beer and enjoying ourselves, while we rode for hours in pasturelands and into the middle of nowhere. It was getting dark out and the stars lit up the sky; more stars than I had ever seen before. We were far out in the country, somewhere in North Carolina. Way off in the distance, we saw some lights and the Dare Devil Dudes began hooting and shouting out the windows. The Sky Divers Club was just up ahead.

We walked in the club behind our new friends who knew almost everyone there. Being the only girls in the bar, many men treated us to drinks and wanted to know all about us. Zoe and I just said we were passing through and took the Dare Devils up on their invitation to see this place. These guys can party it up! Some of the skydivers invited us to jump with them in the morning, but no way was I going with them. I always wanted to sky dive, but knew that these guys were going to be very hung-over come morning. When I sky dive I will do it with sober people, thank-you. I may have been a runaway, but I showed flashes of good sense, now and again.

Later on, the four of us drove to the other side of the field to an old farmhouse. The farmhouse was charming, with large rooms and beautiful, old woodwork. We laid around in the living room smoking hash and listening to music. Eventually we fell asleep on various couches, curled up on the floor, and in chairs. I woke up earlier than the others, walked outside and was struck with beauty. The farmhouse was located in a lush, green field, spanning hundreds of acres. The sun was just coming up and the dewy mist was lifting from the valley floor. This place was heavenly. Zoe woke and came outside with our coffee and also enjoyed the tranquil view. Being in a truly peaceful place gave us a foreign feeling of deep calm. It was time to hit the road again and our new friends drove us back to the highway. We thanked our sweet, Dare Devil, friends for the precious time and wished them well.

Thumbs out again and savoring how relaxed and happy we felt.

Zoe was so excited to be going back to her hometown that she was jumping out of her skin. I was ready for a change myself. She missed her boyfriend terribly and she hadn't spoken with him the entire time we were gone. Months earlier, we had agreed not to make any phone calls on the off-chance that the phone lines were tapped.

We were picked up and driven to Baltimore, Maryland, by two guys that were crazier than us. They were in their early twenties and joy riding. We told them that we had some cocaine to sell and they arranged a meeting with their friends. We met up with them at the far end of an enormous mall parking lot. The friend of these guys pulled his car up to the window and we made the deal. I held out one hand with the coke and the other hand to take the cash. He placed his hand with the bills in my hand, while taking the coke with his other hand. Then he snatched the money back. These guys' friends drove off, ripping me off, and there was nothing I could do about it. I learned a few lessons and was angry, mostly with myself for trusting them. I thought about doing drug deals differently in the future. I was bitching and moaning, while Zoe and I got out of the car. We thanked the guys for the ride and we did not have to mention how pissed I was over the cocaine deal. I had made that clear.

What an overload of culture shock, walking through a giant shopping mall with Zoe. The mall was brightly lit and filled with shoppers moving along to elevator music. It was a surreal shift in reality for me. Zoe and I went into a boutique and she stole a shirt. I wasn't in the mood to steal anything, especially with me carrying drugs. I still had some coke, pot, hashish and 2 hits of real acid. I should have stolen some shoes though, I left my only sneakers in Fort Bragg and was bare foot. It was apparent that we were trouble; untamed was written all over us. Mall Security was closing in and breathing down our necks. We decided to run for it. We bolted out of shopping mall and got away.

We were walking towards the highway and saw women's clothes hanging on a clothes line. The clothes looked like they would fit us so we snuck into the yard. We quietly took a few items and snuck away, breaking into an all-out dash as soon as we were on the street. I had new, green army pants! Zoe gave me one of her old shirts I liked, because she had her new ones. We were feeling pretty slick and free about our life while we walked to the highway ramp.

Thumbs out and away we went.

We were promptly picked up and taken about an hour north. A short ride but we were relieved to be out of Baltimore. Zoe and I were enjoying making plans for our future and decided to take a hit of acid and just enjoy walking down the highway for spell. The acid came on and we started laughing at everything, kidding about purple armadillos coming to get us and spent hours gazing at the sky. What a hilarious break from traveling; simply roaming along the highway. After enough of walking, we stuck our thumbs out. This next ride was from a nice businessman going to Scranton, Pennsylvania. We hopped in his car and Zoe and I slept the whole way.

Scranton was grey and dreary on this day, gloom loomed. We walked over to a truck stop to get something to eat, both, Zoe and I were ravenous and gobbled down the meal. While we were enjoying our omelets a man chatted us up. He was a truck driver who had his sixteen year old son and his sons' best friend with him. They were having a "Guys" truck driving trip together. He paid for our meals and invited us to his hotel room to use the shower. His son and his friend were shooting pool downstairs and we thought, why not? He seemed nice enough and was, after all, traveling with his son. Zoe and I went up to his hotel room and Zoe began to shower first. I waited, smoking a cigarette and sitting at the dining table. The man told me that he was going downstairs to get his son and friend. He told me that they would be back in a minute and that they were going to have sex with us.

I could not believe this man's attitude and what he said, so casually. He walked out of the door. I banged on the bathroom door, got Zoe out of the shower, half naked in a towel, her clothes in hand. We ran outside, as fast as we could, and hid in the bushes. Zoe got herself dressed, while I told her what the man said. I knew they would search for us. We caught our breath and prepared ourselves for a run onto the highway ramp. We launched out of the bushes and ran like lightening. The boys were chasing us and their father was right behind. They were dangerous lunatics and flailing their arms around like Barbarians. We had some real trouble with these men.

We got onto the on-ramp, which was brightly lit with plenty of passersby. The guys backed off and walked back towards the truck stop. Holy Shit, was that a close one and would have been gruesome.

This father was going to rape us with his son and sons' best friend. 'The world has plenty of sick fucks' I thought to myself, shaking my head. We were picked up within minutes and happy to be out of there!

Finally, we arrived back in upstate New York, in a little town, forty miles outside of the city where my family was. Zoe took us to her friend's house, Lisa, an older woman living in an even older farmhouse. Lisa was looked upon as a grandmother to a group of older teens in the town. Lisa's door was always open to them so she had many houseguests. Zoe had known this woman for years and stayed there many times before. I got a weird feeling from this woman and did not trust her like the rest of the gang did. Zoe was reacquainted with her love, Chris, and I never saw her happier. They acted like a married couple, as if no time passed since they were last together.

We stayed in this little town for a few days and visited many of her, long time, friends. I liked being in Zoe's territory and meeting some of the people that I heard so much about. The weather was perfect and the town was lush with beautiful, tree-lined streets. We were invited to a big party and were looking forward to it. There were at least fifty of us, high on acid and coke, smoking joint after joint and drinking tequila. The music was blaring, a rock-n-roll frenzy, with people dancing everywhere. The party went on into the early morning hours and we stayed until the end. I curled up in the corner of the living room and slept. I woke up and discovered that someone ripped me off. Some pot, hashish and money were taken from my pants pocket while I slept. I was enraged that someone would rip me off at Zoe's friend's house and by her, so-called, friends. I was cursing and stomping my feet: pacing the floors and wondering how to get my stuff back. Zoe was shocked that her friends did such a horrible thing to us; it was half hers' too.

Zoe's lover has a best friend, Paul, who I liked a lot. Paul was handsome and quietly showed his intelligence. Zoe and I convinced Chris and Paul that North Carolina was full of money-making opportunities. Zoe and I talked up Fort Bragg, the perfect weather, music shows, and how nice it was to be away from New York. The guys decided to join us in hitchhiking south, and the four of us departed the very next morning. 'Maybe I will actually get to the ocean this time' I thought.

It was early in the morning, about 5:00, when the four of us hitchhiked into the city. I had them wait for me on the block behind my parent's house, while I snuck into my house. I tiptoed up the stairs to my bedroom and grabbed some clothes, and stopped at my mother's purse and took her cash. I was on my way out the door when my father heard me. He jumped up and ran after me, but I was long gone. He had no doubt that it was me and the police were called immediately. I ran through the backyard to my friends and we swiftly made it to the highway. Because there were four of us, we thought we should split up to raise our chances of getting rides. We agreed to meet in North Carolina at the gas station where Dan works.

Paul and I decided to give Zoe and Chris the first ride and off they went. Paul and I were walking along the highway, just south of the city, when a State Trooper pulled up. The Trooper began to ask Paul, "Where we you going?", when I darted off into the woods. As soon as I ran, Paul was put into the police car and the foot chase ensued. I ran through high brush and climbed over two fences, just to be tackled in the swamp. The policeman had a hold of me and took me to the car. I was handcuffed and thrown in the backseat with Paul.

Paul and I were driven to the police station and immediately separated from each other. Paul was older than sixteen and would, most likely, be let off. Paul did not break any laws, technically. He was just hitchhiking, not wanted. He was a nice young man from a middle class home and graduated high school, more than I could say for most of our friends. I, on the other hand, resisted arrest, ran from the cops, and was a runaway. There was no way that I would be let off.

I was arrested and booked, then driven to the Juvenile Detention Center. I was admitted, took the lice bath, and was shown to my room by the guard who locked the door behind me. This time, I felt much differently about being locked up. I was used to being entirely free and had more angst in my blood than ever. I was mad and wanted out! I wanted the whole system, the police, and my father to leave me alone. I wondered about Zoe and how would she ever know where I was? I wanted to be there, free in the South, with them. I hoped their future together will be wonderful and began crying. I cried myself to sleep.

During the night, a guard knocked on my door and said that Zoe

had been arrested in Pennsylvania and was being transported there
now. In the morning we were let out of our cells and told to line up
against the wall. There was Zoe, tired and looked like shit. Zoe and
I had tons to talk about and did so throughout the day. She said that
the State Troopers got her, too. Chris was booked into a
Pennsylvania jail and released after they ran checks on him. We knew
that we were in really big trouble this time and even slightly worried.
I was not only in legal trouble, but ended up with a deep Southern
accent. I formed the accent in Georgia and it solidified in North
Carolina, embarrassing me.

I went to court that day and saw my parents for the first time in
months. Seeing them was very emotional for all of us and I wanted
to go home, more than anything. My lawyer was there. She didn't
like me very much, saying, "You need a good spanking." I laughed
at her which did not make things any better. She was a court-
appointed lawyer and thought all delinquent girls should be sent to
Catholic detention schools. My probation officer was so far out of
the loop on this arrest that she wasn't even at court.

I missed my mom and siblings very much and wanted to see Will
and Eileen. I would have gone home long before this, but resisted
the temptation, knowing that my father would lay his control freak
demands on me. My dad was over the top with keeping me cooped
up, but now I couldn't blame him. The tension between my father
and I was thick; boiling enemies in the same room. I was sentenced
to go back to the detention home for the next three weeks, while the
court appointed psychiatrists coducted tests on me. Back to the
"Home on the Hill", as, us juvenile delinquents called it.

I knew that Zoe has been through a lot and was heartbroken right
then, but that did not explain everything about her behavior. She
looked sicker each day and had less energy as time went on. One
morning Zoe couldn't come out of her room because she felt too ill.
She was brought in to see the Detention Center's doctor and he ran
some tests. She had hepatitis and was quarantined from that moment
on. I waved and smiled at her through the little window of her cell.
Zoe made goofy, loving faces at me, but looked bored to tears in
there. She had to stay in quarantine for at least a week and it was a
miracle that I didn't catch it from her. We shared joints, glasses,
cigarettes and a hairbrush. It was truly amazing that I was healthy,
despite the runaway diet. She was taking powerful medication and

getting better every day.

The Guards were the same ones that I knew from before and felt some comfort from that. They expressed their gladness that Zoe and I were OK. The Guards had known Zoe for years before they met me and seemed to sincerely care about her. It was a full house at the Detention Home and nothing like the Country Club treatment we had in Florida. The other teens and Guards enjoyed hearing about the country club we were locked up in. I told them all about shooting pool, sunbathing, water fights, and great food. The Guards knew Beth and didn't like hearing how she had ratted me out earlier, landing me in Solitary Confinement. Our memories and storytelling helped the days pass, seemingly getting longer and more dreary.

The long, legal journey of deciding what to do with me began. I went to court every ten days, or, so, and each time I was sentenced back to the Detention Center. My parents saw me once a week at visiting time and it was always emotional. My father was doing all he could to persuade the Judge to send me home but it was not going very well. The Judge, my lawyer, and my probation officer were all tired of my complete disrespect for any kind of authority. Now, they wanted to find out, "Just how crazy is she, really?"

No other teenager in the Juvenile Detention Center had a caring parent at court. Nobody wanted these teens anymore. Granted, some of them were real trouble and I didn't see much good coming from their behavior. Some of the crimes committed by these teens were pure evil, no other way to put it. Jealousy began to grow against me with the other inmates, because I was still loved by my parents.

Melody was the biggest bitch of them all! I met Melody there before and we never got along. She was a white toughie from the ghetto and in lock-up for violating her probation by turning tricks on the street. She was a real sleazy woman who hated me. She started a rumor that the only reason I haven't been sent up the river, meaning to a long-term detention center, was because I gave the Judge blowjobs in his chambers. OK, that pissed me off! She would walk by me and call me "slut" and other nasty things. I would have pounded her little ass and loved every moment of it, but knew it would be catastrophic for my release negotiations. This is when the dodge ball games got fun. I slammed Melody, for blood, and got an enormous amount of my anger out.

Meanwhile, I began to feel tenderness in my abdomen and did not think much about it, at first. The days went on and the tenderness turned into severe pain. I told a Guard about my discomfort and she made an appointment for me to see the doctor who works there. The doctor asked me some questions, palpated a bit of my abdomen and prescribed Maalox. The doctor said that I have an ulcer and need to drink this nasty liquid at every meal. A Guard brought me my Maalox at every mealtime, when she walked around the dining room with her tray of medications, handing them out to many inmates.

In the morning, the Guard unlocked my door and ushered me out, to line up in the hallway for breakfast. I could not stand up straight because I was in too much pain. I told her that I needed to stay in my room because the pain is too much to walk. The Guard was well-acquainted with me and my big appetite, and what a social gal I was, so she knew right away that my condition was serious. The Guard was not sure what to do and told me to rest while she called the doctor. I curled up in fetal position and tried to sleep the agony away.

The Detention Center Doctor was unavailable that day. He was there only one day a week and this was not it. The Guard liked me a lot and knew that I was very sick. We both thought that I could die, but neither of us said it. She decided to take control of the situation herself and broke the rules. She telephoned my father and told him to meet us at the hospital. She drove me to the hospital, where my father and my younger brother met me. Why my father brought my little brother along to such a dramatic event is beyond me.

I was walked into an examination room while my father was outside dealing with the paperwork. The doctor examined me, I gave a urine sample and then he took a pap smear and felt my abdomen. The Guard waited outside the examination room door with my father and brother. A nurse stayed with me the whole time and waited for the test results to come back. The test results showed that I had a severe infection. I had very advanced gonorrhea that had turned into "pelvic inflammatory disease." Another nurse entered the room with a big syringe of antibiotics. "I do not do shots!" I screamed. I threw a huge temper tantrum about the shot, refusing and fighting the nurses back.

The two nurses were not strong enough to hold me down and called for help. The Guard and my father came bursting through the door and a doctor was right behind them. My father told me that I would die without the shot and I told him, "I don't care, I'll die then" and kept fighting them off. I was overpowered by the doctor, who took a no-bullshit manner with me. I got the shot in my butt and the commotion stopped. Suddenly the room was quiet, for the moment the doctor wrote my prescription for antibiotics.

The doctor said, "You will, most likely, not be able to have children, because of the scar tissue formed by the advanced infection." My father seemed concerned for me when he heard this news from the doctor. He topped it off with, "You had only two more days, tops, before you would have died."

My poor brother came there to overhear his sister screaming, swearing, and given a shot. I never had a chance to speak with my brother and the whole ordeal drained me. The Guard took my arm and we said good-bye to my father. We walked out of the hospital room and down the hallway, waving to my little brother as I was escorted past him. My brother looked worried look and he didn't know much about the conditions I was under. He is so sweet and I loved him deeply. My heart grew heavy when I saw his face and I longed to be home with my family.

The Guard had saved my life! We were back into the car and at the Detention Center, ending the dramatic episode. I stayed in my room the rest of the day and slept. I was glad to have had the antibiotics and started to feel a little better, despite my needle phobia. The next morning, I was in the breakfast line, still feeling tired and had a tender tummy. It took about four days until my energy came back. Nothing was ever said about the Guard having to break the rules to save me or about the doctor that gave me Maalox for a serious infection and almost killed me. Life is bizarre some times and this baffled me.

The Judge ordered me to have a psychiatric evaluation with a psychiatrist downtown. Two Guards drove me to my appointment. It was great to be out on this beautiful, warm sunny day and I loved the drive through the city. The Guards kept a very close eye on me because they heard how slippery and bold I could be. The three of us entered the waiting room which was empty of patients and decorated in raunchy, cheap modern. The doctor came out and introduced himself to all of us. He was a short, middle-aged man and wearing a dark suit. He had no detectable sense of humor and I got a cold intuitive hit from him. The Guards waited for me in the waiting room and I followed him down the hallway.

The doctor took me into a tiny office, only about 10x10, with two plastic chairs and a small table. The room did not have any windows and the walls were painted white. Being in the tiny room with the doctor made me feel uncomfortable; even more so since I did not want the evaluation in the first place. We sat down and he asked me a bunch of questions about my ambitions, intentions, my past, and the present circumstance that I found myself in. He gave me a long test, with me looking at different black ink shapes on a white background. The Dr. asked me to describe the thoughts that came to my mind as I looked at each picture. He listened to me and took notes on every word I said. His pen never stopped. Afterwards I was brought back to the waiting room and told to have a seat. I chatted with the Guards, read a magazine, and waited. The doctor reappeared and called me into a different office this time. This office was large and sunny, with big windows and lush scenery. One window was opened and a refreshing breeze came through. He sat behind his stately desk and I sat across from him.

The Psychiatrist told me what his recommendations to the Judge would be, as he thumbed through my file. He was going to tell the judge that I needed psychiatric treatments and was not fit to be released to my parents. He said that he thought I needed supervision and was out of control. I yelled, "You're fucked", swiped everything off his desktop, and jumped out of the window. I ran like lightning, escaping into the city. Downtown offered me many places to hide out while making my way over to Dina's.

Wow, was Dina surprised to see me after all those months. The first thing we did was smoke a few joints and catch up. I explained the trouble I just caused for myself by escaping but I felt it was the psychiatrist who was mentally ill. Just because I would not let people rule me, authority figures labeled me as a problem and I was baffled by this. We visited for a while and I realized that I should turn myself in. Dina and I hugged goodbye and I told her I would be in touch soon. It was sad to leave her but we wished each other the best.

I walked a few miles to a different side of town and phoned my mother. She had already been notified about my escape and she begged me not to flee. She was relieved to hear that I wanted to meet her and visit awhile before turning myself in. She jumped in her car, picked me up, and we went to one of our favorite restaurants. She called the police and said that she would bring me back to the Detention Center in two hours. I could always tell my mom how I was feeling. We talked about the changes that will be made regarding my relationship with my Dad. Basically, my mother told him to stop picking on me and to be reasonable for a change. I promised her that I would be a very good girl if they ever got me back. We had a wonderful lunch and a constructive visit.

My mom drove me back to the Detention Center and I was readmitted. The Guards were furious with me for running away on their watch. I did not think about how much grief they were going to catch for losing me. It was about a week before the Guards treated me with their normal caring affection.

The days seemed to be getting longer and dragging on; I wanted out! I was one of the only kids locked up that had a chance of being free in the near future. Watching the other kids made me more thankful for my family than ever! Mealtimes were entertainment for me. Besides loving to eat, the "teen watching" was a hoot. The girls got all made up for lunch, wearing makeup, their cleavages visible and tight jeans showing every groove. I never understood why they wanted to impress the boys in there, anyway. One day a new boy showed up, Ricky, and he was cute. He was short, blonde and animated. I changed my opinion about the "lunchroom-strut." He was so upset to be arrested and locked-up; he cursed non-stop during lunch. Our eyes met and we smiled at each other. I liked him from that first glance.

We also had a new girl at our table and all the Guards knew her so she must have been a regular. The new girl was just released from solitary confinement. She looked frightening and angry, I was thankful that she wasn't seated near me. She was skinny, with pale white skin, and had short red hair. Halfway through lunch, she went animalistic, jumping all around, screaming and then she flipped the long table over. The food, plates and all went crashing to the floor and all of us girls jumped away. The Guards had a hold of her in seconds but that's all the time she'd needed to trash the entire place. She was whisked away and put back into solitary confinement. I heard her screaming during the night from her cell and wondered what she did to get locked-up in the first place.

Spades was the card game of the joint and I played with the guards every day for a few hours. I got to know and liked the Guards; actually they got to know me, because they were limited to only speaking about work. One of the rules about being a Guard was that they were not allowed to share their personal lives with us. This was for their own protection. Zoe did not like playing cards very much and she spent her time drawing pictures and writing. Soap operas were on the television every day, with the radio constantly blaring on the other side of the room. I was not in a dancing mood, but liked watching the other girls dance, and I knew I picked up some hip moves.

Zoe and I did not know what was going to happen to us, but one thing for sure, she had no home to go back to. Zoe was going to be sent somewhere until she turned sixteen in six months. I felt sad that she never had a visitor and she painfully missed her boyfriend. She still managed to laugh a lot and we had so many fond memories to carry us through.

One day we were given our chores and I was told to mop some floors and the stairway from the cells. I filled my mop bucket with water and reached up to get the ammonia from the shelf. The shelf with the ammonia was high enough that I had to nudge it forward with the tips of my fingertips, tilt it off the edge, and catch it. This would have been fine if someone had screwed the cap back on the ammonia. I successfully poured ammonia directly into my eyes. Knowing the thing to do was wash my eyes I ran to the sink and did just that. My eyes burned for the first hour and turned very red, bloodshot to the extreme. I washed my eyes for a long time and thought that I would be fine so I didn't bother mentioning it to the Guards.

Guards do not miss a thing and seeing how red my eyes were they assumed that I had drugs of some sort. One Guard went up and searched my room for drugs while the other Guard asked why my eyes are so red, and told me to hand over the drugs. I explained the ammonia accident. They were mad at me for not telling them about it immediately. This was Visiting Day and the Guards knew my parents were going to see my eyes. They were right.

My parents came to visited me, like always, but had some great news this time. Right away, my parents wanted to know what happened to my eyes. My mother, the nurse, was very concerned but there was nothing she could do about it. I told my parents that I could see fine, that the irritation would pass quickly, and not to worry. I wanted the good news and not waste time talking about my eyes. The judge was considering releasing me to my parents, but with many conditions. One condition was that our whole family has to go to the psychiatric hospital for counseling, every Wednesday for the next year.

"Good grief," I said. I thought about life back home with this going on. My siblings would never agree to this on my behalf; why would they? We were, however, happy to hear any mention from the Judge about me going home, with conditions or not. I had a hard time sleeping that night, too excited and thinking about being home again.

The day before court, a Guard told me that I was going to be released, so bring all my belongings with me to court. I was thrilled beyond words, which was a good thing because the other girls did not want to hear about it. There was a lot of jealousy towards me and even a little from Zoe. Zoe and I cried a lot together that eve and vowed to find each other again. I was hiding how happy I was, saying a sad goodbye with my insides dancing. The Guards and I said our goodbyes, as well. They wished me all the best and told me to keep out of there.

Court Day arrived and I felt like my time in the nightmare was about to end. We lined up for breakfast and Melody walked by me and whispered, "judge fucking slut" in my ear. I could not help myself when I hauled off and punched her in her face. I walked on to the front of the line, acting as if nothing happened. There was some uproar with the girls and the Guards saw it all. Melody held her face, screaming and standing where I hit her but nobody came to her aid. She finally shut up and we all walked in for breakfast like usual. Nothing was said to me about the punch, so the Guards must have kept the incident to themselves. The Guards might even have thought that I deserved that moment to teach her a lesson.

Court was busy that day and a big paddy wagon had to be called in to fit us all. Two of the boys were in handcuffs but seemed relaxed. Court Day was the only time we were allowed to smoke cigarettes and most of us were craving them. We were told that we could smoke after court, if everyone behaved, because there were no windows in the paddy wagon. The inmates were so angry that I thought a mini riot was about to break out. No way did I want to get caught up in any violence with nowhere to go, cramped in a paddy wagon. The entire morning in the courtroom waiting area the feeling was uncharacteristically tense. There were extra police officers in the waiting area and hallway because they had heard talk about someone planning an escape. A tall, fat boy in handcuffs was seated next to me on the long wooded bench. He looked like a man, even had whiskers, but was only fifteen. I asked him, "What did you do to get yourself handcuffed?" He told me that he was being tried as an adult and probably going to prison because he broke almost every bone in a boy's body. He was calm and nicely sat there on the bench. It shocked me that he had committed such a violent crime and yet was sitting next to me and seemed peaceful with the whole thing.

I moved to a bench near the back of the room when my parents and lawyer arrived. We had a meeting about what I should expect, harshly scolded by my lawyer, and told to be demonstrably remorseful. My lawyer told my parents that I needed to be spanked more often and was a spoiled brat, as usual. I shrugged my shoulders and promised that I would be the sweetest girl in the world and show plenty of respect to the Judge. It seemed like an eternity went by before we were called in. The Judge sentenced me to the weekly psychiatric sessions with my whole family and eighteen months' probation, with weekly probation officer meetings. The Judge yelled at me, expressing his disgust and his warnings at me. I could have cared less what the Judge said; the important thing was that I was free! Feeling like I was in a dream, my parents and I walked out of the courthouse and got into the car. We were all so glad that this was over, or at least partially. My dad and I each lit up a cigarette right away.

It felt so good to be back home and I stood in the middle of my bedroom, knowing exactly how lucky I was. I freely roamed around the backyard and admired my mother's gardens. My brothers were glad to see me, but they didn't trust the tranquility around the house for a minute. My brothers said, "Hi" and kept doing whatever they were before we came home. My sister came home a few hours later and had a lot to say to me.

My sister and I went up to her bedroom and I began to tell her about my adventures, when she stopped me. She said, "You are from New York and you better talk like it or I will beat that southern accent out of you!" I said, "What I am supposed to do about it, you think I like it?"

She told me how pissed off she was about having to go to therapy with the family and what an asshole I was. I apologized for running away and told her how the circumstances grew out of control. My sister slapped me upside the head and said, "Do you know how much grey hair mom got while you were gone?" There is no question that everyone was angry with me for disturbing their lives and worrying them sick. I was paying the price both for my father being unbearable for me to live with and for me being addicted to adventure.

I can only imagine how much my being away tore my family up and certainly didn't leave much head-space for my parents to shower on them. My friends and the neighbors must have kept asking what was going on with me and they were tired of the questions. I was on my sisters' "shit list" and the rest of the family had me, sort of, walking on egg shells. I did tell my sister about some of the things I experienced, thinking that she cared. She stared at me like she did not even know me anymore, seeing how the episode changed my personality. My first dinner with the family was a dream come true, literally. In all honesty, I had about enough punishment and planned on being as a good as I can.

My big brother told me that while I was away someone had gone down in the basement and stolen my bicycle. I was bummed out big-time and amazed at the boldness of the crook. My valuable bicycle was not only in the basement, but locked to the water pipe. The crook knew exactly what they wanted and with bolt cutters in hand, took my bike. I had a feeling I knew who it might be and also knew that someone would tell me who it was. Our paper-boy had his eye on my bike and I suspected him first.

I walked to the corner of the street and marveled in having my freedom back. I looked at the trees as if they were long lost best friends which they were. Here came Will! We were ecstatic to see each other again. He shouted, "When did you get out?" We did some catching up and I told him a few stories of my life in the South, especially about the trailer park in Atlanta. He was in shock, listening carefully and just thinking about it all. He told me how much he worried and wished that I never ran away with those girls. He was teary eyed when he said that and I felt terrible for what I must have put him through. I was so busy surviving my present situations that I didn't consider how I affected other people. Our reunion was an emotional one and he felt better when I told him about my plans to be good.

Sleeping in my own bed was heaven and I fell asleep thinking how lucky I was. My door was unlocked and I could pee when I wanted to, Wow! My values whittled back to basics, in many ways. I did not notice my values shifting while it was happening; only after being released it became apparent. Being locked up does bring one down to reality and adds to being appreciative. My adventure has been a "Giant One", indeed.

CHAPTER 10
LUCKY ?

I was enjoying a humid evening, happily sitting on the front porch when a car pulled up. It was Will and a new friend. I asked my parents' permission to go out with them for a while. I could see the fear in their faces and promised them I was coming back. Then the three of us drove around the neighborhood, stopping at the usual places where our friends met. I was treated like a celebrity and amazed to be partying with my friends again. Wills' new friend was the lover of a girl in our group, whose house we often partied at while skipping school. The summer was seeming like it would be great.

I had a serious conversation with my parents about school and the fact that I barely went the whole previous year. The school told my parents that they would take me back again, but that I would have to repeat the 8th grade. No surprise, I knew this was coming and I fully deserved it. A topic that dove-tailed off of the school issue was that my parents were afraid of me having too much time on my hands. My father recommended that I attend a, conservative, private academy for summer school. The academy was about a half hour drive away, out in the country. The academy idea sounded perfect and exciting. I felt eager to get my life going in a positive direction.

My father was going to drive me there and pick me up, every day. Just the idea of spending time with my father every day in the confinement of the car was a giant downer. This would give him plenty of opportunity to put me down and tell me how to live my life. Here he was, being giving of his time, acting as if he cared about me. He lived to control me. He still never uttered an encouraging word; not one positive statement came from his lips about anything I was doing, or my interests. He was, oddly, obsessed with breaking me down. I agreed to attend the academy, knowing it would be a completely different scene from the schools I attended.

Dad was pleasant on the drive to the academy for registration and a tour. We walked through the beautifully manicured campus and were warmly greeted by the principal. He was a large man, had a warm handshake, and seemed to be quite happy with himself. The teens I saw were all white, dressed in the latest fashions, and looked remarkably healthy. Registration went smoothly and I signed up for two classes, American History and Study Skills.

Summer school at the academy was a very good idea and the study skills class changed my life. Speed-reading was a turning point for me, reading in pieces and skimming skills was just what I needed to make my comprehension simpler. I enjoyed reading and studying more now that I was faster and more efficient at it. I was the only student standing under the trees smoking cigarettes on the breaks and I ate my lunch alone. Everyone was nice to me; actually they were nice about everything and behaved in the perfect way. Yuck! I felt as if I jumped into Fairytale Land. My father was right though. I did stay out of trouble and was getting back into the school mode without my friends around.

The summer was filled with wonderful times and the funniest moments with my friends. Will and his new friend, Dan, were the main people I spent time with, along with the friends we visited. Dan loved to drive around and take us to our favorite swimming spot. About a half hour drive away was a small dam where the water flowed into the rocks, forming perfect pools for swimming. It was a well-known party place and we spent whole days there, and sometimes into the night hours, drinking, smoking pot and goofing around. Dan decided he was in love with me and did not hold back telling me. Dan went on and on about how great he thought I was and how he wanted to spend the rest of his life with me. I never even kissed him. I had just met this man and thought he was coming on too strong. I was flattered, just the same, but wasn't going for him.

Many summer nights were spent with my friends visiting on our front porch. One night I began kissing Dan in our backyard and he told me he wanted to marry me and spend forever together. He was five years older than I was and I thought he was a mental case for moving so fast with me. The marriage talk, coupled with the fact that he just met me, made me recoil. There was no way I was going to have sex with him which was what he wanted. I told him that I did not want to be his girlfriend and that was that. The threesome, Dan, Will and I went on but Dan stopped pressuring me about being his lover.

A neighborhood boy showed up after being gone for years. I had never thought about him or wondered where he went. He returned all right, gorgeous and sweet! He sent my heart fluttering. His name was Peter and he had been living at a Boys Academy/Farm, in the corner of the state. Peter quickly became a part of our gang and spent lots of time with us. Peter and I became close friends and I spent more and more alone time with him. I was excited by him and thought about having sex with him. One day we were cuddling in his bed and almost had sex but he just wasn't' going there. He stopped short of taking his clothes off and I knew that I was more into him than he was of me.

However, I talked him into hitchhiking to Florida with me that night and we headed towards the highway. We passed by a friend's house and there was a big party going on, so we had to go in and check it out. The home was owned by a family of, tough-ass, ghetto dwellers, ones not to be messed with. The biggest one, Roy, was a tattooed biker guy who liked me a lot. I knew him through Dina and had partied with him for a few years. He took me aside and told me not to run away with Peter and to just go home. Peter and I got too wasted to run away anyway and we both went back to our homes. Sliding under the sheets in my own bed never felt better! Thank goodness for Roy and his life-shifting advice. My father punished me to the house for two weeks for staying out late. He would have choked to death if he knew how close I was to leaving again. Peter and I broke up the next day because I was too wild for him. We made better friends than lovers anyway, and our group of friends thrived on, with our fun times.

I turned my attention to decorating my bedroom. I hung some Indian fabrics, made macramé plant hangers, and burned lots of incense and candles. My bedroom made me feel happy. My sister bought a stereo and gave me her old record player and all was cool in my world.

Two nights later, I was asleep on the living room couch. I was drunk and had never made it up the stairs to my bed. I could hear pebbles being thrown at my bedroom window but I could not get it together enough to see who there. I just laid there wondering who it was and being too drunk to move my butt off of the couch. The next thing I knew my father came running down the stairs in his underwear and headed out the front door. I heard yelling and recognized Peter's voice. I jumped up in time to see my father grab his arm, but Peter broke loose. My father latched onto his leg and Peter just kept walking, dragging him in the street. I was screaming, "Stop!" as loud as I could. Dad finally let go and Peter took off running down the street. My father ran into the house and called the police. He was deranged, standing in his underpants, cursing me. He told the police, "I want you to find him and bring him back here!"

I could not believe what I woke up to and was so outraged with my father that I stomped my feet and swore. I yelled, "I vow to never forgive you for calling the police on my friend, who had not been doing anything except wanting to speak with me!" The police showed up about fifteen minutes later with Peter in the car. My father said that he is going to press charges against Peter for trespassing. I made myself very clear, screaming at the top of my lungs, "You let him go or I will never speak to you again, I mean it!" I meant every word and my father knew it. He let Peter go and told him to never come around the house again. One more friend I was not allowed to see added to the list of Dina, Sarah, Sally and Zoe. My father screened all my phone calls and I was really only allowed to speak with Will and Eileen, as always.

I managed to be happy anyway and sat out my being confined to the house by drumming and working on my dark suntan. Back to my drumming was fabulous! Eileen came over to tan with me and we decided to climb out onto the roof, over the study so we could smoke pot and have our privacy. The roof was perfectly safe with only a very slight slant and easy to get to from my parents' bedroom window. We were having a fun time until my dad showed up. He popped his head out the window and told us to get off the roof, shouting, of course. He interrupted anything I was doing, especially if it was fun and he could not monitor every spoken word. I told him, "No, we are fine and too bad, we are staying." He was furious about my defiance and stormed away from the window. He was too much sometimes. Eileen did not like to tan with me anyway because I turned a deep brown and she burnt up in minutes and had to stay covered up.

This summer was special because I became certified in CPR and loved the learning experience. It was empowering to know the information that could save lives and it was cool. The CPR class was taught at the Public Safety Building downtown and taught by the mother of the two girls who lived across the street. I visited with the girl my age across the street a few times before, and I liked her older sister too. I was one of five girls from our block that took the class and it was rare that I joined them for anything. This time was different and I liked being included for once.

Through Will I met a boy who used to live down the street from me but who had moved away when I was about nine years old. When that family lived nearby we were told to stay away from them. The family had six boys and a mother who had no control over them. The police pulled up in front of their house, more than once, the sounds of fighting could be heard out on the street. One day, an ambulance showed up at the house and carried someone away. We never heard much about what the family was like or who went in the ambulance, but the family moved shortly afterwards.

Will and this boy, John, were currently good friends and we could do whatever we wanted to at John's house, where there was no supervision. Peter, Will and I went to John's almost every day and partied it up. John and I became lovers and we were thoroughly happy together. He was a genuine hoodlum, in every sense. He was two inches shorter than me but I didn't care; so was my last boyfriend. His mom sat downstairs at the kitchen table and literally was "checked out", she ignored the boys most of the time. The six boys put her over the edge and she dealt with being overwhelmed by drinking Schlitz Beer. John's mother remained oblivious to many foolhardy acts we did in the house and the assorted people coming and going.

John was a grease monkey and loved restoring his cars. He was restoring an old Malibu at the time and helped his friend, Axe, with his hot-rods. Axe was someone I knew from earlier years and we got along like brother and sister. Those two had a pre-dawn gig delivering the newspaper bundles to the paperboys drop spots. Sometimes I rode around with them and, often still awake from the night before. Axe was a strong big man, monstrously crazy, and pretty much everyone was afraid of him. He was one of the "regulars" in John's Party Palace and the guys took care not to get him angry and set him off. His powerful hands were people crushers and he knew it. One of his favorite things to do was show us how he could tear telephone books in half. We lived in a big city with a thick telephone book. Axe liked me a lot for some reason.

I did a lot of drugs at John's house and loved each and every moment of it. There was a drug business going on there, so plenty for us. We mostly snorted lots of cocaine, occasionally dropped acid, and smoke pounds of weed and hash oil.

I never told my parents I was at John's house, because my father had told me to stay away from that whole family, since my childhood. The family had a reputation for being law-breakers and low-lives. My dad could smell trouble brewing somewhere; his senses became keen with his past experiences with me. Will and I would leave the house and not be too specific about where we were going. I told my father we were going to the park or down to the university, but I was with John every day!

John's mom was not happy with me being around there so much and especially late into the night. She knew exactly what we were doing as lovers and would not let me upstairs with the boys. It was easy to sneak by her because she always sat in one of two places and neither of them had a view of the front door. When she knew I was there, she would scream like a lunatic and come running after me with a broom. She was out of her mind and trying to smash me as I ran out the door. She only caught me in the house a couple of times and the tantrums were loud and lengthy.

John's bedroom was enormous, in a finished attic and really more like an apartment. It had high ceilings and big windows beaming in lots of sunlight. He had his own refrigerator, television, two couches and numerous big chairs. There was an alcove with his bed in it and another little room off that. There was always a party scene going on there and we had many enjoyable experiences with drugs in that room.

I met John every morning before school in his Malibu, parked in his backyard. We met, smoked some pot, and had wild sex together. I kept my sex life to myself and was distant from all, but a handful of the kids at my school. I skipped into school for second period and, before long, ended up dropping out of my first period class. First period was my typing class which I had no interest in anyway. The school teacher thought that I was just over sleeping and coming from home so they never called my parents about it. John and I became an "Item" which the whole neighborhood knew about except for my parents.

I spent my time with a few groups of friends and hanging around with my old boyfriend, Jim, and with Sharon. Our friendship was a completely different type of relationship, than mine with John and Will. The four of us spent many Friday nights during the winter playing chess at our science professor's home. The four of us played chess for hours on end and I loved it. We walked to our professor's house even during the worst snowstorms of the season. Playing chess and being relatively wholesome on occasion felt like the right thing to do for myself.

Hanging out with Jim and his best friend (my ex-boyfriend) usually took place during the day when I was skipping school. Jim had a couple of guy friends that joined us often and lived nearby. These two guys were more than a year older than us and seemed strange, in fact a bit scary. These two were brothers, very developed for their age, with deep-set eyes and one long black eyebrow growing across their head. The brothers were too quiet in a creepy way, yet I knew they were very present. One morning the five of us skipped school with a boy named, Scott. I never liked Scott because he was a sluggish, whiny, spoiled white boy and very straight. For some crazy reason, we decided that we were going to become burglars and began to roam the neighborhood streets looking for a house to rob.

Scott told us about a house where some college students lived and said they might have some drugs. We looked like a real gang coming down the street, six young hoodlums looking for something to steal. We went around to the back door of the home Scott recommended and found that the door had a dead bolt. We were the worst burglars ever in regards to efficiency and being quiet. We had to break into their garage to find a crowbar to, loudly, chop through the door. We broke the door into pieces to get inside, leaving the signature of amateurs. The six of us split up and looked around for drugs and didn't find any, except for some animal pills in a cupboard.

Like the cuckoo kids we were, we took all sorts of stuff we had no use for just because we could. Scott took a big TV. I took some jewelry and the two jewelry boxes, a clock radio, a Moody Blues album, and a fur coat. The others took whatever they wanted and we left. Scott went in the other direction from the rest of us, to carry his

TV home. I went directly to my house and threw everything I stole on my bed. I sorted through the jewelry to see what I had and which things I liked most. The jewelry was mostly silver and semi-precious stones, no diamonds or expensive stuff. I did not even like fur coats and what would my parents say if they saw me wearing it? I took the goods for the thrill of it, not because I actually wanted anything. A pound of pot was what I was looking for-- not a clock radio. I stuffed everything into my closet for safekeeping and didn't tell a soul about it.

The next day, I gave John the clock radio as a gift and told him about the rip-off. John thought the robbery was ridiculous and he was right. So right he was! Wimp Boy, Scott, was caught with the TV right off the bat. How was he going to keep a big TV a secret from his parents? Scott was a nerdy jerk and told his parents the whole story. I knew nothing about the fact that I was squealed on when the police car pulled up in front of our house that evening. My mother answered the door and the police said that they have a warrant to search the house for stolen property. My mother said that they were mistaken and that I would never do anything like that. The officers came in and went directly to my bedroom and searched it. A policeman opened my closet door and there was everything, gleaming at him.

My mother could not believe it and stood there with her hands on her face while the policemen carried the loot out. The police put me in the backseat of the cop car and we took a drive instead of going to the police station. The police officers said that I was in serious trouble and that I should be very scared. I was told that if all the property was returned that the victims would not press charges. I knew that John's house was full of partying kids and lots of drugs. I imagined what would happen if I bring the police there and felt sick to my stomach. I made the police promise to stay in the car while I ran into John's and got the clock radio. Amazingly enough, the police did stay in their car and I returned the radio. I was taken down to the police station and sat while the report was written. I was released to my father's custody and told that my probation officer would call me in the morning.

My father was so mad and in complete disbelief of what kind trouble I was involved in. My mother was disappointed, to say the least, and very sad. My parents thought that I was doing great and turning my life around. The police told my father that I took them to John's house and this news flipped him out. I was told that I was not allowed over at John's again, ever. My father thought John put me up to the robbery, but he was innocent. I was punished for two additional weeks and hoped the courts did not want to send me away again. Violations of probation were dealt with sternly and this was a definite violation.

The police called my father and told him how lucky I was because the victims did not press charges. I had to report twice a week to probation instead of once in an effort by the authority to keep an eye on me. The two brothers that robbed the house with us were over sixteen years old and ended up doing some jail time. I felt bad for them and assumed it was not their first offense since they were jailed so quickly.

The family counseling was going on every Wednesday at 4:00 and nobody complained about going. The two psychiatrists were skilled and delightful people and they sincerely cared about our family getting along. The third time we showed up for our session the doctors asked us if they could film our therapy sessions. We had our therapy sessions in a big room with one-way windows and we were being tape-recorded. What were the doctors doing here, research on us? The male doctor was careful in how he told us that we had some classic family disorders and dynamics. The doctors were thinking that our family film would make a useful teaching tool for psychiatry students. We looked at each other, shrugged our shoulders, and agreed to it.

The sessions gave us, each, a safe place to talk about my father's controlling ways and his yelling being too much for us. My mother was on the verge of leaving him because he would not fess-up to anything, let alone ponder civility. My siblings had their own grievances with my father and thought he was the root cause of my running away and violent behavior. My dad did what he always did, saying, "You are all crazy and have rocks in your head." The doctors would try to get dad and me to reach some constructive agreements, but to no avail. My father and I were both born as equally stubborn and neither of us would back down, even a pinch. After each therapy session we went home feeling better but dad and I were still locked in stalemate.

My parents and the doctors never knew the extent of my drug use and it was escalating weekly. I was an expert at sneaking out of the house at night without getting caught. I went to John's at some point every day and did one kind of drug or another. I was selling pot and had a nice, little business that was growing. I sold ounces of pot to the teens at school and to their older siblings. If I could get away with it, I took a little pot for myself and sold slightly underweight bags.

I was still a tomboy and my close friends, except for Eileen, Dina, Sally and Zoe, are all teenage boys who treated me as an equal. I gradually saw less of Cindy and Sharon. Slowly, I started hanging out more with Will and saw less of these guys; growing apart I guess.

Our core group of friends met at John's most nights, where we goofed around, got wasted, and relentlessly jived each other. Axe drove us to our favorite swimming spot and to keg parties in the country. Axe was a maniac and drove like he was in the Indie 500, revving his muscle car engine and squealing his tires. He preloaded the engine until the car jumped up and down and the tires would smoke on takeoff. He gave us mobility and upped our entertainment threshold; we wanted to cruise!

Sally's mom moved the family to the South and that was that. Sally and I lost contact with each other and she became a fond memory. I missed Sally and the friends that she introduced me to, including Scott who since faded out of my life.

I still hung out with the Hippies and they were a lucrative part of my pot business. I found out that some of these Hippies had begun to do some very strong drugs, both pharmaceuticals and street drugs. The Hippies spent some time with a doctor downtown and they often traveled to NYC for rock concerts. I listened closely to their stories and wanted to be included in some of their heavy drug experiences. I thought about trying this one drug they often spoke of, Dilaudid. The stories of being high on this drug sounded like you go way "out there" with pleasure. Dilaudid is made from morphine and was an opioid analgesic so my fourteen-year-old brain figured it is harmless enough.

I knew there was no way those friends would let me do Dilaudid so I did not bothering asking. The Hippies thought of me as too young for experiencing a few things, including sex and hard drugs. I told them about my drug use in the South and the present, but they were not like the drugs these guys were doing. I wanted to try

Dilaudid so much that I went into my friend's stash and took two pills and a syringe. I had heard about shooting up the drug but had never done so before. I thought I would try shooting up, just once, so I would know what everybody was talking about. I am not clear how I formed my strong beliefs opposing needle use and drew this as my line to never cross. For as long as I could remember I knew that needles were bad and "Out". I still wanted to experience something transcendent, if only once and thought this would be the ticket. I took the syringe and pills to John and showed him. I told John the stories I heard about the pleasurable high with these pills and he was intrigued. John and I were alone in his bedroom and deciding on whether to shoot it up or throw it in the trash. John felt the same haunting way as I did about needle use, bad.

I was talking him into it, saying, "one time, only, and then we'll know for ourselves." I told him that I knew how to cook it up from watching the junkies in Atlanta. John agreed to try it with me, not because he wanted to, but because I was going to do it anyway. I got a spoon, some cotton balls and a candle. I lit the candle and put a tiny bit of water in the spoon, added a crushed up pill and cooked it slowly. I drew the liquid up into the syringe through some cotton, squeezed tight, just like I saw them do it in Georgia. Then I held the syringe up and looked at it. John said, "No, I am not going to do it." I wasn't going to shoot up if John wasn't going to and I put the syringe down. We decided to squirt the syringe full into a glass of water and we split it. John and I split the other pill and drank it down.

Within just a few minutes I threw up, barely making it to the wastebasket in time. I instantly became wasted and traveled off to another land, within and without. I completely lost awareness of John and where I was. John was going through a similar experience on the couch a few feet away. I sat back in a big, soft lounge chair and passed out for the next three hours. A doctor may have said I was in a coma because I very well could have been. My first thought was that I was so glad that we hadn't shot this stuff up. I am 100% certain that we would have instantly overdosed and died. Thank goodness John had shown good sense at that critical, last moment. We both knew that we were lucky to be alive after my brilliant idea of the week. My fantasy of trying needles, even once, vanished that day. What could I say to John? I said I was sorry, but Geez Girl!

My parents took us on a family vacation to Florida. We visited my
parent's friends in Georgia on the way down and then met up with
my grandparents. My grandparents rented a condo next to ours, for
two weeks of sunshine, beach time and fun. I was excited about
going to Florida and being able to actually experience the ocean,
finally. My sister stayed home because she landed a new waitress job.
I knew she was happy to have the house to herself, who knows what
that Preacher's Daughter did? The five of us piled into one of the
smallest cars ever made and drove south. My brothers and I calmed
down after our initial squabbles and territory issues got solved.

The drive to Florida was surreal for me since we drove the same
route I hitchhiked with Zoe. It had been a year since I was down
there and the fresh memories ran like a movie in my mind. I
daydreamed out the window, speechless, for hours at a pop. My
being quiet was rare and I knew my parents picked up on my
contemplation. I told my father to buy his cigarettes in Fayetteville,
N.C. because they are the cheapest. I swayed him into stopping at
the gas station where Dan worked and where I had spent so much
time; the same gas station where my life was saved from being raped
and killed. I went into the gas station and, although it was early for
Dan to be in, I wanted to leave him a message. I asked the attendant
about Dan and was told that he didn't work there anymore. I asked
if they knew how to get in touch with Ron. The woman looked
concerned and said, "Ron is missing, nobody knows what happened
to him." I thanked her and quickly got back into the car.

Dad had his cigarettes, we were gassed up, and drove away. I did
not share any information about this gas station with my parents and
saw no need for it. Numbness came over me, thinking about what
could have happened to Ron since he was a rip-off. He sold phony
drugs and his life was bound to get ugly someday. He had raked in
the dough, so maybe he moved somewhere exotic. It was a blessing
to be with my family and driving away from here for good. My body
knew how lucky I was to be alive even when my wild mind drifted in
adventure fantasy. I knew that I did not want to repeat any scenes
like I had in the South. I swear that I did not even want to stop in
Georgia to pee!

We visited a couple my parent's friends they met years ago at church and who moved to Savannah, Georgia. Their house was plantation style, big and beautiful. Our tour of the city was nice enough but I was eager to put Georgia behind us. My mother liked Savannah so much that the adults discussed real estate opportunities over wine and into the night.

I was glad to be staying there only one night, because I had developed an unexpected nasal condition. I was a cocaine addict but never thought about what it meant to be away from it. I had always had access to cocaine and hadn't really realized that I was an addict. My nose started to run like Niagara Falls and nothing would stop it. I had not brought any coke with me, only some pot. Pot was not going to be helpful with this crisis. I would need to be at our condo before I would have a chance to smoke, anyway. I talked my mother into keeping me well supplied with Robitussin by blaming my runny nose on a cold. I knew my nose was feeling the ravages of the snorting I did. My nostrils must have been numbed out from the drugs and were now falling apart. I consumed bottles of cough syrup and used boxes of Kleenex, chafing my nose.

The ocean, finally! I loved my grandparents and was happy to be spending our vacation together. The condos were across the quiet street from the beach, ocean, white sand and peace. Us, kids were at the beach within minutes of arriving. The first thing that happened to me was that I had walked into the ocean and straight into an underwater riptide. I was a strong swimmer but knew nothing about the power of the ocean or how to approach it. I pinned myself against the bottom while resisting being dragged out to sea. I tried hanging onto the sandy bottom for dear life, scratching the ocean floor on my way out. Of course this wasn't going to work for long. I knew that I was about to drown and needed a breath of air, now! A comforting sense of calm came over me and I was surprisingly level headed while I thought my goodbyes to my family and friends. I swam towards the surface and had to take in a breath but was not at the surface yet. I fully expected to breathe in water and drown. I took in a breath and, to my shock, it was air. I was miraculously spit out of the top of the surf, at the exact nanosecond I needed to be.

I will never forget expecting to drown but then being popped out of the ocean instead, touching on primordial vibes. I made it to shore gasping for more air, only to find out that my older brother was going through the exact same experience. He was just a few yards away from me and not as strong swimmer. Chills ran through my body with the thought that my mother almost lost two of her kids in a swift moment. My parents had no idea what had happened to us and how the vacation was really beginning.

We did all the Touristy Florida stuff, saw The Kennedy Space Center and ate plenty of lobster. My mother had a green thumb and she was in awe of the cactus that lined the roadways. One night my mother had us kids out, with scissors, knives and any cutting utensil she could find, slicing off pieces of cacti so she could bring them back to grow in New York. Cacti are not friendly! Cactus stickers and breaking the law; of course we did it for our mother. So much for the law-abiding Preacher's Family. The Florida trip was fun but I could not wait to get home and see John again. This was the longest we had been apart since we met and I missed him painfully. I missed him because I loved him, not just because my nose was still running like Niagara Falls. By now, I did want cocaine and my satisfaction with cough syrup was long gone. Plus I wanted to show off my suntan. It was great to be returning home; excited and relaxed at the same time.

Being back with John made us both happy and our time apart strengthened our loving feelings for each other. I also missed Dina, it had been a long time since we had seen each other. I decided to go over to her house after my Florida trip and I should have known better and stayed away. We took off to visit her old man, dad-like friend at the gas station. Dina was not the druggie I was, but she liked to drink her whiskey. We drank some whiskey, roamed down to her regular restaurant, and arranged for a ride to the gas station. I was already going to be in trouble for staying out late, so I thought, 'screw it, I'll just stay out.' Dina and I had a great time at the restaurant and I enjoyed seeing my old buddies. We ended up at the station about 2:00 am., very drunk and being silly. Her friend was overjoyed to see us and we all visited until sunrise, when his work shift ended.

The night was a long one for us and we were invited back to Dina's friend's house to sleep a bit. His place was a room with a twin bed, a hot plate and a tiny bathroom. The place was gross but I was drunk and just passed out in a chair. I woke up and could hear Dina having sex with him. Shit, he was almost sixty years older than her and yucky. I noticed there were cockroaches roaming all over everything and I lost it. When I heard they were finished humping, I got up and went outside. I lit a cigarette and told them I needed to get to John's house as fast as possible.

Dina and her friend dropped me off at John's and I wished that I had never stayed out. I should have guessed that she was "giving it up" to this old man. I was so naïve. Why else did he bring her presents and spoil her? The cockroaches changed everything for me and I was not going back there anymore. I had lots of fun with him, but now saw that he was a dirty old man, living in a dump.

I knew that I was going to be in trouble for staying out so I hid at John's house for a few days. I loved being with him and wanted to live with him forever. There was always action with John and we were in love. Our fantasies about our future together were delightful and not too farfetched. He worked on cars and sold drugs, did not pay rent and things seemed fine. John's work schedule was in his own hands which gave us complete freedom for entertainment.

I adored being out in nature and often spoke with John about the Adirondack Mountains. We planned a backpacking trip in the mountains; as long as I was already a runaway. We packed our gear together and Axe drove us, hours, to our trailhead. The hike we chose was about seven miles to a lean-to and a pond according to our map and I thought it would be paradise. We thanked Axe for the ride and made the plan to meet him four days later, in the same place and same time. John and I hiked up the mountain trail and it was gorgeous, nourishing our every sense. We hiked mile after mile and neither of us knew how far we already went, but were getting tired.

After it became clear that we hiked well over seven miles, we knew that we were on a different trail than we thought. The trail was steep and moderately difficult, but our backpacks were heavy. I suggested that we make camp before it got too dark and go back down the trail in the morning. I love setting up the campsite; it's so primal and romantic. We pitched our tent, found firewood, made a toasty fire, cooked some dinner, and started drinking shots of tequila. We were in heaven even thought we were lost in the Adirondacks somewhere. My legs needed the night's rest more than the rest of me.

I had more experience camping than John so I let him know about the bears. I made our bear bag and stressed the importance of having all the food, even gum, in the bag. We hung the bag from a tree limb about thirty yards from the tent. We stayed up quite late considering how tired we were. During the night I heard something big walking around outside of our tent. I nudged John, but he was drunk asleep and I wanted to keep quiet. I knew it was a bear and could hear it breathing at the side of the tent. I was terrified and grabbed the tequila and guzzled it down. If I was going to be eaten by a bear I was going to be drunk when it happens. I listened to the woods being explored and especially loud sounds coming from the direction of our bear bag.

The tequila worked and I passed out until the morning light. Then, first thing, I told John about the bear in camp and it scared the crap out of him. John marveled at the footprints around the tent and under the bear bag, very glad he had slept through it. The bear bag was untouched and our breakfast was extra delicious. Campfire cooking makes food taste better, somehow. We packed up camp and headed back down the mountain to the highway. We thought, so now what? We hitchhiked about thirty miles to Blue Mountain Lake and called Axe. John and I spent the day at the pristine lake, swimming and relaxing in the sunshine. The Adirondacks are magnificent and the idyllic place to be with John. Axe drove up to the mountains to rescue us, and like a true friend, had no trouble telling us we are dumb asses. Axe laughed at us for going to the wrong trailhead and almost getting killed by bears. He thought the story was worth the drive up there, mocking our "nature loving" attempt. The short trip was an experience that we would always remember: the smells, tastes, beauty and romance. I also liked being somewhere that I knew the police would not find me and dreaded going back to the city.

Zoe showed up again and became Axe's lover -- how perfect! We cruised around in Axe's convertible, being rebellious teens and enjoying life. It was a beautiful day and seemed like everyone in the neighborhood was outside. The streets were filled with kids playing and teenagers hanging around. We drove past a large group of black teenagers standing in the street not very far from John's house. For some incomprehensible, stupid reason Zoe yells out to the group, "You Fucking Niggers!" I almost died and knew we would probably be brutally killed for her big mouth. Zoe was hanging around the wrong people if she was racist because we are all against bigotry in any form. What a huge problem to deal with, out of the blue and spoiling my day.

We drove to John's and soon afterwards the gang of insulted black people showed up, in larger numbers and were rightfully outraged. Zoe was acting as if she had no idea what had made the crowd act like this. The people gathered on the street and sidewalk in front of the house and screamed hateful things to us. One guy said, "Bring your white asses out here, we are going to beat you bloody!" The crowd cheered him on and similar things were shouted. The situation was heated and growing dangerously worse. The crowd was about to combust with hatred any second. I knew that the house would be stormed and us beaten. I grew up with many of the people outside and they knew that my family was not racist. I hoped the angry people remembered me when I was standing in front of the mob. I knew I had to do something, so I went outside and spoke to them. I recalled that it only takes one link to break a chain and thought this was our only chance of surviving this mess.

I stood there feeling small, yet invincible, and began to speak. I told them, "You know I am not prejudiced and neither is John, I've known you all my whole life." I pointed out some of my buddies in the crowd and told them how I thought they were very cool. I said, "Zoe is drunk and stupid, having no idea what she was saying, being an idiot and she is truly sorry for saying that." Things were cooling down and there was a lot of talk between themselves, with others shouting to bring Zoe out. I begged them to let Zoe slide on this and trust that I would take care of her. I told them that she did not live around here and was leaving anyway. Finally, a black teen said about me, "You know her, she's cool, not prejudiced, went to King School and is friends with many of us here." Whew, the group agreed and began walking away. Holy Shit, that was close! I warned Zoe about what she did and told her people get killed for that and less.

The police showed up at John's house a few days later, with a search warrant and looking for me. The police found me hiding in the bathroom shower. I was stuffed in the police car and taken to the station, booked, and driven back to the Juvenile Detention Center. Once you have been locked up, the police just lock you up again, no questions. The days when I was intercepted from the police by my father were over. I went through the usual intake process and was shown to my room.

I spent three days locked up with no court date or any information from my lawyer. It was getting stranger by the day to be there and knowing zero about my case. Visiting day rolled around and my father showed up, alone this time. He was extremely serious and diabolical in his voice and manner. He told me that if I did not agree to never seeing John again that I was going to stay locked-up for a very long time. It was clear that he was using the police for his personal agenda and I became infuriated about that. I did not answer my father's question and glared in anger at him. I called for the Guards to take him away and let me back into my room. I could not believe what a monster he was being about me seeing my friends. I did not care what my father said, I wasn't agreeing to that crap.

After sleeping on it, I realized that I burned myself and should have just lied to my father. I asked a Guard if it would be OK for her to arrange a phone call, under the circumstances. I was able to call my dad and I told him that I realized he is right and that I would not see John again. What do you know? I had a court date the very next morning and was released to my father's custody. Now, the most attractive person for me to be with was the "forbidden" John. I was not allowed to leave the house for a month, so I skipped school and snuck out of the house at night to see him.

After the month inside thinking about my options, I came up with an idea. I used the name of one of Sharon's friends, Julie, and her phone number to construct my new set of lies. Sharon was sweet and studious, so my parents were pleased when we visited. I figured that a friend of Sharon's would be OK for me to see, parent-wise. One Friday, I asked my mom if I could stay overnight at Julie's house with Sharon and she agreed. I spent the night at John's instead and we had a big, wild party. The scam worked out so well that I did this same thing every weekend for the next few months. One Friday night, my mother called Julie's house to ask me a question. Julie's mother answered and told my mother that I wasn't there. The conversation went on and my mother found out that I never spent the night over there and her mother didn't even know me.

When I returned home, my father asked me where I had been staying and who I was with. I stood in the living room and spoke out loud to myself. I said, "Hmm, should I keep lying, or simply tell them the truth, hmmm", and stared up at the ceiling. I decided to tell them the truth. I said, "I have been spending the weekend nights with John." My father almost fainted because he thought John was out of my life since he threatened me with being locked-up. I was ordered to my bedroom by my father, which suited me fine. An hour later, my father called me downstairs for a talk. My parents agreed that I could see John but it was more important that I tell the truth about my whereabouts. Again, I was punished.

Will and I decided that we wanted to spend the evening wandering the neighborhood after snorting some PCP. I told Will that I knew where John kept it and it would be alright for me to take a ¼ gram for us to split. I went over to John's, got the bindle of PCP and met Will at my house. Will was a part of our family by this point and was invited to stay for dinner later that evening. Will and I were up in my bedroom and I convinced him that if we snorted the PCP now, went downstairs and ate dinner, that we would be coming on to it just as we left for the evening. Two things, first, I only thought I knew what a ¼ gram looked like and, second, I did not realize that we would be ripped on the PCP within seconds after snorting it.

Will believed me and we snorted a ½ gram each, thinking it was 1/8 gram each. We went downstairs for dinner and sat at the table with my whole family. We silently, picked at the food on our plates. Both, Will and I usually ate like horses and were quite talkative too. Neither of us said more than two words the long five minutes we could stand being there. I looked over at Will and saw that he turned white as a ghost and knew I had to do something drastic. I asked Will if he was ready to go out and he nodded. We stood up and walked straight out the front door. My parents knew we were wasted on something and I don't think they wanted the details. My parents did not say anything as we left which was highly unusual. What a lesson in drugs and measurement that episode was, indeed. I became the most careful drug measurer after that.

Partying at John's one night with two of our great friends we decided to entertain ourselves. John already knew all about hot-wiring cars so we decided we would go for a "joy ride." We picked out a car to steal, just around the corner. We agreed to ride around until the gas tank was nearly empty and return the car to the same parking place. The four of us figured it wasn't stealing a car, merely borrowing it. John did his magic and it was running in less than a minute. The weather was horrific; snow was coming down by the feet and no cars were on the road except the snow plows and us.

It was around midnight by then and we drove to parking lots and spun 360's on the ice. We were speeding down the road by the creek when we spun out of control and ended up on top of a four foot high snow drift with three wheels in the air. I ran down the street in the night and crept up onto the front porch of a house and stole their snow shovel. I ran back with the shovel and we dug ourselves out. We were drunk and laughing like the crazy kids we were. I was nervous about getting stuck in the drift because we were two blocks down from my house and the shovel was from a neighbor whom I played badminton with. We got the car out and parked it back where we found it. We never heard anything about this "joy ride", even though our tracks were visible in the snow.

John started working for a man named Fernando, restoring his vintage car. The car needed some body work and I helped John with that. I loved working on cars and adored learning about fiber-glassing and finishing. Fernando and his wife, Marcy, ended up becoming our good friends and we spent days on end at their apartment. We did a lot of drugs with these two and their friends. WOW, did we get "out-there" on some news drugs. We experimented with Quaaludes. My second experience with smoking any drug other than marijuana was with these two and it was opium. The "trips" took each of us into our own inner world. John finished the restoration of the beautiful car and Fernando was thrilled with the outcome. Not too long afterwards, Fernando and Marcy moved away and we lost touch with them. It turned out that Fernando was a slick businessman and owed some folks money. His nickname became "Swindle". I was thankful for some educational and high times, but did not miss him at all. I did not miss them because their lack of integrity had begun to show.

Big changes were occurring. John and Will were hired at a

restaurant, along with two others from our gang. John borrowed one of Axe's cars that he was working on and let me drive him to the restaurant to pick up his paycheck. We pulled up to the back door and I made a big, embarrassing mistake. I was nervous and pressed the gas pedal instead of the brake, hitting the building with a loud Bang! Many of the employees came rushing out to see what happened because the collision rocked the whole building. I sank down in the car seat and tried to be invisible, but that didn't work. Everyone working at the restaurant was laughing their fannies off, except for John and myself.

I crunched the front end of Axe's car and John already knew better than to let anyone drive his car without his permission. I had no money to pay for the car repairs. Axe was the "Crusher" and I assumed he would simply squish me to pieces when he finds out what happened. After we returned to John's, he called Axe and told him about the accident. Axe arrived and looked his car over and was quiet about it, so quiet that it was eerily unsettling for me. I could not tell what was going through his mind, except that he could have one of his violent blowups. He was much angrier with John for allowing the accident to happen than he was with me. Axe told me to never drive his cars without his permission and the car was a piece of shit that he didn't care about anyway. He let me slide and I kissed the ground that I could still use my legs to stand on.

CHAPTER 11
SWIMMING IN OPPOSITE DIRECTIONS

Life around our house was turbulent and for a change it was not due to me. My father had a problem-riddled, series of events unfold on the Indian Reservation, which had a huge effect on the whole family. It all started off as an argument between the Chief and the Longhouse wanting a man and his family off the reservation. The argument grew out of control when someone burned this unwanted man's family home to the ground. Times of upheaval are when people seem to reach out and contact their priest. My father received a phone call that lasted a long time and sounded intense from his end. My father was instrumental in housing the burned out family while he orchestrated the rebuilding of the torched home. My father attended numerous late night meetings with some Indian men and they pulled their plan together. The Chief and Longhouse became extremely angry with my father and the Indian men from the church who helped the arson victim.

As I mentioned earlier, my father has some very interesting friends and he contacted some of them for assistance. His Underworld ties knew about construction; a few phone calls were made and he had the construction materials donated. He was able to have the plumbing and foundation work done with some mysterious donations, as well. The workforce of Indian men, my father, and other volunteers had the home rebuilt quickly. The Chief and the Longhouse had a squad of thugs working for them who terrorized the workers, my Father, and our family. The thugs tried to sabotage the construction site so my father and others kept their guard up. With the home completed and the family moved back in, my father thought the task was over, and he could rest.

The Chief and the Longhouse were livid with my father and threatened his life and the lives of us, his lucky family. The Chief and the Longhouse targeted others on the reservation and found ridiculous reasons to evict them. My father, his Indian friends, and his Underworld connections managed to have some rural property donated, off the Reservation. My Father, younger brother, and the rest of the concerned people, built two homes on the property and relocated the threatened families. My father was able to secure a generous union donation and all the building materials appeared. He was also given a lot of assistance from the Marine Corp. I do not want to make it sound like this was an easy process. It consumed my father's life and the lives of others for months. Meanwhile, our family was in danger over my dad's good deeds.

The contrast of my father helping these families to be safe while endangering us in the process was bizarre. The more media attention my father received the more incidents of carloads of armed thugs parked in front of our house. I wasn't thrilled with the media coverage when it meant standing outside for the ribbon cutting ceremonies of the new homes. My father blessed the homes and all of the people who built them gathered around to watch the first family enter their new, safe home. The television crews came, interviewing my father, the family being given the home, and the construction helpers. I, along with the rest of "The Preacher's Family," stood there watching and this appeared on the news. I didn't know how to respond when people recognized me from the news story and told me how wonderful my dad was. Dad was wonderful for everyone except his family and I was doing everything to keep him away from me.

The danger of being murdered became very real to us when the bullets started flying. My father was fully aware that he was a "wanted man" on the reservation but continued to risk his life by going there. My father was as stubborn as they come and continued his priestly duties, driving to the church regularly. The threats against my father's life escalated and bullets just missed him while driving. My father decided to drive my mother's car to the reservation, because everyone loved my mom. My father returned home with bullet holes in my mother's car. That was when our family stopped going to the reservation for church. We decided that it was too risky for us now and I left the congregation without being able to say goodbye. My father continued as the priest on the reservation, but went without the rest of us. We never knew if he would be returning and our home was under constant watch by the thugs and the police.

The Episcopal bishop met with my father often to try and settle the deadly problems we were having but I never knew what was going on. I am certain that my parents discussed many options to keep us alive but, us kids, never heard them. The energy around the house was tense and I often escaped into the world of partying with my friends. On the surface it seemed like life as usual but we all knew Dad could get wiped out any minute. I saw the thugs parked outside and walked out of the house just the same. There is much more to this story and I will continue it later as the events themselves unfold.

I kept so busy with my friends and my inner thoughts that the reservation problem felt distant, somehow. I was upset with my father for making Mom a target and worried about her safety all day long. My brothers were even-keeled, concealing their concern, and went about their lives as normal. My sister moved into an apartment with her boyfriend and began her career so she wasn't around very much. Eileen, Will, and many other friends asked me questions about what was going on but I didn't have anything to tell them. I could only say what I knew; that my father helped a family whose house was burned to the ground on the reservation and now some Indian thugs were trying to scare him away or kill us. That was about the extent of what I knew and played down my under-lying fears for my mom's life. My "Wild Child" lifestyle was going strong and took my attention off of my family's future.

Maybe it was the forbidden part to the relationship with John that kept it hot, like an obscure magic ingredient. Not long after I was permitted to see John, I lost interest in him. I had begun summer school and was enjoying it. Especially when I met an attractive and pleasant guy there, who had his eyes on me. We lived near each other and started walking to and from school together. He was electrifying! We became a loving couple, rapidly. His name is Kevin, and he was tall, thin and had flawless, olive toned skin. He was soft spoken and semi-hid behind his long, brown hair. As soon as I knew that I had fallen in love with Kevin, I broke up with John and he did not take it well. He made leaving him easy when he asked me if we could still have our morning sex-rendezvous in his car. John was disgusting to ask me such a dumb question. I was a lot of things, but a cheater was not one of them. I was a faithful girlfriend and would never consider it. After John's sleazy suggestion and realizing he did not love me as deeply as I thought, I dumped him forever. My mind was made up, after returning from the south, 'I will never cheat on my lover or ever be with a friend's sweetheart'.

Kevin hung out with a much healthier group of friends than John's and I already knew most of them. He lived in our neighborhood and was also friends with Will. These summer school days were filled with excitement, and I was taking marvelously interesting classes: Chemistry and American Government. Kevin was the highlight of my days however and we grew closer and closer. I had met Kevin's main group of friends before, with Cindy, and had a blast with them. The neighborhood where Cindy and I went to keg parties was with Peter's gang of friends. They all went camping and snow skiing every chance they got.

Kevin was one of the only boyfriends that I ever brought to my house and he came over almost every day. My father approved of Kevin, much to my amazement. His father was a prominent businessman in the city and they had a big Catholic family. I was allowed to go on camping trips with Kevin and these friends, because I was getting A's in school. They may have been afraid that I would have gone without permission, anyway. An hour drive away was a popular pond, where older teens camped and were free to indulge in altered states--did lots of drugs. Each weekend, about ten of us would go camping, pitch our tents, and get super ripped. This group of friends knew how to camp: eating the best foods, drinking quality booze, smoking top-notch weed, and getting wild in the woods.

Three hunters approached our campsite one evening and we invited them to stay for a cocktail. These guys seemed nice enough and had been out shooting rabbits all afternoon. The hunters stayed at our camp for dinner and well into the night. I dropped a hit of acid along with the rest of our friends but we kept that a secret from the hunters in case they were cops or straight. The campfire was extra colorful and vibrated swirls of color through my entire body. The rowdy group of us were drinking whiskey and smoking pot, too. I walked off into the woods to pee and passed out in the bushes somewhere, a first for me.

Next thing I knew, I woke up in the woods with twigs in my hair and wanting some coffee emergency-like. I wandered back to the campsite and heard about the nightmare I had missed by passing out in the forest. It is a very good thing that I slept when and where I did because I would have done something bad-ass for sure. I heard that the hunters' mood changed from tranquil to mean and they picked a fight with a couple of my friends. Fighting broke out all around the campsite but I did not hear a peep. The hunters pulled their guns on my friends and took their money. Kevin paddled them across the pond in his canoe at gunpoint. The cars were all parked in a lot on the other side of the pond. He took the hunters across the pond in the dark and let them off at the car lot.

Circumstances took a turn and Kevin had gotten into a fight with the hunters as well, ending up with a black eye. One hunter pulled out his gun and put bullet holes into our cars. Kevin was driving his mother's car and it was filled with the most bullets. The hunters eventually let Kevin go and he paddled back to our camp. I woke up minutes after Kevin returned and heard everyone screaming about what happened. Kevin was in shock and the other guys were deciding on what to do next.

It's unbelievable that I slept through all that commotion and the gunshots, even on drugs and booze. I was an alert, light sleeper due to being on the road for a few years. I know myself and I would have surely gotten in the middle of the ruckus.

After a quick breakfast and pots of coffee, we packed up and headed back to the parking lot. One friend walked to a nearby farmhouse and called the police to come check out the crime scene. The police arrived and took notes of our stories and the descriptions of the hunters. We all must have looked mega-sordid after the long night and no showers. I am glad the cars were not mine because of the tedious court procedures my friends had to go through to get their car repairs paid for. Two of the charges against the hunters were attempted murder and armed robbery so a serious and drawn out legal entanglement ensued.

Summer school ended and we were back at school. Kevin was in high school and I entered the ninth grade. Cindy didn't hang out with me very much and most of the kids at school were afraid of me. My reputation of arrests, violence, and drugs made most kids think I was dangerous and crazy. I really can't fault anyone for thinking about me like that. I was nice to the usual folks at the smoking corners, but that's about it. My satisfaction was coming from my grand plan: to be passed out of that school soon by making up my required units in other ways. Attending the past year at summer school had not been required but let me get two extra classes out of the way. I went to night school, which really took place right after the regular school day and got another class out of the way. The first half of the year was easy for me, now that I was happily working on my grand plan to exit early and prove my father wrong. My father was convinced that I would never graduate high school and there was no way that I would let him be right!

Kevin and I were having a close relationship and saw each other every day. Almost every evening Kevin came over to my house and we played chess in my bedroom. I loved playing chess, but that's not all we were doing. Hey, I am a Preacher's Daughter and "naughty" is expected from us-- my birthright. We made a point to be out in nature often: camping, fishing, and hiking with our friends. My relationship with this group of friends was twice as healthy as the one with John had been and I was filled with vitality. This group smoked quality weed and hash, ate quality LSD on occasion, and snorted the purest cocaine. PCP and raunchy pharmaceutical drugs were not a part of these folks life. The gang would meet at the park for lively games of touch football and soccer, even in the mud. This group was filled with kindness and wholesomeness and I thrived on it. The teenagers were from wealthier families than mine and were all good students, which helped motivate me to complete my academic plan.

To be very honest, two of the best things my dad ever did were to put me down and remind me that my life was hell. If I brought up my accomplishments at school and plans for my future education he said, "You are not graduating high school. You are going to end up in prison." My older brother was the brain and achieved the Valedictorian honor at the same school I was attending. My older brother never did anything wrong and had some interests in common with dad; Boy Scouts and the Military. The other great thing my father did was say, "Why don't you be more like your brother." His attitude triggered the rebellious streak in me and I was determined to prove him wrong. I was focused on graduating high school even earlier than my original class, the one from before my flunking the eighth grade.

Christmas time was especially splendid; Kevin and I were in love. He gave me a beautiful chess set; the pieces were finely carved mahogany from the Philippines. We played chess together five nights a week and Eileen played when Kevin wasn't. Kevin started working at a small pizza place not far from the house and he liked the money. The first thing he did was to buy an old van that was a rough powerhouse with no back seats. Like any father of a teenage daughter would, my father turned green when he saw the van and a mattress in the back. Peter and I had a great time with the van and often drove to the country, fishing and such.

�

School was a different story, because I was having a terrible time with algebra class and the teacher. We thoroughly despised each other. We did not mix well and I could not grasp any of the information due to his style of teaching. Personally, I think just hearing his voice shut me down and seeing him made my skin crawl. He gave us a test and I wrote across the front page of it, "I will do the test when you learn how to teach." Needless to say, I failed the test and the course. I was scheduled to take the same class over again and dreaded the thought of it.

I counted up my credits and saw that I took everything I needed to for the ninth grade, except two classes. I hoped that I could take algebra from a different teacher and at the high school. It was clear that I could start with half a day at the high school, if I could explain my position properly. I made an appointment with a guidance counselor and pointed out the credits I achieved by taking extra classes. I begged her to let me start taking classes at the high school explaining that the math teacher there might be a better match for me. It was quite easy to talk the principal into letting me go to the high school part-time; he did not want me at his school to begin with. It was all arranged and I split my days between the two schools. I kept with my academic plan and went to night school and summer school for another year, racking up my credits.

✦

I was still a pot dealer and did a lot of drugs when I wasn't at school. The main achievement in my parents' eyes was that I wasn't running away from home anymore and was pleasant. Dina's mother moved the family outside the city limits to an industrial nasty town. Dina and I grew apart, although we had many happy memories of thrilling adventures, I'll say! The news of Dina's move came as a huge relief for my father.

The psychiatric evaluations and therapy sessions with the family were over and I had six months left on probation. My father was still obsessed with having me go to "shrinks" and he took me to see a phone book's worth. He hit pay dirt one time, taking me to see a social worker who knew just what to do. I liked Joy a lot and saw her once a week for four months. I walked to her office through a beautiful neighborhood and my time alone did me a service after our sessions. I needed this time to reflect on the accomplishments made in therapy and relax before arriving back home. Joy drew up a contract between my father and me that saved my parents' marriage and the family's sanity.

Joy asked my father to come to a session and hash out the contract. She asked my father, "What do you want from her?" He explained that he wanted me to get straight A's in school. She asked me, "What do you want from your father?" I explained how I never want to speak with my father or have to ask his permission for anything. Thus, a contract was made in writing and signed by both of us! My father would not have any say over my actions. Only my mother could deal with me. In return I would get A's in school and did not have to come home as long as my mother knew where I was.

Peace and freedom at last and the contract was placed on the refrigerator door for a constant reminder. I got the straight A's in school and my father had no say in what I did. My mother was relieved beyond belief to know where I was and with whom. I was free and had no reason to lie to my mother anymore so I gladly told her.

I was still hanging out with Will and we were having more fun than ever. We loved to go to the outdoor concerts at the university and at the Square downtown. Will and Kevin quickly became close friends and our groups merged, making the parties bigger and wilder. Will and I did not snow ski but Kevin and his friends were devote fanatics. I went skiing with the gang and fell down a bunch, embarrassing myself thoroughly. Kevin was incredibly sweet and patient with me, teaching me how to ski and staying close by. Being on the gorgeous ski slopes made the bumps worth it though.

The night of my first attempt at skiing, I dreamt that I was paralleling perfectly down snowy slopes, smoothly and with ease. In my dream I skied with the grace and comfort of someone who had skied for their entire life. I went out skiing the next day and was an instant pro, just like in my dream. I became a great skier overnight. I know this sounds weird but that is just what happened. I became a "hot-dog" skier that same winter, flying down the slope in speed tucks and doing "spread eagles" off the jumps. Kevin was amazed at how miraculously I learned to ski, too.

Our whole gang made a point to be at the ski resort for "Friday Night Freak-Outs". On Friday nights the ski resort stayed open until midnight and we were there! Each person in our gang had their own wine skin, filled of course, joints and sometimes we did a hit of acid. We were all great skiers and joined up on the slopes to party in the Winter Wonderland. The craziest among us had their own primal screams that could be heard echoing through the mountains. The ski runs sparkled in the lights and were seemingly magical. Skiing was expensive. All my friends had season passes, but I had very little money. I skied up to the chair lift with all the confidence in the world and hopped on. If the lift attendant seemed like they were going to say something to me, I would jump in first with a question. By the time they had answered my question, I was on the chair lift and gone. I asked the lift attendants things like, 'what time is it?' or 'how late are you open today?' It worked like a charm and I skied two seasons for free.

Soon, I wanted my own skis. I knew just the skis I wanted but there was no way I had that kind of money. I was bold and so started a new business. I ran off with a pair of skis a week and sold them to kids in the neighborhood. First, I stole myself a pair of K2 Comps and changed the serial numbers with my father's engraving tool. It was so easy that I just kept doing it. I easily made enough money to buy my ski boots and was really ready for the slopes. I never got caught stealing the skis but started to feel bad after a half season of stealing so I stopped. I shared a ski locker at the resort with my true love, Kevin.

Kevin gave me a ski trip to Killington, Vermont for my birthday! My parents didn't want to let me go because I was only turning sixteen and they knew we would have sex. The conversation was useless because I had my mind made up and would go anyway. My mother told me that she did not want me to go because of the winter driving conditions and that I was too young. With a firm tone, I told her what I was going to do. I told her that she might as well let me go because I was going no matter what. Out the door I went and we had a fantastic birthday vacation together.

I could not have been happier with five days of skiing at Killington, in gorgeous Vermont and with loving Kevin for my birthday. The resort was, by far, the biggest and most majestic ski resort I had ever been to. Killington's slopes proved our local ski resort to be the mere bump that it really was. The tall mountains glittered with the spring sunshine reflecting off the snow and showed how magnificent they were. The long drive there and back was breathtaking with beauty and the road conditions were clear. Mom was glad to see me return in one piece.

I had my driving permit and was legal driving with Kevin because he was eighteen. My mother let Kevin and I drive her car to the ski resort to clean out our locker for the seasons end. Our whole gang went by the carloads out to the resort to do the same. There was a bar on the way back from the resort and this night they had a twenty-five cent, draft beer special. We liked this bar because they served minors, was filled with country dudes, and had pool tables. There were three carloads of us out there and Eileen was with us. Eileen was not allowed to be with me since she got caught sneaking out partying with me, when our parents thought we were camping out in our backyard. This night was the first time in six months that Eileen was allowed out with me, and it ended quite badly.

The ten of us piled into the bar and started drinking drafts. Kevin had a rare treat for everyone, including the bartenders. The treat was chocolate mescaline that his friend brought back from Colorado. The whole group of us started "tripping", including the bartenders and some of the local guys. Insanity! A fight broke out and these local guys dragged my friend outside to beat him. I ran outside and jumped in front of a lacrosse stick about to be smashed over my friend's head. I said, "He is wasted, sorry, let me handle it, we are going now." I was stuffing my friend into my car while fending off these two big galoots, when my friend pulled a gun on one guy. He shocked the crap out of me, almost literally. We were not a gun carrying-gang and I had no idea that he was this "sicko."

I grabbed the gun from his drunken hand and threw it under the car. I told him to wait in my car while I got Kevin. He got out of the car and was causing more trouble with the locals in the parking lot while I was inside. The bunch of us headed for our cars, trying to leave before someone got hurt. One of my friends pulled out of his parking place and came very close to hitting my mother's car, pissing me off. I jumped out of the car and started yelling to my friend, "Don't you, or anybody, get near my mom's car or I will kick your ass." Kevin told me to slide over on the seat and that he would drive because it was snowing heavily. To be honest, the chaos left me too frazzled to drive.

I decided to let Kevin drive but he went directly to the corner and ran off the road into a deep ditch. The same moment my mother's car was pointing down a ditch in a heavy blizzard, the volunteer fire department sirens in the tiny town went off. Sirens blaring and police cars with their lights flashing filled the bar parking lot and the streets. This must have been the biggest thing that had happened in that tiny town for a long time. The police arrested every one of us, one after the other, as they could round us up. A tow truck came for my mother's car and I had no idea where it was being taken. I was in panic, freezing and angry with Kevin for driving into the ditch; royally pissed off and screaming.

The blizzard was a big one, visibility was almost nothing, and it was 3 o'clock in the morning. Everyone was under arrest and in a warm police car, except for me. I was left standing alone, cold in the blizzard, in a rinky-dink town, and with no way home. I tapped on a police car window and asked the police officer if I could get a ride to the city. The police officer was mean and nasty to me, he said, "Get out of here or I will arrest you too." I backed away from the window and wondered what to do next, stuck there and cold. I tapped on the window of the car again and asked if he would call my parents for me. The cop got out of his car and arrested me, too, forcing me into the back seat. The back seat was already full with my friends and I made a fourth.

We were being taken to the hospital, in the city, for various blood and urine tests. Kevin was in a different police car and there were three police cars of us in total. One of my friends in the car asked the police officer for his name and badge number, like he saw in the movies. This police officer lacked any sense of humor and said nothing. My friend kept on demanding to know his name and the police officer told him, after a while. Now, remembering we were all still tripping on the chocolate mescaline, the officer said, "I am Deputy Duck." Oh no, hearing this set us off in hysterics and our belly laughs were uncontrollable.

We laughed until tears poured and repeated his name, "Deputy Duck" and roared all over again. Tripping made it impossible for us to stop laughing. We would stop laughing for a few seconds but then somebody would gasp, starting the laughter again.

Deputy Duck became infuriated and emotionally snapped and pulled the car to the side of the highway. My friend, who had asked the deputy the questions, was yanked from the car and slammed against the side of it, hard. The deputy threw him back into the car and smacked his head on the door jam in the process. The whole carload of us went silent and looked at each other with sobering glances.

The policeman took us into the hospital, where we were met by the rest of our friends. The friend of mine, who had the gun and had started the fighting in the first place, was dancing around the waiting area and hallway grabbing nurses butts. He tried to lift up the dress of a passing nurse and the police tackled him, threw his arms behind his back, and hand-cuffed him. He was the first one of us taken in for blood and urine tests. A policeman walked along the line of us waiting and pointed out which of us are going to have and urine samples taken. I was not one of the ones pin pointed for drug testing, but I was going to be taken to the police station for booking. All of us were under arrest, for at least being a public disturbance.

I was tired of waiting in the brightly lit hallway so I went to the bathroom and then walked outside. I decided I would wait for everyone else in the police car where it was quiet and dark. I never thought that waiting in the police car would make such a huge problem. The policemen noticed me gone and they began searching for me throughout the hospital. A policeman searched the parking lot and saw me sitting in the back seat of the police car. He said, "What are you doing?" I told him that I was just waiting for everyone. He told me that I was not allowed to move from that chair and escorted me back inside the hospital. My friends were shocked that I didn't just run off. It was late, freezing outside and I knew the police had my ID, so running was just going to cause me more trauma. I just wanted to get to my bed.

The mescaline was wearing off and I felt trashed. I sat in my chair, holding my head in my hands while leaning my elbows on my knees. I heard the voice of Kevin's father and looked up to see him speaking with the police officers. A minute later, Kevin and I were told to get up and leave with his dad. His dad saved our butts! I am so glad that I did not run off into the freezing night and that I am Kevin's girlfriend. Kevin's father was furious and blamed him for the trouble we were in. His father was flared up, red in his face and yelling at Kevin about how stupid he behaved. His father made Kevin get out of the car at my house and told him that he must explain what happened to my father and apologize.

Kevin and I walked onto my front porch as his father drove away. I told Kevin that he did not have to come in and face my father and to jump off the porch and cut through my backyard. Kevin insisted on bringing me inside and I knew this was going to be hell for him. My father screamed at both of us, telling us what big idiots we are and kicked Kevin out of the house. My mother was sitting in a living room chair crying and didn't say anything to Kevin. After Kevin left, my mother hugged me and said, "I am so glad that you are not hurt!" My father sent me upstairs to bed and said, "You are going to school in the morning and I am driving you there." It was already morning, leaving me only forty minutes to sleep before school. I was drained to the max and could not yet comprehend what had happened.

Timing is everything sometimes and this was the worst night to have gone anywhere. This was the day I had to take my exams and it required hours of concentration. I was fried but miraculously kept my eyes opened, with an evident brain fog from the mescaline and fiasco. Surviving through the exams was rough and my main goal was getting back home to my bed. I did OK on my exams, but this was not my intention. In going to the ski resort, my plan was to be home and asleep by 11:00 pm and waking up refreshed.

Man, did I mess up and get sucked into a "three stooges" type catastrophe and totaling my mother's car. I was having a horrible endless day. My mother received a phone call from Eileen's mother, telling her that Eileen was eighteen and arrested, her father beat her with a belt, and she was never allowed to see me again. The first night she was allowed to see me after months and "this" had to happen. I felt horrible for her. My parents decided to make a "family night" out of visiting my mother's car at the tow yard by taking us all go out dinner afterwards. When we drove up to the tow lot a surprising thing happened. My mother told me that they were going to wait in the car a few minutes and let me go on ahead of them. My mother said, "Get everything out of the car that you do not want us to see." I was shocked at her reasoning to the possibility of finding what they did not want any knowledge of.

I went to the car and picked up two beer cans and pulled the roaches out of the ashtray. My mother was extra thankful for me being in one piece, as she looked at her smashed car. Mom said, "Well, let's go, I needed a new car anyway." Going out for a family dinner was a poor idea with the shape I was in. My brothers razzed me relentlessly for being a dumb jerk and laughed about how much trouble I was in. Bringing my brothers along could have been part of my father's plan to make me miserable. I was falling on my face tired and the men of the family made too many bad jokes about my driving skills, even though Kevin was driving the car. No justice came my way and they did not know the half of it; the gun. I was never so happy to get home and bury myself into bed.

I started my first job, working at a large department store where many of my fellow high school students worked. I had to keep the shelves stocked, make keys for the customers, and cut the custom sized, window shades. My mother was a darling and drove me to and from work. I enjoyed the job OK, but didn't take it too seriously. As an employee, I had a discount on my store purchases and kept seeing things I wanted. I thought this was a good time to start my "Hope Chest" for my first apartment.

My job required spending time in the warehouse, where I priced the merchandise and unpacked the big boxes. The warehouse was huge and I was there alone, for long periods of time. I brought a sleeping bag that I planned on buying that evening into the warehouse. Throughout my work shift I hid smaller things I wanted inside of the sleeping bag. At the end of my shift, I took the sleeping bag and a few other things through the cashier's line. The cashier poked around at the sleeping bag and unrolled it, finding my stash. Plainly caught stealing, with no other possible explanation that would fly, I was fired on the spot!

When my mother came into the store to see why I was late coming out, she was told that I was caught being a thief. The store manager said, "We will not press charges if she never comes into this store again." I was thankful that no charges would be brought against me and the fear in my stomach subsided. I was sixteen now and would be treated as an adult by the court, with my "Youthful Offender" being my only last chance. My mother was demonstrably disappointed in me and scolded me all the whole way home. My father yelled at me and told me what an idiot I was. I didn't care a speck about the job and I had no regrets over trying to steal the things. Somehow, I could justify stealing from stores, if I ever gave it one thought back then.

Who wanted to work that summer anyway, Kevin and I had big plans for camping. Our friend, Joe, did some research and came up with the perfect camping trip plan for us. We reserved two canoes and a lean-to at the Newcomb Lake Nature Reserve. Our reservation was for twelve tranquil days and many of our friends would be hiking in for the adventure. Kevin, Joe and I drove up to the Adirondack Mountains and arrived at the reserve about midday. The hike was nine miles down a fire road to a mansion, built by the industrialists and kept in perfect condition. The log mansion and the surrounding grounds felt like heaven on earth.

Our canoes were locked in the boathouse and our keys were issued when we checked in at the Ranger Station. We loaded our gear into the canoes and paddled seven miles to our campsite, where our log lean-to awaited. The beautiful chained lakes were completely still and looked like glass. The relaxing sounds of our paddles in the water, fish jumping, and birds singing were all that was heard. The three of us barely spoke during the canoe trip and just absorbed the magnificent surroundings. The lean-to was built on a rock outcrop, overlooking the lake and the campfire pit. The three of us were as happy as could be and had the place to ourselves for the next three days, then our friends would start arriving.

We made camp and started our glowing fire, pitched our tents and gathered up firewood. We all helped with cooking our steak dinner and mixing cocktails. We drank a lot, smoked joints and joked around under the star filled sky. Being the only people around for miles was a primal rush and I never slept better. The peacefulness of being in nature and so far away from daily tasks let me finally reflect on my life.

I was awake before anyone else and took a canoe out to catch our fish for breakfast. The morning mist rising off of the still lake and listening to a pair of loons calling to each other was paradise. I caught some sunfish to grill with our eggs and the guys loved them. I had an arrangement with the guys about the fish; I catch and cook them and they clean them for me. Cleaning fish is too gory for me and the trade-off for cooking them worked out tasty. We spent hours in the canoes on the never ending, wandering lake, exploring and appreciating the beauty of the reserve. I paddled by beaver dams and saw more hawks than I could keep count.

We partied hearty around the campfire in the nights, being as free as we wanted. The three of us took some acid and had laughter filled times! The owls had a lot to say about us--hooting throughout the night. During the twelve days, Will and many other good friends hiked in and spent some days with us. This was the best camping trip of all time! A magical experience and the memories will stay in my heart, forever.

With a truly great adventure behind me to keep me going through the rest of the summer, I began my summer school classes. Plus, Will made some new friends and introduced them to Sarah and myself when three of us went to their house one afternoon. This was one sexy guy, a few years older than us and was living with the prettiest blonde woman I ever met. Our visit was interesting because they were unusual. Ricky was recovering from an accident and had only been released from the hospital a few days prior. Ricky had his left arm and hand bandaged up but did not mention what occurred to get that way. Ricky caught my eye for a few reasons, all superficial. He was tall, sexy, had the coolest leather jacket, and played guitar. In my sixteen-year old brain it was like meeting my idols, David Bowie or Joey Ramone. I walked on the clouds. Ricky was already hooked up with his beauty and barely noticed me at all. Just as well, it was going to be hard enough to focus on school and Kevin as it was.

I was hired as a cashier in a neighborhood drugstore and liked it a OK, even though it was boring most of the time. Eileen was working there too and that added a little more excitement. The timing of the job could not have been better. My parents planned a family trip to Boston and because of my job I was allowed to stay home. Having the house to myself for a full week of entertaining Kevin every night was splendid. Will popped over a couple of times and the three of us enjoyed those evenings. Kevin, Will, and I played house together and found it was relaxing. Will was an exceptional cook and had worked in a restaurant for the past two years, so we shared many yummy meals together. I decided not to throw any wild parties while my parents were gone, mostly because of my work schedule.

My co-worker and friend, Eileen, came up to me at work one afternoon and asked me to front her a pack of cigarettes for an hour and then she would pay me. Eileen was having a nicotine fit and pressured me relentlessly, so I agreed. Due to her being a co-worker, I thought that I could trust her and my boss would never find out. Before Eileen returned from cashing her paycheck and paying me for the cigarettes I was fired for stealing. The store security men were watching me from a one-way mirror placed near the ceiling.

The security men did not believe me that Eileen was going to pay for the cigarettes and said that I gave them to her. My co-worker returned and told the security men the truth but the store manager still fired me. My parents returned home to find me unemployed. It would have been a tragedy for me if the store pressed charges but they didn't. My father actually believed me and tried to get me my job back. However, even he couldn't get my ex-boss to change his mind.

Kevin and I spent lots of time together and our relationship seemed to be going along smoothly. Suddenly Kevin dropped out of sight for two days, then another day, until eight days went by with no telephone call from him. I was pissed off and could not wait to hear his explanation for being incommunicado. I was sitting on my front porch the afternoon that he drove up. He parked his van, walked over, and sat down beside me.

He acted as if nothing happened and thought zippo of not telling me what he was doing. I told him that I refuse to be treated like this and broke up with him, then and there. I told him to shove his head up his ass and went inside of the house. He looked sad and confused, as he drove away. I got a little talking to from my mother; who thought I was being too hard on him. My parents adored Kevin for some reason, probably because I was staying at home more. I listened to her carefully and still believed that I did the right thing, dumping him. 'What else would he think was "fine" if disappearing for days was?', I thought.

Sarah met a friend at high school, named Pat, who was studious and looked conservative but she had a wild streak. Pat knew some "hot" young men that lived in a tiny town about 50 miles away. When I say tiny town, I mean population eighteen. These three guys lived together in a rundown old farmhouse on twenty-five acres with an empty barn on it. Pat and her older sister each had one of these untamed country dudes for their lovers. Sarah and I just had to take a trip up there for a weekend and check them out for ourselves. Pat came with us and we camped out on the beach of a darling little lake. The three of us could not have had more fun together: swimming and crying with laughter.

We drove to the only bar in town and met up with four of the country dudes. The seven of us got thoroughly wasted, while becoming well acquainted, before we all went back to our campsite. We whooped it up all night long; snorting lots of cocaine while the joints went around non-stop. Dancing and swimming in the moonlight! The night sky was filled with stars and the temperature was a balmy perfect. We made wonderful new friends that night and enjoyed spending the time in the nature's beauty. All the guys had a witty sense of humor that I found refreshing, pure, and innocently hilarious.

The country dudes threw an enormous party every year at the farm, called "The Blast". The party guests all camped in the huge field and the musicians' stage and beer kegs were inside the big barn. Sarah, Will, and our whole gang were invited to the party and knew it was going to be a memorable time. Will and four carloads of us drove to the country for the big party weekend. The amount of acid eaten by the crowd made for the liveliest dance floor I had ever witnessed. Being single added a special zest to meeting and dancing with some hunky and available men.

A close friend brought some acid there to sell but he got too wasted to conduct business, so I took over for him. I was given the acid and began selling it. I had a line of excited customers forming, just like when I was dealing down in N.C. As high as I was, dark as it was and with my customer line, I remained acutely alert of my surroundings.

In the midst of what I was doing with the band playing super loud, I suddenly had a strong, tingling sensation run through my body. I felt a strange urgency to know where Sarah was. I looked over to the other side of the barn and saw her back as she was walking out the barn door. The place was jammed packed and most of the people were out of control. I saw a man walk out the door the moment after Sarah did and I just knew he was trouble. Every cell in my body told me that this man intended to rape her.

I quickly left the line of customers and headed towards the door, picking up a three foot long 2X4 that was leaning up against the wall. I fled the barn walking fast and caught up to them right away. Sarah was walking out into the field to pee and this man was closing in on her. She was so wasted that she had no idea she was being followed in the pitch black night. I came up behind the guy and told him to get the fuck away from her; more than ready to smash him with the board. He ran back into the barn and Sarah thanked me in the biggest way she knew how. We put the event behind us and I partied on, dancing with full abandon.

I danced with a cute country dude and we quickly got hot and heavy with each other. I was not alone in my tent that early morning. My sexy, country, dance partner woke up before me and left. The fellow who stayed with me was one of the guys involved with organizing the party and had to get the breakfast set-up going. This was going to be a long day and I was pleased to have gone back to sleep for a few more hours. Just as I was crawling out of my tent, I felt something in my sleeping bag. I felt around and pulled out a fat roll of money. I counted the money, totaling $1,500.00 and knew it was the party money. The party cost each person $25.00 to get in, and this money covered the beer and band expenses. As I was holding the wad of money, I thought 'my tent guest must be going insane looking for it'.

After I found my way to a much needed cup of coffee, I returned the money to him. I held up the roll of bills and said, "This must be yours." The relief on his face showed how much panic he was feeling. Gracious words of "Thanks" for my honesty bubbled out of him. He treated me like an angel that saved his ass. That party was rocking and rolling early, loud and lawless. Being in the middle of nowhere and not a policeman for miles allowed the crowd to let loose. The collective buzz of us all and our drug consumption was insanely fun. Our new friends and this mega party was a stellar way to wind up my summer.

The seventy, or so, of us partied for three days straight and I looked beat up and tired beyond description. I was going through the movements of walking, yet felt like I was falling on my face with complete exhaustion. I looked so ruined when I returned home that my mother didn't even ask me any questions about what I was doing. I slept for fifteen hours straight before slowly coming back to life. I had some recuperating to do and it took three days before I regained my normal energy back.

This was the best summer yet and it went by fast. I loved beginning school because my plan to graduate early was coming along perfectly. Knowing that I was proving my father wrong gave me tons of satisfaction and a passionate drive. This was the year that I was going to finish my plan and be done with high school in December, six months ahead of my original class.

I became a short order cook at a steak house at the Mall. My boss wanted me to sweat blood for him and he treated me and the other woman without respect. The manager let the male cooks verbally harass me. One day a fellow cook, a teen boy from my high school, called me a slut bitch and I lost it. I grabbed his hand and put it on the grill top and let him scream. What did he expect; that I was going to stand there and let him abuse me? I did not stay at that greasy job more than two months and my mother helped me write my accusatory resignation letter. My mother was so upset that a boss would be so mean to an employee and she supported my decision to quit.

Not long afterwards, I was hired at another nearby steak house, this time taking the customers' orders. The restaurant was organized so that the customers walked down a corridor that was lined with the framed menu. By the time the customers walked up to the counter they had their orders ready for me. A mother and her very young son came walking down the corridor and looked at the pictures of meals. The mother and son were picking out their meals and the boy wasn't giving his mother much feedback about what he wanted. I was watching this woman and saw her yank, hard, on her son's arm and pushed him around, yelling mean things at him.

When the woman approached the counter she was still hurting her defenseless little boy. I told the woman to never hit her son while in this restaurant and I should report her for child abuse. This woman became outraged and screamed to the manager that I was telling her how to raise her son. My boss came over and told me, "Don't you ever comment on what the customers are doing with their children again, or you will be fired." I firmly said, "That's child abuse and you are telling me to let it go on?" I was told to be quiet and do my job or else. I was shocked at my manager's wimpy stance with the mother and ordering me to be silent about child abuse. The older I got, the more complicated the world seemed to become.

A week later, I was trained to serve the customers their meals and restock the salad bar. Being able to mingle with the customers suited me better than standing behind the counter. I knew many of the customers and my friends could come in and see me, too. The uniforms were short dresses for the girls. The Woman's Rights Activists would have slammed this company for exploiting us young beauties. There was one afternoon that I would never forget. The restaurant was busy as usual and I was serving meals to the customers. I heard a woman screaming, "Help!" She was sitting just a few feet from me and I saw her husband was choking.

Just like I've seen on TV, I got a pure adrenaline rush and pulled a very heavy and long wooden table away from the man, pulled him up to his feet, jumped behind him and squeezed him. Repeatedly, I squeezed and lifted this huge man, with no noticeable effort on my part. I gave him the Heimlich maneuver that I learned two years ago in CPR class. The man was an American Indian, about 55 years old, tall and heavy set. I thrust the man against me so hard it raised him off his feet until a piece of steak flew out of his throat. The concerned customers gathered around and watched us. His wife was screaming the whole time and she pounced on me with hugs and thanks when the piece of steak popped out. The man was catching his breath with tears in his eyes and gave me a big smile. The two of them left the restaurant and I just stood there for a moment, frozen in place.

The restaurant returned to it's normal atmosphere soon after the couple left, but that was when the shock hit me. I had reacted without thinking and the intensity of the emergency was overwhelming. I stood there and thought, "What was that?" My boss came up to me and told me to stop standing around and get back to work. I told him that I just saved a man's life, was in shock and needed a few minutes to regroup. He was so mean and cold about the near death of this sweet man that I disliked him after that day. His "child abuse" non-action and now this void of feeling reaction to me was pathetic.

My business selling pot was going fine and growing. This way of making money had so much more excitement and fun attached to it, in comparison to working at a restaurant or department store, plus the pay was better. Most of my business took place at the high school so I had to hide the smelly pot and it wasn't easy. Every day, the same group of us met at the back door of the school and smoked cigarettes. Most days, somebody would light up a joint or pass a pipe with weed around. On this particular day I was the one who provided the pipe full.

The bell rang and I stuffed the pipe into my pants pocket and started to walk down the hallway to class. The principal saw me put something in my pocket from a distance but wasn't quite sure what it was. I started to walk past him and he reached out and put a crushing "Spock Hold" on my neck muscles. I cried out with pain but the principal didn't mind my agony one bit and brought me to my knees. He said, "I know you are doing something bad, you always are, and I am taking you to my office to empty your pockets." He had a tight hold of me and there was nothing I could do except to go with him.

The school cop came into the office with us and listened to the whole conversation. The principal sat behind his desk and ordered me to empty my pockets and I loudly refused. I said, "It is nobody's business but mine what's in my pockets." The principal stood up and took a big book off his bookshelf and opened it up on his desk. He flipped to the page that says he has the right to search my pockets. He had me come over to his desk and read the caption for myself. I read it and slammed the book closed, saying, "That is just a dumb book and too bad."

The school policeman was transferred to the high school from my junior high school and we'd known each other for the past few years. The cop and I were friends and flirted heavily, with both of us knowing it was just play. Unfortunately, the principal was also transferred from the junior high school and, not only knew me, he knew my father. The principal told the cop to tell me what was going to happen next, if I did not empty my pockets. The police officer explained that a policewoman would arrive and strip search me but then the subsequent punishment would be out of their control.

The judge would be fit to be tied with me for giving zero respect to authority figures and laws, as was my norm. They had already telephoned my mother who had left work and was on her way to the school. I had a bigger problem, a ¾ ounce bag of pot in my other pants pocket. I knew if the woman police officer strip-searched me the bag would certainly be found. So, I said, "OK, here is what is in my pockets" and took everything out, except the bag of pot. I was wearing corduroy pants and the bag of pot made a visible bulge, so I knew this strategy was a long shot.

The Principal and police officer looked over everything from my pockets and focused on the smelly pipe. There was a tiny bit of pot still in it and a buildup of resin. My mother arrived and was very concerned with what was happening. With my mother now in the room, the legalities of searching me shifted. The Principal told the cop to pat me down and my heart sunk. The cop patted down my pockets and he put his hand directly over the bag of pot. My guts twirled and I'm sure that I turned bone white when he touched it.

Nevertheless, the policeman said, "She is clean, that's all she has." Wow, he really was a friend and obviously cared for me. I was arrested for the pipe and having drugs at school. The resin and grains still in the pipe were counted as possession of a controlled substance. I was abruptly arrested and suspended from school. My mother was crying as I was released to her and told we would be notified of the court date.

This was a tricky situation, due to the fact that the mayor just put out a warning that there was a crackdown on drugs at school and the "book" would be thrown at the next kid caught. The city was officially determined to make a point with the next kid busted, being me. My father was on the phone, strategizing, with my lawyer every day until my court date rolled around because this time was serious. I was under the microscope of the Mayor and the School Board now. My father called every friend he had in the legal system to try and help me out of being the example for the city's crackdown. For a while it looked like I was going to get more probation added on, but then the negotiations started to turn bad. The Mayor was not messing around and I could easily get three years at a Girls Reform School for this. Shit!

The morning of court began when my parents and I walked down the long hallways to the hearing room. The police officer that I kicked in his balls during a chase from Dina's a few years ago recognized me. I knew so many police officers' faces by this point in my life that I could not place which bust they were a part of anymore. He walked along beside me, gripped my neck with his big hand, leaned into my ear and said, "It's a good thing that you are with your parents. When I see you on the street, I will kill you." His words made the hair on the back on my neck stand up and there was a scary strength behind them. He walked away. I was amazed that he came over and threatened my life right in front of my parents even though they didn't hear his whispers.

We continued to the hearing room and for once I was frightened to go inside. Court dates had been a joke for me in the past but I was sixteen now and the court system was clearly sick of me. The Mayor was calling for an example to be made out of me and the whole school board was involved this time. I went before the furious Judge, who screamed at me when he told me that I was going to be sent away for a long time. The Judge said that I used up all the favors I was going to get and that having drugs at school was worse than any runaway stunt. The conversation between the Judge, my lawyer, and my parents got super-duper intense. I was just hoping I wasn't getting "sent up". The Judge called a recess and we were told to wait outside in the hallway.

My mother and I sat on a long bench while my lawyer and father stood talking over the possible outcome. My lawyer was sad and dismayed. Just the night before she had been told that I would get more probation and not be sent away. My lawyer said that it didn't seem to be going well and that she had never seen this Judge so upset and forceful. The Judge was under the mammoth pressure of the mayor, school district, and the public was watching. Abruptly, the tables turned against me and I knew what to do next.

My lawyer stepped away for a moment and I leaned over and whispered in my mother's ear, "I am going to Canada now." I explained that there was no way that I was going to sit on this bench waiting to be handcuffed and taken away for three years. I was going to be sent to a home for girls called "Holy Angels." My mother begged me not to go and to please wait and see what happens. My lawyer returned and said that she thought it would turn out OK for me, but it wasn't said convincingly.

I stayed and went before the Judge. He was still as angry as he had been earlier by the tone of his voice. The Judge said that I need a hard spanking and that if they searched me right that minute that I was probably carrying drugs. I did have a pipe and a bud in my pocket and hoped he was just threatening a search. What a scandal that would be! The judge went on to say that my saving grace is that I am a dedicated and good student. My sentence was unusual and the outcome uncertain. I was to plead my case in front of the City School Board and convince them to let me continue with school. The Judge said that if they agreed to give me another chance that he would go along with their decision, this once.

He yelled at me for a long time and made his point well known. He said that the next time I get arrested I would be tried as an adult and this case has used up my one time, "Youthful Offender" privilege. My heart was pounding and I knew that his conditional sentence was a miracle for me.

The meeting with The School Board was stressful beyond belief; I knew I was notorious for making trouble throughout the school system. My parents and lawyer sat at the long conference table with the board members and myself. The tension in the room was heavy and I knew I had to do some fancy talking, or else. With a cold nervous sweat, I made The School Board every promise I could think of and made sure they knew how sorry I was for the incident. The Board listened to my parent's testimony of the improvements I made over the year and how this event was a real wake up call for me. The School Board ruled and I was allowed to stay in school! Thankfulness and relief filled my body with knowing what a close call to hell this was.

I was not sorry for smoking pot at school in the slightest, but was determined never to be caught again. The Judge left me realistic about my future if I didn't quit being a Bad-ass. Locked in jail was the last place I was going to end up! I made a vow to myself; pick my crimes carefully and always weigh out the consequences. My carefree, spontaneous, and reckless behavior was dangerous to me now so I reeled-in myself a bit.

✷

Working with wood always attracted me and I took every wood shop class that the school offered. I loved seeing what I made. It was deeply fulfilling for my soul. The class I was taking this time was "House Construction" and my dream house fantasies ran wild. I took all the drafting classes offered at the high school as well, and this class let me make what I learned to draw. I was the only girl in this class, just like in all the other shop classes. We had to work in teams and I picked my buddy who took the drafting classes with me. The two of us were the only white kids in the class and it made no difference because we were friends with all the boys in there, having known them for years.

On the first day of class we were given a test to see how well we could measure. I looked at the test and thought it was ridiculously stupid. The test questions were line drawings of marked rulers and we had to write down the measurement, 5-1/8 inches etc. I handed in my test first and asked the teacher why we had to do such a simple test and he told me that he had to give it. I was blown away to watch how the kids, other than my partner, grew more and more frustrated.

The test was too difficult for some of the kids in the class and three of the boys actually stormed out of the classroom. Some of the boys tore up their test papers in anger and just sat at their desks. These kids did not know how to read a simple ruler and measure an inch, not even to mention rulers of different scales. I was aghast to know that I would be graduating high school with kids who are so poorly educated. The school system obviously pushed these kids through the grades just to be rid of them.

Our class assignment for the semester was to build a miniature house, complete with each joist, sill, beam, and all. My teammate and I sawed, measured, sanded and nailed together the most gratifying house. On the last day of the assignment, we were putting the final touches on our project and so proud of what we built together. The other boys in the class spent the semester goofing around and barely started their houses, understandable because measuring was the big part of the project. The teacher left the room for a few minutes and told us to continue working on our project.

A notoriously dangerous boy came up to our shop table and tore a wall off our house and started to take it for his own. Other boys lined up to dismantle and steal our project as well. There was no way that I was going to stand for it! I, simultaneously, snatched the lead "Bad Ass" by his shirt collar and pulled him close to me, while picking up a power drill with my other hand and revving it at high speed in front of his eyes. I screamed, "You put that back, or I am going to drill you in your face!" He almost shit his pants and dropped the wall on the table. If you would ever have seen a black boy turn white as a ghost--this was It! He backed up and kept screaming, "You are fucking crazy!" All the boys backed up and left me alone, forever after. The teacher returned, overheard the conversations and asked me what happened. I told him everything; even that I had revved the drill in the boy's face. The teacher replied, "Brilliant, glad you did it." My reputation went through the roof after word spread about what I did to one of the most feared boys at school. Oh, well, what can I say? I got an "A" for my house project!

I became friends with a new girl at the school, Lisa. She was a hot mamma and knew how to strut her young self. She became the lover to a bad boy and a longtime friend of mine, Steve from the "John Days." Her boyfriend was not only a friend but someone I had done business with for years. The new girl in town had been living in a group home for girls and was presently being released. These two "Love Birds" rented an apartment and moved in together. One sunny afternoon, I was visiting with Lisa at her new apartment. We were laughing, drinking some wine and getting high together. Her sweetheart was out with a few of his friends and they returned; stoned and belligerent with booze. Steve was not acting like he usually did and I had never met these scoundrels he brought home.

Steve was acting like a total jerk, picking on Lisa, and saying the meanest things to her. He was standing in front of her and calling her names: bitch, whore, slut and other nasty things. I did not like what was going on and was getting increasingly upset with Steve. Steve hit Lisa in her head and threw a glass of red wine on her, all over her white angora sweater. I yelled to Lisa, "Kick him in his balls, he deserves it!" Steve came over to me and snatched my neck with his strong hands and held it. I warned him, through my gasps, "Get your hands off me or I will kill you!"

He let go of my neck, laughing a cynical snicker and walked a few feet away from me. He turned around and came back after me, grabbing my neck again, Lisa shouted for him to let me go. The dirtbag guys were sitting there laughing at the whole abusive drama and I wanted to kill them too. I went into a craze, so fierce that I even frightened myself, and broke away from Steve. The power surge in this crazed state made me burst and I sent the chair I was sitting in flying across the room when I broke loose.

I picked up a thick, wood curtain rod that was on the floor and I swung the pole at Steve's head with all my strength. He ran out the door just in time and the swing missed him by only a smidge. I would have killed him if that blow connected and I didn't give a damn. I ran after him and was calling him every swear word I knew. He ran as fast as he could out into the street and looked back to see if I was following him. I smashed his truck with the pole twice and dented it good.

I hollered the meanest things at Steve as I went back in the apartment and picked up my things. Lisa was crying and trying to clean the place up from the brawl. I saw how she cowered before Steve and showed me how afraid of him she is. I told her that I loved her and walked out the door. I bitched about Steve the entire three-mile walk home. To think that Lisa was choosing to be with a man who would treat her so badly was truly baffling and unsettling for me to witness. That was the first and last time I went there to visit Lisa, because it was sad and dangerous for me.

CHAPTER 12
PERFECTLY ENTWINED: BEST AND WORST

A whole new life was beginning for me: "Punk Rock." The punk rock scene was growing rapidly in the USA and I started to see these new bands popping up in the city. The few "new wave" bands we had in our city were becoming more energetic on stage and it was fantastic. There were two bars downtown that I was able to get into using the voter's registration card of my older sister, even though she was known at one of the bars. I met some students from the university and was invited to some "after-hour's parties" and was thrilled to go.

I took to the punk rock scene immediately, as it appealed to my rebellious nature perfectly. The Ramones, The Police, The Kinks, Joe Jackson, and many other bands came to town and I saw them all. Will, the neighborhood kids and everyone I knew, except the hippies, were trying to understand what I was into now. Punk rock was new, high energy, anarchistic and I loved it. I understood why most people found us threatening, we did look like trouble and ready for unruly thrills. The punk style complimenting me dressing like a boy in combat boots, torn clothes, spiked bracelets and my cherished black leather jacket. I'd finally found somewhere I fit in and felt refreshed and welcomed by my new friends.

Something terrible happened to my ex-boyfriend, Kevin, he fell off the roof of a three-story house, gashed his face and shattered his heal to sand on the pavement. Kevin was renting an apartment from my very good friend's dad and traded some home repair work for his rent. He was partying on this day, using speed to be specific, and then went up onto the roof to make repairs. The home was built in the 30's and was falling apart at the core. Kevin tied a safety rope for himself to the chimney and figured he was protected. He lost his balance and went sliding towards the edge of the roof engaging the safety line. The chimney was so old that it broke apart into pieces, sending Kevin to the ground. He was taken by ambulance to the hospital and had emergency surgery for his pulverized heal. I knew that Kevin was going to need a lot of care and I still had a special place for him in my heart. The day after Kevin was back at his apartment, in a full leg cast, I stopped over to visit him. I made him dinner and we ended up falling in love again. I visited him daily and within two weeks I was living with him.

This time in my life was a dream come true, doing something I had been wanting for a very long time; moving out of my house. Not only was I living with my lover, I had been working for many months now and finally felt some personal freedom. The best thing of all was that I finished with my high school requirements except for ¼ credit in social studies. My Russian History teacher liked me a lot and we enjoyed sharing our fishing stories. He fished at some of the same spots where Kevin and I fished.

I explained to my teacher that I had all the credits to be out of there, except needing the ¼ credit in social studies. He was gracious and smiling, handed me a thick, hardcover book, told me to read it and write him a report about it. He said he will give me the ¼ credit when I turn in the paper. I gave my "all" to completing the social studies book report and wanted my teacher to be proud of the work I handed him. Life was Grand!

The high school guidance counselor called me into her office and asked me, "What classes are you going to be taking next semester, because you are not signed up for any?" I sat back in the chair and said, " Count up my credits. I have enough to graduate." The moment I planned for and worked hard towards, for two and a half years, was here at last! The guidance counselor counted up my credits and saw that I was short the ¼ credit in social studies, then tried to verbally slam me. When I told her about the assignment I have to earn the ¼ credit in plenty of time for graduation, she went into a weird frenzy. Agitation doesn't fully explain the meltdown she had and said, "We are going to have a meeting with your parents and the principal."

Gladly, I did not have to wait long for the school and parent meeting: it was held the next day. My parents were amazed and had never seen it coming. The principal said, "You are not mature enough to graduate high school" and the guidance counselor never liked me anyway. I said, "Count them up, I have what is required and a 94% grade average. I am out of here!" I raised my voice and told the whole group that they were not being fair and I worked hard to get school behind me. The meeting ended up with the school not able to protest my graduation, providing I turn in the book report, but they were not happy for me, either. The relief and giant sense of satisfaction I felt was truly liberating.

Living with Kevin was delightful and with many fun times. We held poker night on Wednesdays and the same five of our friends would come and play. This is when I learned how to play poker and I picked it up fast, winning enough for my season ski pass on my first night. I enjoyed the banter going on during poker night with the guys, with me being the only female.

Trying out my cooking skills was yummy although basic. I was proud to serve Stovetop Stuffing and master Rice-a-Roni with fried chicken. Living as a couple in love suited me and Kevin was recovering very well. Although, still in his cast, he bummed out when his friends picked me up for skiing, oh well. I had a blast and was falling deeper in love with him each day. Kevin was given a knee cast and finally had more mobility. He became increasingly moody as the two-month mark passed. He was tired of his leg cast and missed the skiing trips, but that was no reason for him to become snippy with me. Kevin would nitpick over nothing, slacked off on any domestic chores and started treating me like a slave.

He was taking advantage of me with his condition and expecting me to be Betty Home-Maker. If he thought I was going to do all the house cleaning, grocery shopping, cook all our meals, and shell out the dough, he was nuts! I came home from work with groceries to find the sink full of dishes and the beer I bought the day before gone. He sat on his ass all day, waited for his "maid" to come home, and could not even be bothered to save me a beer. I let him know that I expected some cleaning to go on while I am out making the bacon. Kevin tried to defend himself and admitted that he should have saved a beer for me. Dissatisfaction was growing inside of me, as I became familiar with the day-to-day chores of keeping up a household and not having help from the significant other; the lazy ass acting like a King.

I was particularly irritated this day because of my boss at work, the worm. My female co-workers told me the manager put his hands on their butts and breasts when they were putting food away in the walk-in cooler. I heard the stories of the skinny, weasel of a man groping the girls but nobody said a word about it to others in management. This was the day when I was told to put the salad bar food away in the cooler and I flashed on the stories about the manager. I have no time in my life for taking any abuse from this guy and knew just what I would do if he tried anything with me.

I was in the cooler putting the containers up on the shelf, when the manager came walking up behind me. Before he had the chance to touch me, I turned around to him and told him, "If you touch me I will kick your ass." He just looked at me for a second and walked out of the cooler. Maybe he wasn't even going to try anything, but I had heard enough and somebody should scare him into being respectful. I finished up my shift, just as I normally would, and went home. Kevin had no idea about my bad day at work and how it amplified my impatience for his laziness.

Three days later, a freak, spring snow blizzard hit during the night and the roads were a mess. The snow plows and salt trucks were busy but only the main streets were passable. The time it would take for a taxi to get me to work would have made me much too late. I walked a few blocks to the main street and hitchhiked to work, trying to avoid being splattered on by cars. I was ten minutes late getting to my job and freezing cold.

My wormy manager, the same guy with the cooler groping history, fired me for being late. I knew that he was waiting for me to do anything wrong so he could get rid of me ever since I threatened to kick his ass. It was a miracle that I had made it to work at all in the middle of a blizzard and he knew it. He thoroughly enjoyed firing me. It was clear by his face. Honestly, the job was wearing thin on me and I preferred my pot business, which needed more of my attention anyway. Plus, I finished my book report for school and would be handing it in the next morning!

The next day I returned home from turning in my book report and lit up a joint in celebration. I kicked back on the sofa and was catching up on the day with Kevin. No more high school! I was thrilled beyond my wildest dreams! Kevin decided it was a fine time to tell me that I had a visitor while I was out. It was Sally and her family had returned from the South. I already knew Sally was back and had visited with her. She was living with her mom just a few blocks from my parents' house and was enrolled back at high school.

She was as "cool" as ever, had become a talented artist, and looked beautiful.

Kevin also calmly mentioned, "Oh, we had sex." He used a tone that implied, "Fuck You, See, Idiot." My insides floundered while I sat on the couch and took in what I just heard for a moment. I thought, 'Asshole!' Then I thought, 'I could run over and leap out of the attic apartment window, die on the ground below, and then he would be sorry.' As fast as the thoughts came, I realized he was not worth my life, my love or anything from me ever again! My dream of living with my sweetheart blew up in my face and the emotional pain was mixed with bombastic anger.

I telephoned my mother and told her what happened and she invited me to return home with opened arms. I quickly packed up my things, including the toilet paper that I bought, and left. My dear mother said, "I knew you would be back soon, that's why I wasn't too worried when you moved out." I was glad to be back home and able to blow off some steam over Kevin and Sally. Sally seemed like a loyal, longtime friend, but Oh No. I was infuriated at the whole city when I woke up the next morning and walked out of the house in a storm of angst. I decided that I would join the Navy and be done with this place and everyone in it. In a fury and cursing my head off, I began to walk down the street towards the recruiting office. I yelled just what I was thinking; screw it all, which was my attitude.

Who drives up beside me and asks, "What's up?" but Kevin's older brother. I was close with his brother and he was a skiing, camping, and poker regular. I had known him for at least five years and felt comfortable bursting out in tears. He told me to hop in the car and we drove to a favorite party spot with an overlook view of the city. The overlook ended up being the perfect place for the conversation of joining the Navy or getting my life together where I was. He was firm, "Do not join the Navy when you are in this mood, you cannot take back your signature. Sleep on it at least."

We smoked so many joints and laughed about the crap life can deal us, that I needed to just go home and take a nap. When I woke up I scared myself, having remembered how close I came to joining the Navy. I almost made the biggest mistake of my life; I would have crumbled into a frenzy-ridden woman and locked in their jail within the first week. Kevin's brother was an angel in my life and there was no better person to talk me out of the emotional pit that I was in than him.

Life was looking up, and by a giant margin, especially the next night. I was at the neighborhood bar shooting pool with Sarah and Will. Sally walked in and acted as if she was my best friend asking me, "How are you doing?" Without saying a word, I punched her in the face and sent her flying to the floor. I yelled at her, "You whore, betraying slut" and repeated other curse words. She was shocked and assumed Kevin would never tell me about them having sex. My heartache vanished quickly after that appropriately placed punch.

My new Sidekick, Martha, was a trip and had spent the past five years living between a city park and a drug dealer's house. Martha was a street urchin by the sleaziest definition, with uncanny manipulation skills. She lied her ass off about almost everything and she stole anything from anyone, including her friends. Martha was a serious drug addict and had some sexual preferences that were beyond my desire to fathom. Martha was so low sometimes that she stole from me. She visited me over at Kevin's apartment once and stole my favorite shirt and a family heirloom, cameo pin. I confronted her about my missing things and she denied knowing about them, while wearing a smirk on her face.

Martha looked like trouble and she would do almost anything. I still liked to pal around with her, even after she robbed me, because she took me to visit some entertaining people in drug-filled homes. This is the frank truth; she was wild and we did lots of drugs together with her screwed up friends.

CHAPTER 13
LIBERIA TO OBLIVION

On the home front, my Father was given a new assignment . . . in Liberia, Africa. The Bishop of the church was under a mountain of pressure from the Indian tribe to get rid of my father and he did a thorough job of it. My father was being sent to Liberia to be a Professor of Theology at the University and to do his priestly duties at the only church. My parents were not missionaries in any sense but he agreed to the three-year position. My mother worked hard to secure some grants to buy medical equipment for her new life in Africa. She was setting out to teach Labor and Delivery at the hospital and to the nursing students in Liberia.

The Bishop didn't like my dad much, obviously, and sent him into a war zone just ahead of a bloody coup. With many meetings, paperwork, and negotiations out of the way, my parents began to make their plans. First of all, my younger brother was just entering high school and was given the choice; go to boarding school or come to Liberia. He decided to go to Liberia mostly because he did not want to spend his summer vacations with our grandparents. My parents decided that my father and brother would leave six months earlier than my mother to set up the house. The family home in New York would be rented out for the three-year contract and what they weren't taking with them would be stored in the attic.

My older brother took matters into his own hands and joined the Army without saying a word about it. My brother made his announcement at the dinner table and my father's jaw dropped. My father assumed that he would join the Marines and went into a weird state of pouty disgust. The fact that my brother didn't discuss his plans with my father was a big deal. The boy who never did anything wrong dropped a bomb on us with an articulate and calm delivery. He waited to say anything about his departure until it was close, only two weeks away. It was smart to let us in on his plans without giving my father too much time to give him grief about it.

Just like that, my older brother left for boot camp and never returned, ending up being stationed in Germany. Personally, I felt happy for him and knew he was getting out of there. He had never had a girlfriend and stayed to himself a lot; reading and playing war games with his friends. Big Bro was an Eagle Scout and in school clubs from time to time but, other than that, he was usually in his bedroom. Little did anyone suspect that he was busy plotting his departure. Off to the Army he went. Thankfully we were not presently at war and it was back in the days when the military actually educated their troops. After his stint in Germany he graduated from M.I.T., Massachusetts Institute of Technology, and made a successful career for himself.

Deciding on what I wanted to do was simple, I wanted to be an architect and go to a small college in the mountains. My parents loved my plan and we worked out the details over the next few months. My parents made it understood that they wanted me to join them but only if I want to. I was told that arrangements would be made so that if I changed my mind during the next three years the church would fly me to Liberia. The reality of being in New York, alone in the mountains and without family was not really setting in yet, with all the partying I was doing. Liberia huh?

Time flew by and I made my college arrangements, having been accepted at Adirondack Community College. My parents and I made a road trip to the college and met with the Dean, took a pleasant tour, and checked out the town. The Dean sat us down in his office and proceeded to reassure my parents that there was no drug problem at the college or in this beautiful town. It suddenly dawned on me that my life as a college student was going to be drastically different. I was ready to change my life around or at least thought so. Enrolling in the architecture program was a milestone for my parents being able to go off to Liberia with peace of mind. We met with a charming, old lady and rented a room for me in her spacious home. All secured with my college schedule and living space for the next few years, I then began my personal preparations.

The bishop decided to host a going away party for my parents' and my little brother at his palatial home. Our family was there along with many priests, deacons, and the bishop. The bishop's wife had recently been committed to a mental hospital and the bishop had a new girlfriend. The Bishop was hooked up with a very young, beautiful blonde and was shamelessly flaunting her. I could not help myself and loudly asked my mother, "Is that his wife or his daughter?" At which point, my mother kicked me under the table and I said, again loudly, "Ouie, why did you kick me?" The whole room went silent and my questions were left unanswered. I loved the moment being a brat and showing that I was not happy about losing my family.

Graduation Day was approaching and I wanted a dress for the first time in my life. I told my mother that I was thinking about wearing a dress for graduation and she thought she heard me wrong. She said, "What did you say?" I told her that I wanted a dress for graduation. This was music to her ears. She never thought she would see this day. Mom said, "Get in the car, we are going shopping." My mother was in a hurry to get me in the store and buy a dress before I changed my mind. I picked out a seersucker skirt suit with a matching vest. We bought a white linen blouse and a bow tie to wear with it.

This was my first time wearing woman's clothing, so I did not have a slip, pantyhose or shoes. My mom was thrilled that I was realizing that I was a woman and let me pick anything I wanted to wear. My grandparents were coming for my graduation and this would be the first time for them to see me in a skirt. No doubt, my grandparents, brothers, teachers and schoolmates would all be stunned to see me dressed up. My father and younger brother left for Liberia and missed the sight of me in a skirt. I wished my father had watched me graduate from high school after his years of discouragement.

Graduation was a miraculous achievement and I had plenty to be proud about. I was not dead or in jail and I loved proving my father and the principal wrong. The principal was shaking hands with each student and wished them well, while he handed out the diplomas. I walked tall across the stage to receive my diploma and the principal squeezed my hand so hard that my knees gave out a little, but I didn't care, I graduated!

After the ceremony, I skipped the high school parties and went to a club downtown to see my favorite punk band and party it up. My high school years seemed like a lifetime ago by the time I went to graduation and I didn't hang out with those teens much. I showed

up at the club wearing the seersucker suit and felt the eyes move on
me. People were staring at me and my friends commented on how
nice I looked. The complements were hard for me to take and I
knew I blushed bright red. Maybe being a woman wasn't as bad as I
always thought. Even so, I cherished my combat boots and would
never give up wearing my bad-ass, leather jacket.

During this week I fell in love with Ricky, whom I'd met the
previous summer with Will. When I first met him he was living with
a gorgeous blonde girlfriend and had just been released from the
hospital. Ricky was tall and thin, with a sparkle in his eyes, and wore
a hip leather jacket. I met many of his friends and his apartment
mate, all of them living in a nearby, small town. Ricky disclosed to
me why he was hospitalized and his story was gruesome. He had
shot-up some drugs that were cut with some kind of milk sugar and
that caused deadly injury to his veins.

He had to have half of two fingers amputated and it was a miracle
that the doctors were able to save his arm. He swore to me that he
gave up using intravenous drugs, forever. It was easy for me to
believe him while I was looking at his partial fingers. Ricky and I
snorted a lot of cocaine every day and saw the sunrise regularly. I
told my mother about my new boyfriend, Ricky, but I never
introduced them. Kevin was the only boyfriend that I ever brought
to my house and the others were afraid of my father, and rightfully
so. My mother did not seem concerned about Ricky in my life
because I was leaving for college in a few weeks.

The afternoon before my departure for college, my mother and I
were driving downtown to pick me up some last minute items. We
drove as far as the corner of our street when I broke the startling
news. I said, "Mom, I don't want to go to college." My mother was
extremely surprised but kept her cool unbelievably well. My mother
said, "Nobody is making you go to college, only go if you want to.
When I have a problem with you it is when you do something that
you do not want to do." Her words came across as a huge comfort
and I felt at ease with telling her about my desires.

I told her that I was in love with Ricky and wanted to play drums
in a punk band. Mom said, "Do it then." We drove back home and
she telephoned my landlord at college to tell her that I wasn't
coming. The switch in my plans cost my parents a lot of money:
apartment, books, schedule and supplies. My mother was an angel

and never said one word about the financial consequences of changing my mind. I was feeling on top of the world and couldn't wait to tell Ricky that I was staying in the city. My thoughts swiftly went from going to college and becoming an Architect, to playing drums in a punk band, being Ricky's lover, and selling drugs.

Ricky and I were in love and spent almost every moment together. He was working at an auto repair shop downtown and drove a vintage car that he restored. I was making enough money with my pot business for my own drug use and hanging out at the bars, every night. The music scene was getting more exciting with new punk bands starting to spring up. I had major challenges with becoming a punk rock drummer: not owning a drum set or a vehicle to transport them in. Ricky and I spent time with Will, Martha, and some of their new friends. My life was a non-stop party and I thought I was "happening" with my drug business and Ricky's love.

My business was growing faster than I planned, or ever planned on for that matter. I began to sell a variety of drugs: cocaine, speed, LSD. My business meant that I had to do my regular rounds at some of the roughest bars in the city. I had made friends all over the city and they were always waiting to see me for "the goods". My mother was about to move to Liberia and needed to know that I had a safe and healthy place to live and a career plan, at the very least. I was out every night, getting home about six o'clock in the morning and wasted on some drug or another. My mother woke me up this morning and said, "You are not doing nothing, get a job and register for trade school today." I said, "OK, I will" and went back to sleep for an hour.

I enrolled at BOCES Trade School, for Gourmet Cooking and House Construction. My classes interested me, especially the house construction course. There was one other woman in the class filled with older men and she wanted to learn how to build a barn. The teacher was a big old man, a burly type, with a friendly smile. The teacher liked my enthusiasm and was impressed with my knowledge of using the tools of the trade. I was thrilled whenever he asked me to demonstrate how to use a specific tool for the class: a router, planer, etc.

Gourmet Cooking was inspiring and I had always enjoyed cooking. Kevin would, justly, tell you that there was a lot I could have learned about cooking. The class was all women, except for one man, and a lively bunch we were. We ate our creations at the end of every class and seemed like having a dinner party. I felt different from everyone else, yet we all liked each other and had a good time. My mother was happy about me enrolling in school and never expressed her disappointment with me for not going to college. She was the most understanding and supportive mother anybody could ever have.

I met another new friend, Gail, and we rapidly became confidantes. Our conversations flowed as if we had known each other for years. When I was not with Ricky, I was mostly with Gail having a jovial time. I laughed with Gail about many things and we were creative together. Gail had a plan a minute and was enormously enthusiastic about life, even to a manic extreme. We experimented with some artistic career ideas, one after another, until something stuck. We made a short, goofy film with a movie camera her father owned. We made stained glass artwork for a few weeks, without any masterpieces to show for it. The fact of the matter is we were not very good at either pursuit; nor had the discipline to perfect our skills. Gail and I had big dreams for our future together, as best friends forever; like sisters.

My mother was leaving for Africa soon and rented out the house to a family while they were gone. I had to get an apartment right away and did not have a job or enough money. Gail and I spoke about my situation and we decided to get jobs and an apartment together. That very same day, Gail and I both got jobs. She was hired as a waitress at an Italian Restaurant and I was hired as a bartender/waitress at a bar/restaurant about twenty miles outside of the city.

There is an apartment building not far from Ricky's apartment and we moved in there within three days. Gail and I moved in some furniture with her father's station wagon and set up our new home. We laughed at how fortunate we were to have made our dream happen so fast and knew that lucky stars shined on us. Having an apartment together worked out smoothly and our partying commenced.

I was promoted at my job within a week and made generous tips. Ricky picked me up from work and Gail dropped me off because I did not have my own car. Throughout my shift I snorted lines of coke so it's no wonder my boss thought I was the fastest waitress he had ever seen. I had my own bar and cash register in the kitchen area; mixed my own drinks and rang up the customers checks. It took me about two weeks to figure out that I could pocket a lot of the money and drink whatever I want. I began embezzling around $100.00 a night.

This job was great for me. The bands they booked were a pleasure and I made it pay well but my drug business was suffering. Working weekends and not going to my selling points every night began to hurt my profits. Gail and Ricky grew tired of me working so far away and not owning a car of my own so I ended up quitting my job. I kept a lie going with my mother about me working because she was leaving in a couple of days and would majorly, freak-out. My mother would have been suspicious about how I was planning to pay for the apartment and she did not need to worry about me while she dealt with her upcoming trip.

My mom left for Liberia and it did not set in immediately just how alone I really was. My older sister and I were close and we spoke on the phone often, taking the edge off missing my mom. I trusted my sister and told her everything, maybe too much at times. She was worried about me getting into bad trouble with the police or at the sleazy dives I frequented. I was unaware of the problems I could have and saw myself as the "party queen" without a concern in the world.

I needed help with my business and Gail agreed to be my partner and our secretary. I explained to Gail that by us working together we could easily pay our bills. This was before cell phones so someone had to stay near the telephone. That was Gail's job. Gail had an old Sky Lark car and I drove it for the business. I made the drug pickups and tended to the sales around the city and we flourished. The business grew and so did my inventory of essentials, all illegal. My drug dealer, Dan, gave me limitless credit and he watched the money I was making sky rocket.

I sold crystal meth, acid, black opium, hash oil, cocaine, Quaaludes and pot. I was a very popular woman and the phone rang constantly with potential buyers. We lived in a police dead zone; near a small township and between law enforcement jurisdictions. The traffic in and out of our apartment would have been noticeable in the city, but the apartment complex was big enough that my visitors did not stick out too much. The neighbors complained about our late night dancing and music even though I tried my best to keep the noise level down. Gail and I had fun together and met the wildest people.

Martha showed up after disappearing for a month and we walked down to the punk club to visit our friend who was the soundman there. The "Punk" scene was still new and met with some resistance and conflicts. Some tough guys would often arrive at the shows and pick fights with the crowd. This night was no exception, except the trouble makers picked on my friend. These two big thugs, who looked like they were from the movie "Deliverance", punched our friend in his face. I could not believe what I saw and, like a reflex, I hit the attacker in his head with a bottle.

The whole bar was filled with screams as other fights that promptly broke-out.. I ran to the pay phone and called the police on the tough guys, gave their descriptions, and told them my friend was attacked. The second I hung up the phone, I was escorted out of the bar because the bouncer saw me hit the guy with the bottle and he was bleeding all over the place. I yelled curse words at the tough guy as I was being carried out the front door. Martha followed me. The violent clash emptied out into the street in front of the club and some dudes from the disco next door came to join in the punk rocker bashing. The Disco crowd and the Punk Rock crowd were no strangers to violent clashes; it happened almost every weekend.

Martha climbed up on the roof of the disco and threw bricks at the disco dudes that were trying to beat up our friends. Martha was crazier than I was and she never had regrets about the mean things she did. She hit one guy in the head and suddenly the entire crowd's attention went to her. Because Martha was a street urchin she knew the back alleyways and short cuts quickly escape. The police pulled up with their sirens blaring and gave us the distraction we needed to escape. Martha and I ran as fast as we could and easily ditched the disco mob. The mob was afraid to chase us into the dark back ways, where we had an advantage. Meanwhile Gail and Ricky were at the apartment waiting for us to return and were not surprised about the bar fight. I started chopping up lines of coke and we visited till the sun rose.

The amount of drugs I was using each day kept growing and the quantities I dealt in grew too. My clothes closet was a drug super-store! My reputation spread further than I suspected. Now I needed to be careful of rip-offs and my evil competitors. The stakes were higher now and I grew a hardened attitude. I laid down the rules of transaction and my customers had to follow them or I would stop selling to them. To tell a drug buyer that you cut them off was devastating for them so they complied. My main rule was that buyers had to come to our apartment alone and without people waiting for them in their car. I dealt with some "cut-throat" dealers, thugs, serious junkies, and even white-collar workers. I was too big a dealer to not have any protection and I felt it in my blood.

A man was coming over to buy some acid and I told him to come alone, or no deal. This was a guy I had known since high school and I was looking forward to seeing him again. I happened to be looking out of the window when he drove into the parking lot and I saw that he had three people with him. The parking lot was big and he parked at the far end of it, not knowing I saw him pull in. He rang the doorbell and I pulled him into the apartment by his shirt and slammed the door behind us. I told him that I said to come alone and you did not, so no drugs for you, ever. I went on to tell him that I would shoot him if he came back and that went for his friends too. He pleaded with me and told me that the people in the car are his close friends, but I would not change my mind. He told me that he was surprised how mean and dangerous I had become since high school. I led him out the door while cursing at him. This was not enjoyable for me and I did not want to be such a hard ass with him. I felt that I needed to make a strong example for his friends. These people came from the Southside, the Ghetto, and familiar with rough drug deals, killings, and such. I had entered the big leagues of drug dealing within three months of graduating high school and was setting my boundaries.

That night, Gail, Ricky and I stayed home and enjoyed a yummy dinner. Afterwards, we snorted lines of cocaine, laughed about various silly things and listened to music. Around ten o'clock I noticed three concerning cars parked in front of the apartment. The cars were at opposite corners from each other and looked like undercover police cars to me. I turned out the lights and kept an eye on them from a corner of the window.

As I watched, two men got out of one car and walked behind my apartment building. Ricky said, "They just want to take a piss, don't be so paranoid." The bottom line was that the reality of my vulnerability suddenly set in. I saw another unmarked cop car pull up making four cars in total. I knew in my gut that something was very, very wrong. The apartment did not have a back exit and I was in possession of enough drugs to get twenty years behind bars. My closet was filled with ounces of coke, thousands of hits of acid, pounds of pot and hash, ounces of crystal meth and black opium, plus Quaaludes. I suddenly understood the situation that I made for myself and felt terrified. This was too big of a drug stash to effectively hide in the apartment without being found. I sat in front of the window all night long and watched for any movement in the parking lot; not taking my eyes off these men. Ricky stayed by my side and we discussed what I should do next. Ricky and I decided that if we made it until morning without being busted then I would store the drugs somewhere else.

The anxiety rushing through me made it hard to think straight and eating food was the last thing on my mind. The unmarked police cars drove away at the same time around 6:00 am. I jumped up and down with joy that we made it through the night! I had already packed up my drug stash during the extra-long night and was ready to get them out of there. After just enough time to drink a cup of coffee, Ricky and I drove to his apartment complex. I waited in the car, with the stash, while Ricky went inside to get a shovel.

We packed the drugs in garbage bags and took the shovel with us into the wooded area behind his apartment complex. The thick wooded area was dense enough for safety, yet close enough that I could get to it when I needed to sell some. We dug two big holes, buried the drugs and impeccably covered up our tracks. In knew in my heart that I had a close call with jail and vowed to never keep that much inventory again. Ricky and I were able to finally get some sleep and feel safe, even though it took me hours to calm down.

Gail had enough excitement with the police and our lifestyle. She moved out of the apartment that same day, back to her parent's house. I moved in with Ricky and his roommate that evening and left our apartment unlocked with the keys on the kitchen counter. After the scary night I did not care what the landlords thought about my exit. The important fact was that Gail and I were seemingly safe and both happy with our new living arrangements.

The next morning I needed to get my drugs and make a sale, lots of sales, and get rid of them. I went out to the woods only to discover two empty holes. I freaked out! Someone must have seen us bury the bags and dug them up, ripping me off. What was I going to tell the dealer who fronted me the drugs? I had to tell him the truth and I knew that I was in serious trouble. I had no money for him either. Ricky came home to find me shaking with fear and cursing the assholes who stole my drug stash. Ricky tried to console me but knew how much trouble I was in and knowing that there was nothing he could do to fix it. I knew what I had to do: first, put the word out on the street for the thief to return my drugs and then, go tell my dealer what happened.

Dan, my dealer, got angry and started yelling at me, "You drug addict. You did the drugs yourself!" I explained the story again begging him to believe me and telling him I was sorry. He told me to come up with the money or he would kill me, adding what a scum thief I was. I left the house frightened for my life and had no idea how I would come up with that kind of money. He wanted payment in two weeks or he would come and find me.

The unheard of happened! My drugs were returned with the exception of 1 gram of coke. I had put word out on the street, "If I did not get the drugs back, I will be killed because they were not paid for." Someone out there had mercy for me but I never found out who had them. To say that I was thankful would be an understatement. I was lucky this time! I returned the drugs and proved my innocence to Dan. He apologized for not trusting me and calling me low-down names. However, he never said if he was sorry for threatening my life, thus permanently changed our relationship. I also ran my drug business differently from that day forward.

After that frightening night, I only kept my personal stash on hand: a few grams of coke, two ounces of pot, and a dozen Quaaludes. When I got an order for drugs I picked them up and made the sale without the drugs ever passing through our apartment. Life was looking up and Ricky and I were back to drama-free love. Getting myself to the trade school for my classes ended up becoming impossible so I dropped out. As much as I liked house construction and cooking, let's face it, I was not in any shape to be a student.

Dancing was my main exercise and I danced endless hours a week. My dancing style was high energy, intense and calorie burning. I was born with great genes and I stayed slender and toned with no effort whatsoever. I ate very well, mostly due to Ricky's roommate being a career chef. Life with Ricky was fantastic and we often discussed our future plans together. I felt like all my dreams were beginning to come true. I wanted to marry Ricky and start a family when we could get our own home.

Still a businesswoman, I had to visit my usual bars and my regular customers. Gail and I often went out together and made hilarious adventures out of the mundane. I danced myself into another world; feeling as if I was an instrument being played by the music. Ricky was not into this type of music scene but he came along with me and we went to his favorite bar too. We shot hundreds of games of pool at this one dark bar and I won many drinks and money. I was a foosball ringer with my slam-dunk shot from the goal. That shot was lightning fast and worked 99% of the time. Some nights I won as many as 35 drinks on credit which came in handy. Business was going just fine although I interacted with some ruthless characters as well as some trustworthy people.

A man from my past, who I met with the older hippies I knew, came into the bar and we became reacquainted. Business dealings through him were great and he introduced me to new friends, Kip and Laurie. This evening I was at their house and Kip asked me if I wanted to try liquid opium. They said that you swallow the nasty tasting stuff but that the high was ultra-wonderful. I was always up for trying something new and said, "Sure." The four of us sat at their kitchen table, held our shot glasses with the opium, clinked our glasses together and swigged it down. As soon as it hit my stomach my insides twisted and I knew it was coming right back up so I leaped up and tried to get to the bathroom. The reaction was so fast that I had no time to speak. It was also my first time over at their house so I was clueless about where their bathroom was. I panicked and opened a door that I thought was the bathroom, at the same time I started throwing up, and that was that. I opened up the closet door. The high was instant. Even so, I felt embarrassment and was very apologetic to my hosts. We were all laughing about it and just closed the closet door, being much too high to deal with it then. The "high" was intense yet smoothly pleasant at the same time. I never did the liquid opium again and they never forgot the visitor who threw up in their closet! Kip and I did lots of business together and enjoyed our friendship, but they disappeared one day. Drug dealers have a way of simply vanishing for sudden and untold reasons.

Ricky and I decided to take a drive up to the Adirondack Mountains and visit the church camp where I went as a child. We packed a cooler of food and wine, had some acid to take in the forest, and set out on our drive. When we arrived I was glad that the same dirt road we used years earlier was still drivable. Ricky was happy to be in the beautiful mountains and loved re-exploring the camp with me. We parked the car at the path that led to the swimming area, each ate a hit of acid, before we walked towards the main camping area. The acid took effect and so did our laughter and the colorful landscape enhancements. We wandered around the camping area while I told him stories from my childhood. The camp acreage was still gorgeous and the memories coming back filled me with nostalgic joy. We walked down the path to the outdoor chapel where I listened to many sermons spoken by my father. I had no idea why I thought such a disrespectful thing but suggested that we could have sex on the altar. It seemed like the perfect way to say "Fuck-You" to my father for his controlling ways, so we did it. I was right, at least for this brief moment in time.

Ricky and I brought our picnic basket and walked along the path to the swimming area and we dined on the end of the dock. The day could not have been nicer. The leaves were turning their splendid autumn colors and there was a cool crispness to the air. We were drinking wine, nibbling food, and just enjoying ourselves, when we saw a motorboat come around the bend. We watched the motorboat stop on the lake and a man began looking over the side, into the water. It was obvious that the man was looking for something in the lake and he spent about fifteen minutes searching. He looked up and saw us sitting on the dock and quickly sped away, oddly.

Being on acid, the stranger seemed like an intruder to our privacy and his reaction to seeing us made me curious about what he was looking for. We both got the creeps and casually packed up our stuff for the walk back to the car. It was starting to get dark out on the dock so it was pitch black along the deep forest path. I knew the way practically blindfolded, like the back of my hand, thank goodness. As we approached our car, a car filled with drunken teenagers drove by us and kicked up a thick cloud of dust. Evidently, the campgrounds had turned into a local party spot and I was afraid they would double back for us. Maybe it was just coming down from the acid but I felt that we were in big danger so we hauled ass out of there.

The trip was a great one but I was coming down hard from the acid. I was extra emotional when I began thinking about how the camp vibe had changed and what a pity that was. I became melancholy and decided to call my sister and tell her about the trip to camp. I told her about having sex on the altar and she was shocked at the depth of my defiant streak. She was not thrilled with my story and became concerned about how high I was and that I could hardly speak a sentence. My bed felt extra comfortable this night.

Martha began hanging around us more often. I knew Martha was a drug addict and that she was shooting up more often so I kept her at arm's length. I was not a part of the needle scene nor did I do any business with her rip-off self. We had many mutual friends and she became friends with Ricky too. I did not know much about when they would meet each other and I was not a suspicious woman so I wasn't alarmed about it. I knew Ricky was in love with me and I trusted him was all that mattered. Martha knew that I would beat her badly if I caught her having sex with Ricky and she knew to be afraid of me.

The bottom fell out of my Dream Life" one evening. I saw track marks on Ricky's arms and knew that he was shooting up drugs again. Ricky promised me when we first got together that he would never shoot up again. The trauma he went through having parts of his fingers amputated had apparently worn off. I drew the line; dumped him that same minute and wished him well. He begged me to stay and promised me that he was never going to shoot up again and that this was a one-time mistake. He pleaded with me for hours and I eventually gave in. I was still in love with him so I gave him one last chance.

I told Ricky's roommate about him shooting up again and he hit the roof. He was going to kick his ass if he caught him with any needles or tracks in his arms. Ricky was worse off than his roommate or I thought and his long drug withdrawal was ugly to watch. The roommate and I decided that Ricky had to stay home and not have visitors for a few weeks until he got clean again. We rotated guard, babysitting, to make sure that Ricky did not get any drugs and he definitely tried. The rest of my life stopped while I tended to Ricky and put up with his angry outbursts. My love for him was used up and I was nearing the end of what I could do for him. One night, Ricky was in the bathroom a little too long and made me wonder if he had found a way to get drugs. My intuition was right. I picked the bathroom lock and found him hitting up. He was relaxed back on the toilet seat with the needle sitting there on the sink. After giving up my life to babysit him, I became furious and had been through enough. I packed up my things and phoned his roommate to explain why I was leaving. I told Ricky, "Have a nice life", and slammed the door behind me.

Gail was a college student now and doing very well. Her parents had a big house and went away for the winter to visit relatives. Gail was so sad to hear what happened with Ricky that she invited me to stay with her for the winter. Being with Gail gave me a sense of deep comfort and gave me a chance to heal from my broken dreams and drug use. Living with Gail was healthier by far than living with Ricky and it was a more stable environment. I missed my mother immensely and could have used one of her giant hugs!

Life with Gail was still action packed as we resumed business together and circulated through the bar scene. Ricky was calling me and trying to convince me to come back but there was no way. I moved passed Ricky fast and remembering the lies he told made it easy. I knew how strong drug addiction could be and knew that Ricky was powerless against it. I also knew that life was too short to spend it babysitting a deceitful junkie.

Gail and I met two handsome guys at a bar downtown who knew some of Ricky's childhood friends. The four of us had a lively conversation and the chemistry between us was electrifying. We invited the fine fellows back to our house to snort some lines and have privacy. Our new friends happily took us up on our invitation.

Gail began a love affair with one of the lovely men; definitely the sexier of the two. I actually was attracted to the other man because he was manly in a Jack Nicholson sort of way. His voice was deep and sexy, he had a mustache, and medium length brown hair. These two guys were "city slickers": fashionable, sexy, and knew how to treat a woman. The four of us spent many nights together. Gail and her lover slept upstairs in the attic bedroom and we slept in my room down in the basement. My bedroom was huge and perfect for our partying area, as it was tucked far away from Gail's siblings. These two guys were much bigger drug dealers than I was and introduced us to some heavy characters.

This particular night was more life changing than I ever realized it could be; with my new boyfriend, Walt, turning me onto "freebase." I am a double Pisces and highly susceptible to addictions, plus I loved experiencing altered states of consciousness. Freebase took me by surprise and I loved it right away. I became a freebase addict within days of trying it and Walt had plenty of it.

My cocaine addiction was getting seriously expensive. I used at least 2 grams a day to snort in addition to the freebase, costing me at least $700.00 a day. Walt and his friend spent quite a lot of time in NYC and Miami so Gail and I were often on our own. We frequented the bar scene, danced liked frenzied animals, and strutted our stuff. We thought we were the coolest women in the city and knew many people wherever we went.

Business was rocking though, at times I made some deals under the influence so there were some mistakes with calculating. I answered the phone one evening and spoke "numbers" with this guy who wanted to make a purchase. He agreed to my price and we ended the call by arranging our meeting. I hung up the phone and double-checked my figures and found a mistake. I meant to make $80.00 off the deal but accidently made $800.00. Nice!

Did I call and correct my mistake? No. My integrity was in the toilet when it came to my business and I would get away with whatever I could. I cut my cocaine with Manitol, lightly, because I wanted the coke for myself. The cocaine I was getting was so pure that it was still better cut than the average coke on the street. I spoke with Gail about all the drug deals and my rationale for how I was handling them. There is no question that Gail, Dear Sweet Gail, was my conscience. She would ask, "Now, is that right?" Gail allowed a small margin for my cutting the product and bumping up prices for the ignorant.

My bedroom was located in a section of the gigantic basement, in a wood paneled room, and I plunked a mattress down in front of the furnace. The winters were too freezing for me and the house was kept so cold that we could see our breath in the kitchen. I became highly addicted to freebase and neglected healthy routines. Thinking of food as necessary nutrition never entered my mind and it was too cold to cook. I seldom ate, but when I did it was usually something simple like steak and eggs. The winter weather was getting me down and my internal rhythm was a mess. Gail and I stayed up until dawn every night and slept until late in the day.

Most mornings Gail fell asleep on the couch in my bedroom. We woke up about the same time and, from under our warm covers, argued about whose turn it is to make the coffee. Neither of us wanted to be traumatized by getting up from the comfort of our beds (her couch). Gail and I made many bargains and trades when it came to preparing meals in the cold kitchen. Gail and I were just like sisters and bickered like an old married couple. We woke up every afternoon and started our party life over again: dealing, bar-hopping, and partying till dawn. We had many memorable times in that basement; especially with the bizarre array of people we invited there after the bars closed. We sure thought that we were the Party Gals with the goods.

CHAPTER 14
BLASTED OPEN: DARK-VS-LIGHT

January 3rd at about 1:30 in the morning "It" happened and I will never forget this otherworldly experience. Gail and I returned home from the bar and went downstairs to my room, like always. We were carrying on about the night's entertaining interactions, sipping cognac for warmth, and feeling quite pleased with ourselves. We returned home earlier and more sober than normally. Gail was sitting in a chair across from me and I was sitting on the couch, with a coffee table in between us. Then "It" happened! A bolt of white light flashed through me and electrocuted me. It shot through my whole body; I shook, and was vibrated to my very core. I could not move or speak, and was physically riveted to the couch. The white light blast lasted for a few seconds and was truly the most powerful otherworldly experience that I ever had. The magnificent energy jolt left me forever changed.

Gail felt the energy blast and saw the white light too. The light white light blast was less intense for her but she saw that I was going through something very intense. When the white light bolt stopped, Gail and I could only just stare at each other. It took both of us a moment to be able to speak again, being in shock because we knew this was a supernatural experience.

I asked Gail, " Do you think this is the feeling you get if your mother dies or something terrible has happened?" My reaction and first words frightened Gail to her bones. Gail's mother was spending the night and we went upstairs to check on her. Oddly Gail's mother was already awake and turned to us asking, "What are you doing up?" We told her about the white light blast and how I was vibrating like a live wire. She told Gail that she could call her father and check on him if she wants to, but that we should go to sleep. Gail telephoned her dad and he was fine. I could not call my parents because they used long wave radio in their African village and I didn't know how to get a call through to them. I assumed my parents were fine because there was nothing else I could do.

We went back to the basement and sat side-by-side on the sofa. For some weird reason I was afraid to have my back to the door and watched it closely while we spoke. Then another freaky thing happened. I began to say something to Gail, but instead, I became an observer to my own words. Out of my mouth flowed a number of strange things, posed mostly as questions. I said, "Why do I know things before they happen? Why have people always commented on my eyes? Why did the bullets not hit me? Why did I know to not get in the car with the men in N.C.? Why am I on Earth?" I rambled off these questions and others, with Gail focused not on my words but on how "out of character" I was acting. Feeling in control of my words again, I said, "Gail, I do not know where those words came from and I am shaking with power surges."

Suddenly I panicked and frantically said, "Your mother is coming to us!" Gail's mother never before came downstairs to my room. I was afraid and practically climbing on Gail by the time her mother came through the door. She came in the room, calmly sat down in the chair and, without us saying a word, she answered the questions I asked in my weird state. Then she stood up and walked back upstairs. Gail's mom's voice sounded unusual: slow, like she was channeling a spirit or something equally as wacko.

My life was getting stranger by the second and Gail didn't know what to think. We both knew that something very powerful and incomprehensible was happening to us. Gail said, "You know, you are strange." Then another bolt of white light hit us both, but this time the energy made us feel serene and fully calmed us. The light lasted for just a couple of seconds and was so comforting that it made us feel safe. Tired after all that, we both slept deeply, and had plenty to speak about the next morning.

The white lightning jolt drastically changed me and I mostly noticed the difference in my intuition and energy level. My body was in a heightened state of alertness and I knew who was calling before the phone even rang. I knew that a psychic portal of some kind had opened up for me. Gail still did not know what to think about me, yet thought this was a provocative gift to have. Gail and I decided to see just how psychic I became and to put me through some challenges.

We spent hours in my bedroom testing my skills by Gail picking a regular playing card and then I would tell her what card it is. It was easy for me to know if it was a red suit or a black one but the royal cards were the hardest to identify. When Gail looked at a card, I saw the card floating in the air in front of her face, it was see-through but I could make it out fairly well. I knew about 85% of the cards at first and got much better at it as the days went by. I asked Gail to visualize anything in the world and she did. She kept the vision in her mind for about ten seconds and I told her it is a big piece of ice or a crystal. Gail said that she was visioning the ice cube in her glass. We were thrilled! Our brains spun with ways to use these powers for our gain and it was thrilling. We were not having a dull life, I'll say!

It was uncanny that I knew what was going to happen next, who was going to call and why. I got giant surges of energy and knew to be at a specific place and time to meet up with someone I wanted to see. Gail was fascinated by our life and the many oddities and serendipity that happened to us every day. For example, whenever we pulled into the parking lot of a bar we frequented, the streetlights would go off. We did not think much of it until it happened every time we parked there for months. Plus, when we walked to the door of a bar, often Gail or I, would find money on the ground and it was always a twenty dollar bill. This happened to us at least three times a week for the rest of the winter.

The weirdest thing was that I always knew where our boyfriends were and when they would be returning. I would tell Gail where to be when they arrived; specific times and places. I knew, to the minute, when they were to walk in and Gail would scream when they arrived, every time. We were comical together, laughing about our secret insights, and other people had no idea what we were giggling about.

Some things stayed the same. I was still a coke addict and running my business. Gail and I made the rounds to our bars and partied until sunrise. The basement bedroom did not have any windows so we were on our own, unhealthy, inner rhythms.

One eerie night when we were falling asleep, I felt strangely unsettled for no apparent reason. Gail was asleep on the couch and I was tucked in my bed on the floor in front of the furnace. I was almost asleep when a pressure came onto my body and the room became extra dark. I did not know what was happening to me, the pressure became a heavy weight on my chest. The darkness was thick and frightening, especially when the furnace kicked on and there was no reflection from the flame. The light on the clock was cloaked by the blackness and I was scared. I tried to move my body but the weight of the blackness was too much and it pinned me down. After I tried to scream and nothing came out, the heavy blackness left and the pressure on me lifted. I thought Gail was sleeping through the whole thing, but she was witnessing the same freaky presence. When the darkness vanished we both sat up and started talking about what just happened. We knew in our blood that this darkness was pure evil and that we were clueless as to what to do about it.

The next morning, Gail called a woman who she knew was a white witch and asked her about our blackness problem. We were told to wear blue pajamas, put blue sheets on the beds, light a white candle, and ask the Angels of Light for their help. Gail thanked her for her advice and we listened. Gail and I found blue pajamas and we split the only blue set of sheets in the house. A white candle was burning at every safe spot in my bedroom; making it look like a sanctuary.

That night the darkness returned with its heaviness. Again, the reflection from the fire of the furnace was not visible through the weighty blackness, and lasting for about two minutes. I did not feel the pressure on me nearly as forcefully as the night before, however I could feel the presence of pure evil in the room. I asked the Guardian Angels of Light to please protect us, just like we were told to do. The thick blackness left and Gail and I shouted out in our relief! We thought that we had the evil presence kicked out of the house with the help of the Guardian Angels of Light and the white candles. It never occurred to use to wonder why this heavy darkness showed up in the first place.

I wanted to have a Turkish tea-leaf reading done to see if I could understand more about what was going on with me. While my tea-leaves were being read the clairvoyant said, "Oh no, Oh no" and then put the cup down. She said, "I am stopping now, I'm too tired and we can finish the reading soon." I begged her to tell me what she saw in the teacup, but she refused in a harsh tone. I was bewildered at her reaction to the teacup and it scared me.

Two days later we finished the reading and it was very disturbing. The cup showed the spelling of a woman's name in one direction and a skeleton with horns when you turn the cup sideways. The woman whose name was written in the tea leaves was staying in Gail's house with us. She was a college student who we've known since high school and she basically kept to herself. The Clairvoyant assured me that I would not have any trouble from this woman and that she will be moving away very soon. The reading showed that I would prevail and that evil forces really were at work. I thanked her for the insights and she wished me all the protection that I need.

I told Gail about the tea-leaf reading and she got the heebie-jeebies about what the woman house guest might do. We thought of horror movies, the Exorcist and Carrie, getting ourselves completely flipped out. Gail and I decided to go upstairs and have a little visit with the woman, who we really liked. She acted normally and was studying at her desk. She was glad we popped in for a visit. Gail asked her about her plans and how she was doing with her studies. The conversation went nice enough and I knew Gail and I were both being a bit strange around her. She had no plans of moving out soon and her college studies were going fine. We wished her a lovely evening and went back downstairs and sat in front of the fireplace.

I was letting Gail know about the changes I was experiencing with my energy field. If I put my hands out in front of me more than a foot or so, my hands would become super electrified and they felt like sparks were flying out of them. I showed Gail what I was talking about and pointed my hand out towards her. She felt it all right and jumped back a few feet, yelling, "Stop it!"

This phenomenon was powerful and I did not know what to do with it. I had to keep my hands close to my body or else electric shocks shot straight out of them. I also was laughing about the psychic occurrences and about me being able to know what people are thinking. I was showing off my new electrical power and wondered what the dog would do if I pointed my hand towards it. I pointed at the dog and the shock waves flew out. The dog turned vicious and showed its teeth growling at me. I put my hands away fast before I got bit. I had never seen the docile dog get upset before and it scared me.

Gail's sister was staying at the house and told me that the woman guest was looking all over for me and wanted to speak with me. I could not imagine what she wanted since we had just visited. I was hesitant to go up to her room but I did anyway. I knocked on the door and heard a deep male voice say, "What do you want?" The hair on the back of my neck stood up. I knew that this was not her voice and it sounded demonic so I ran. I leapt from the top of the staircase to the floor below, not taking the time to walk down properly. I was frightened out of my wits that the devil was in her, or in her bedroom, because of the horned skeleton in the tea-leaf reading. Gail was startled by the loud thump I made landing and came running into the foyer, where I told her what I heard and felt. I did not want to sleep one more night under the same roof with her and neither did Gail.

As Gail and I were wondering how to protect ourselves from the house guest, she came running down the stairs. She said, "I don't know what's going around here, but I saw a ghost and am gone. Bye." She was running from the house with her suitcase. She came over the next day with her boyfriend and picked up the rest of her things. While she was here, she told us that she saw the devil trying to enter her and has never been so afraid in her life. This was the last time she ever set a foot in that house. "Holy Shit" I thought. I was a long way from understanding the supernatural powers in our lives.

The heavy blackness was still coming in the night and we asked the Guardian Angels of Light for their help, wore our blue pajamas, and lit the white candles. With the haunting continuing, we sought advice more from the Clairvoyant and had to keep coping with it. The Clairvoyant called me to say that she had an angelic visitation the night before. She said that her astral body was taken to our house and was she greeted by three angels hovering over the rooftop. When she asked the angels what they were doing here, they said, "We are taking care of Gail and Anne." The Clairvoyant said that what is going on at your house is a big deal and to have all this happening to me was weird. I couldn't wait to tell her about my electric shocking hands and she said, "Yes, very strange." Gail and I felt so much better knowing that three angels were at the house protecting us.

Gail and I were still enjoying our flourishing business and wild nightlife. When we were not with our boyfriends, we were strutting ourselves around the city, snorting and drinking in "hot" outfits. I still had a tomboy streak when it came to shoes and only wore my Converse All-Stars, or combat boots. Gail loved the high heels and satin pants style. The two of us were always up to something and found the constant serendipity in our life entertaining. The street lights in the parking lot turning off when we pull in, daily finding money on the ground, and winning the $20.00 lottery 99 percent of time we bought a ticket and the psychic insights galore kept us ecstatic. We loved our men and cherished the time we spent with them, but we kept our paranormal concerns to ourselves. Our lovers already thought Gail and I were "out there" and the haunting and psychic events would have made them run.

Gail's boyfriend showed up at the bar with a friend of his who we had never met. We invited them over to the house for some after-hour partying and they accepted. After two hours, Gail and her lover went up to her bedroom and his friend snuggled into my bed. He knew about my boyfriend and I made it quite clear that he was just going to sleep; no sex. I told him that a heavy blackness may come but not to worry because three angels are here protecting us.

He was listening carefully to what I was saying and then it came. The blackness filled the room and I pointed out that the furnace flame reflection wasn't visible. This guy freaked out, jumped out of bed, and had his pants on within seconds. He went running up the stairs to get his friend, who was running down the stairs. The two of them said, "Goodbye" and dashed out the front door.

Gail told me that they had been making love, when the entire room flashed with a blinding bright, white light and her boyfriend jumped out of his skin in terror. Gail told him it was just three angels sent here to protect us and not to be afraid. He wasn't going to stay one more second and hauled butt down the stairs. I told Gail what happened in my room and thought we may never see them again. Gail and I laughed loudly over what happened. The look on their faces was real terror and we enjoyed the bizarre episode thoroughly. Our life together was getting intensely confusing and we had no idea what this otherworldly influence wanted with us.

The next day, Gail's lover called her and told her that his friend was released from a mental hospital only the week before. His friend was admitted to the hospital six months ago because demons were following him and he went loony over it. I did not think the experience I gave him was funny anymore, after I heard the horrible story. We still saw them often but never at our house because they were too scared to return there.

Gail received a phone call from a neighborhood friend, saying he got me into a high stakes poker game at a rough Biker bar. We were so excited because I was finally going to get the chance to use my new powers to win. The poker players were big and mostly fat. They looked thoroughly like tough Bikers; large men wearing their leather vests with the "club" insignia and each had long stringy hair. I was acting like a goofball and had Gail walk around my chair three times and wiggle her fingers over it for good luck. I looked about fourteen years old, dressed like a bad-ass boy and was skinny from my lifestyle. I could see the men's cards; their hands were shown across their foreheads, like a holograph, and I knew when they were bluffing.

I won the poker hands, time after time, and the biker guys couldn't understand it. I was being watched very closely and wasn't cheating in a detectable way and baffled them further. I won a particularly large pot and reached over to scoop the money towards me, when a big strong hand got there first. I told the Biker, "Give me my money now!" He just looked at me and the other guys were watching the scandal develop. I jumped in his face and screamed at him, "You better give me money or you will be very sorry." He backed down and pushed the money towards me, while cursing at me the whole time. My attitude was as if I had my hand on a gun; bold and loud. Gail and I decided this was a good time to leave and walked out. I won more than eight hundred dollars that night and liked my new powers a lot! Wow, did Gail and I have a lot to laugh about while celebrating our weird winnings!

It had been awhile since I spoke with my sister and was overjoyed when she finally called me. I filled her in on the details about the terrifying heavy blackness and the angels sent to protect us. Also, about how we are protecting ourselves with lighting white candles and wearing blue pajamas. My sister knew about my freebase addiction and what I told her frightened her. She knew that I hung out with some big-wig, dangerous dealers and drug addicts in the sleaziest of places. However, the evil spirit that was haunting me really scared her and she thought I would need a rubber room soon. I was urged to see my old therapist and get off the drugs but I didn't listen to her. Instead, I talked about how much fun I was having and loving life. There was nothing she could do to help me because I was clueless anything was wrong with the way I was living. We agreed to speak soon and wished each other lots of love.

My addiction grew and the amounts of freebase I was smoking everyday depleted all the money we made. I got a new boyfriend,

Doug, the same man who was at the house and scared off by the heavy darkness -- Yes, the one just released from the mental hospital. I had stayed at his house almost every night since we became romantic. He was an expert freebase cook and had pounds of cocaine at any given time. More than mere drug friends, we shared deeply caring feelings between us, yet our main pastime was staying up all night, smoking base. We smoked ounces of freebase and every few days we went to a restaurant for a big meal.

He had plenty of booze, some coffee, and cookies in the house, but no real food. Gail and her lover would meet with us at restaurants that were having 'all you can eat' king crab leg specials. We dined the 'king crab special' restaurant circuit, yum! The four of us ate a mountain of crab and stayed for hours. We took turns going to the parking lot for a pot smoking breaks. The times we had together at these restaurants were a blast and our lovers treated us like queens. Gail and I got used to this lifestyle fast.

Having all the freebase I could smoke, cocaine I could snort, pot to smoke, and alcohol to drink was starting to show. Eating every few days, when I remembered, was not enough to sustain myself. My internal clock was turned upside down; Sunlight, huh, what's that? I began to have abdominal cramps and they were not menstrual in nature. However, I was consumed with only one thing; getting more freebase. I paid little attention to myself, other than I needed lots of cocaine.

I woke up at Gail's house one morning and we had run out of cocaine for the first time since I became an addict. My addiction showed just how bad and painful it could get and I was desperate. I could not get out of bed because I could not bear the agony I felt and wanted to sleep until some cocaine arrived. I kept moaning to Gail, "Did you call…..(the names changed as I thought about who might bring me coke)." I hurt emotionally and physically, and did not know how to cope with the strength of it. Full Blown Misery! Finally some cocaine arrived and put me back in shape. Now, I knew that I must never run out of freebase again.

My nights out with Gail were full of coincidences and humorous moments with our private jokes about the paranormal activity going on. This odd development in our lives fueled plenty of laughs. For example, Gail and I were chatting at the bar and a frantic man came up to us. He was pointing at me and kept repeating, "You are

Glowing! You are Glowing!" Gail told him it was just an angel buddy and not to be alarmed, then we cracked up laughing. The man just looked at us like we were crazy and walked away, without saying another word. Then, I handed the bartender some money and accidently shocked him by putting my hand out further than my "personal energy field." The bartender said, "Ouch", pulled his hand back and then he looked up at me with wonder. Again, Gail and I laughed at the event, thinking that we were super cool with an extra kicker.

While we were in the bar very late, a snow blizzard was underway and burying the streets. Gail and I decided to leave earlier than usual for some reason and found the parking lot was two feet high with snow. We got into the car and thought that we needed a miracle to get home. As fast as we thought that, the streetlight blinked back on and we knew we would make it home safely. We did safely slide into the driveway, home.

Back in my warm bedroom I began experimenting on Gail with my new energy and she didn't like this one bit. I asked her to tell me what she feels and I opened up my arms and stuck them out towards her. She tried to cover herself and began screaming, "Stop it! Stop it!" I pulled my arms back in and thought I was the most awesome woman ever born. My newly discovered gifts went right to my head. I began thinking that I was even more powerful than the heavy blackness. Wrong!

That night the heavy black presence returned and we prayed to the Guardian Angels of Light for protection. The furnace flame could not be seen for more than three minutes this time and the weight was heavier than it had been lately. Gail and I ran upstairs in fear and feeling that the evil darkness was gaining strength. This darkness was the blackest black that exists and so thick that it pinned me in my bed once. Gail and I had about enough of this demonic presence and were getting desperate for help.

Gail telephoned the Clairvoyant, who we woke, and she told us to find a Bible and open it up. We took an ancient Bible off the bookshelf and opened it up, just like she said. Gail turned the cover back and a white lightning bolt flashed out of it, lighting up the whole room. We both jumped backward with amazement and completely awestruck. We started to giggle and I said, "I guess it is gone now." We took the ancient Bible downstairs with us and opened it up, keeping it as near to us as we could. We attempted to sleep with the lights on, wearing our blue pajamas and white candles burning. With the blackness returning, we were afraid our protective rituals were not doing the trick.

To add to a very bad time, I spent the drug money I made and wasn't able to pay my dealer. My drug use had become very expensive and out of my addicted control. I had no willpower left against the cocaine. My dealer, Dan, became enraged with me when I told him that I mismanaged the money. Before, when I was ripped off, he accused me of being an addict and doing the drugs. I was innocent back then but this time he was right. I owed him $650.00 and did not have it. Plus, if he decides to cut me off from having drugs to sell then I would have a hard time making his money back.

Dan gave me three weeks to get the cash, or else he was going to kill me. I knew more about this guy now and had no doubt that he would have me maimed, just as an example to others. I told him I would get him the money, that I was very sorry, and then got out of his home. I spent so much time doing freebase with my lover that I was incapable of keeping a job so dealing drugs was my career. The stress of owing Dan money was gnawing on me, scarily so.

Gail knew all about the trouble I was in with Dan and she got an idea. Gail heard about a spell that would make him like me, no matter what. The spell idea sounded good and I was willing to try anything to save myself. Gail and I woke up early that morning and performed the spell ritual. Then, we asked ourselves some questions: "Would the spell work? How long would it take? How will we know?" Holy Shit! By noon we knew exactly what happened with the spell.

Dan telephoned Gail saying that he did not know why he had to urgently speak with her and told her what had just happened. He got into his car and started to back out of the garage, and like always, put his car in reverse and pushed the gas pedal. Mysteriously the car's engine revved up on its own, drove forward instead of reverse, and he crashed through the back of his garage. Then he kept saying, "I do not know why I have to tell you this, it just happened." Gail consoled him the best she could and hung up the phone. We both stood in the kitchen looking at each other with our hands over our faces. We burst out laughing and swore we would never tell anybody about this.

Crazy as it is, we tried to figure out what we might have done wrong with the spell ritual and then tried it again. We did it again and waited to hear news it brings and hoping that Dan decided to like me again.

Again, he felt the urgency to call Gail and tell her what happened. This time, he was driving down a busy road and suddenly his car spun around and was heading in the opposite direction. He drove up onto a schoolyard lawn to avoid a head-on collision. He kept saying that he had no control over his car and he thought something very spooky was happening. He still could not understand why he felt that he needed to call her about it. Dan was frantic! Gail told me the news and we both burst out laughing, knowing that he was safe. After we caught our breath, we knew that spells were "Out". Dan hated me just the same as he did before and maybe even more.

Gail's old friend thought that we needed to meet a man she knows who might be able to help us better understand our frightening blackness problem. We were open to all the help we could get and didn't know where else to turn for advice. We invited her friend and this man to dinner, plus two others making six. The conversation was exciting and this man certainly was unusual and seemed wise about the spirit world. He had long hair and a beard, was slender, and around forty-five years old. The conversation steered itself into him explaining about the Tarot to us and I thought it was interesting. He was generous in offering to do a Tarot card reading with me after dinner and I accepted the invitation.

I thought it was odd that, one by one, every person at dinner left the table. Each person said that they were tired and were going to sit in the living room and nap. This strange and interesting man and I conversed at the dining table late into the night. He did more than one tarot card reading with me and gave me his intuitive interpretations of the meanings for me. I was told that I was the Blonde Beast and was meant to be a Priestess of the Occult. I had no idea what he was talking about and he said that I was powerful and could have anything I wanted. His words sounded thrilling to me and gave me something fanciful to think about. We finished our conversation with him saying that the next day he would drop off a book for me to read.

The strange man left by taxi and Gail woke up when she heard the front door close. I told her about the tarot readings; as much as I was able to understand about it. Gail had an interesting insight, and thought the strange man put the house under a spell to make everyone else fall asleep after dinner. I had to agree that is was ultra-odd that everyone, except for him and I, passed out. I slept better that night than I had in a very long time, even though my head had been filled with the majestic thoughts he left with me.

Sure enough, he did come by the next day and left the book for me on the porch. The book was *The Book of the New Law* and I read it cover to cover in one sitting. The book was obviously a Bible of some kind for the Devil Worshipers and I found it hard to comprehend that this stuff goes on. I was oblivious of the occultists in the city and, after reading that book, knew to stay away from that crowd. The things I read in *The Book of the New Law* had no place in my life. The evil spirit already haunting us was enough darkness thank-you. Neither this book nor the strange man gave me any clues about how to rid myself from the heavy blackness problem.

Not knowing where my strong beliefs about this man came from, I just knew not to go anywhere with him. He phoned and asked, "So how do you like the book?" I was honest with him and told him that I thought it was too extreme for me although I had found it highly educational. I left the book on the porch for him to pick up and made certain that I would not see him. *The Book of the New Law* had parts in it describing killing babies and using their blood in rituals and called for people to cause pain and suffering in every way they could. You do not have to be a 'Preacher's Daughter' to know that this is trouble with a capital T.

I moved into the bedroom upstairs made available by the woman houseguest leaving. After seeing her name written into a skeleton with horns in the tea leaves, Gail and I felt more relaxed when she moved out. I was greatly unsettled by the heavy darkness still appearing downstairs after she left because I hoped that it would have left with her. The otherworldly, heavy blackness became more terrifying and confusing with time, and I had nobody to help me. At least my new bedroom was lighter and much warmer. I needed a change and this room increased my chances of seeing daylight.

My body was still vibrating at a high level since the white light bolt hit me but the electrical shocks from my hands had decreased. Still infatuated by my new gifts, I tested myself whenever I could. I sat on the bed and focused my attention on the corner of a poster hanging on the wall. I experimented on flipping up the corner of the poster with my mind. It took no effort to get the corner of the poster to move a little and I got really excited. I ran downstairs to find Gail and show her what I could do.

Gail came up to my bedroom and sat down on the bed next to me. I told her to watch the corner of the poster because I am going to flip up the edge with my mind. Gail waited and stared at the poster, having no doubt that I could do it. Sure enough, the corner of the poster did flip up and this time I gave my intention a burst and the corner of the poster tore. Gail didn't like my trick at all. In fact it scared her.

I was, literally, jumping up and down with joy and thought, 'I am ultra powerful'. Gail begged me to stop messing around and told me that I should stick to poker games. We had no idea what I was able to do with these odd gifts but we had some fantasies.

I was falling asleep that night in my new, lighter bedroom and I finally felt safe. I was almost asleep when my spirit rose up and out of my body. I was floating above and looking down at my body in the bed. My spirit was about four feet above my body and the sensations I felt were weightlessness and tingling. As soon as I comprehended that I was out of my body, I came down fast-- slamming back into myself. I enjoying the grand experience and promptly drifted off into deep sleep, feeling exhausted from it.

I couldn't wait to tell Gail what had happened over our morning coffee. Gail's eyes were opened extra wide while she listened to my "out of body" story. The most significant thing was that we both slept a night without the heavy blackness coming and scaring us half to death.

Gail's relative arrived and was going to be staying in my upstairs bedroom for the night. I was hesitant to go back to the basement room because of the spooky times down there. I thought that the evil spirit might be living in the basement and we should always sleep upstairs. Gail and I were even afraid to go to the basement to do our laundry; knowing the blackness was down there. Gail's sister has an upstairs bedroom, with two twin beds, and we slept in her room that night. Her sister was away at college and would not have minded under the scary circumstances.

I was in that lucid state, just before falling into deep sleep, when I began to hear a deep howling sound. The sound was a tone that breezed through me with a wave of sheer terror. The sound grew extremely loud and thunderous, yet was definitely guttural and resonating. I know this will sound unbelievable, but the walls began breathing in and out in sync with the howling sound. I do not think that I could have been more frightened than I was at that moment.

Then, I saw flashing lights shining through the floor to ceiling windows that faced the front of the house. The lights looked the same as those from a police car and, having a drug dealing history, my first reaction was to jump up and look. A major haunting was going on but the flashing lights had to be dealt with. I started to sit up and was going to go over to the window when I heard a loud male voice say, "Do not go to the window because it wants to throw you out of it and kill you."

So, I yelled out, "I am not going to go to the window and get out of here! Now!" The flashing lights vanished in that instant and the room stopped breathing and so did the bone penetrating groans. I begged the Guardian Angels of Light to take care of us and thanked the voice that told me not to go to the window. This voice had to be an Angel; it came out of nowhere and spoke to me, loud and clear. Initially, I was scared out of my wits and paralyzed then, after hearing the voice, I suddenly felt strong enough to do something.

Calm came over the room and I looked over towards Gail, who was fit for a rubber room. Gail was fully awake and scared stiff throughout the entire event. She witnessed the flashing lights and heard the groans, but did not hear the voice that told me not to go to the window. I asked Gail, "What do you say we get an apartment today?" We had seen enough and she did not hesitate for a second to say, "Yes".

There was no use in trying to sleep after that and with our fear flooding us. Instead, we drank some coffee and started looking in the newspaper for an apartment. We found a cute, two-bedroom apartment in a 4plex in an ideal location. After telephoning Gail's dad for some money, we rented it and moved in enough things to sleep and eat there. Being in our new apartment was truly liberating for many reasons. The relief we both, were feeling was enormous; like we barely escaped the "Exorcist Real Life Movie."

Gail and I were thoroughly comforted by an ethereal, white light cross that was shining in midair and stayed in the hallway leading to our bedrooms. The cross was about 2-1/2 feet tall and shined brightly. Gail saw the light cross too, and we knew that we made the right decision to move and were finally protected.

We settled into our new apartment easily and were having the best times. We made our business rounds and partied up a storm in the city. Our lovers popped back into town and we invited them over for dinner. I developed a new love for cooking and made a crab quiche for the first time. Our sweethearts loved our new apartment and talked about how scared they were to visit us where we had been staying. The heavy blackness, along with my new powers, were a bit much for anyone to take calmly so we understood their fright.

We sat on pillows around a coffee table in the living room, not having a dining room table, yet. I was listening to the conversation when I felt a sharp poke in my right butt cheek. I rubbed my hand over the spot to see if a pin was stuck there and looked if something sharp was in the carpet but I didn't find anything. I ignored it and went back to enjoying my meal. I felt another sharp poke and it was stronger than the first time and I said, "Ouch!" I mentioned the poke this time and I still felt nothing in the carpet or my jeans; it's too weird.

The four of us were having a great time together: catching up and laughing. I was listening to Gail when my head turned to the right, completely by itself, with no thought or muscle engagement from me whatsoever. I knew my neck movement was bizarre and before I could say anything about it my neck turned again. Instantly, I knew that I was under a voodoo spell and that it was coming from the strange man who read my tarot cards and was into *The Book of the New Law*. I jumped up with fear and explained what had just happened, and my thoughts about it. The voodoo attack on me freaked out our lovers and they did anything to change the subject.

I immediately telephoned the Clairvoyant, tea-leaf reader, to see if she could help me with a voodoo problem. Thank-goodness that she answered the phone! She told me that the person who put the voodoo spell on me would need to contact me soon and if I asked him about it, that he would have to tell me the truth. She said there was a set of rules for magic and that he must admit to the spell. I was told to say a prayer to the Guardian Angels of Light to reverse the spell back to him and to keep his energy from coming into our apartment. The Angels did it again! My head turning stopped and no more sharp pokes in my butt cheeks. We all soon forgot about the voodoo incident and I resumed visiting with our Sweethearts.

I received a phone call from the strange man in the morning, just like the Clairvoyant said he would. He called to invite me to a gathering of some friends and thought it would be an enjoyable time for me. The odd thing is that I became an observer to what I was saying. I witnessed myself say, "You mean your cult?" The man was happy to say, "Yes." Then I asked him if he put me under a voodoo spell and he said, "Yes". I was still observing my reactions and the words that automatically popped out of me. I replied, "Thank-you, but I am not interested in going to your cult and your spells will come back to you ten times greater than you put out." Then I hung up the phone. I must say that this phone call was one of the most miraculous conversations I had ever had. If I were on my own I do not think I would have stayed as calm, nor handled the voodoo spell with that tone of authority.

I took a boring waitress job, at a café a few blocks away, that did not pay much. The early morning shifts were rough on me due to my party schedule at the bars every night. However it was a great month because it had the feeling of normalcy. 'Normal' anything was comforting after the supernatural goings-on. My drug business was going great with fewer yet bigger sales, and I still owed Dan money.

Gail went out of the state for a week to visit relatives and I didn't want to be alone for the whole time so I looked up an old friend from the neighborhood, Eileen, and invited her over for some wine. It had been at least a year and a half since we had last seen each other and we had lots to tell. Her older sister came with her and had quite a story to share. A few years back she had broken her arm and had a bone transplant that became infected. There was a strong chance that she would have to have her arm amputated, after already enduring 5 surgeries and a year of antibiotics.

Her mother found a woman who was known as a faith healer and brought her to the hospital to see her. The woman told her to pray to Jesus Christ and to visualize her arm being healthy. The healer woman came each day for a week and prayed over her arm. Within that week the transplant took hold and the infection cleared up. Eileen's sister was glad to show me her arm and how healthy it is. She talked about knowing that miracles do happen and that Jesus Christ is truly watching out for us. I thought her story was amazing and exactly the type of thing that I needed to hear. The subject we were on, at the onset of our visit, was divinely perfect. I figured it was safe to let them in on the haunting stories of "The Black" and spoke about the recent voodoo spell too. They weren't that shocked and knew that otherworldly things do happen. They grew up in a haunted home themselves. Eileen told me that the healer woman talks to the Angels of Light and teaches a class about spiritual protection at a bookstore. Both of them thought that I might want to ask her for advice.

I gave my friends a tour of the apartment; all five rooms of it. As we began to enter my bedroom a thick grey cloud appeared and pushed the women back from the door. This thick grey cloud was keeping them from entering my bedroom and I had never encountered it before. Eileen said, "Crazy, You are right, you need help!" My friends could see the cloud and feel the force of it pushing against them. We decided to quickly return to the living room.

While we were conversing, an intense feeling flowed through me and I thought I was going to explode. My heart began to race and I felt a pounding on my chest like someone was stepping on it. I gasped out, "What is happening to me?" The women had no idea what to do and I was sputtering out, "It is getting stronger." Suddenly I knew that the pounding on my chest was my feeling the footsteps of someone arriving. Then I heard the sounds of someone coming up the stairway and I ran towards the door. I opened it to find an exhausted Gail standing there with her suitcases. Gail said, "My flight was cancelled and it looks like I am supposed to stay here after all." I was so glad that Gail was not going because I was too scared to be alone for a whole week. Gail knew my visitors well so we all had a wonderful time together. I filled Gail in on the grey cloud incident and she found it unsettling. Although she was demonstrably grateful for the information about the faith healer.

A few weeks went by with no major haunting events and the white light cross still shown brightly in our hallway. I never did go to the bookstore to find the faith healer woman because I was too busy: partying, dealing, and satisfying my cocaine addiction. I tried to ignore how energized and clairvoyant I had become; tingles, zaps, knowing what will happen next, until I noticed something distressing. One morning I looked in the mirror at my eyes and they did not seem like mine. It's a difficult thing to explain. I looked at my eyes and it felt like someone else was looking back at me. I hoped this was nothing to get alarmed about and would simply stop. I asked the Guardian Angels of Light for their protection from evil spirits, just like I already did, about eighty times a day. The feeling of looking at someone else's eyes in the mirror persisted for another couple of days, when I noticed that my behavior had also changed. I could distinctly feel when this "other thing" was in me because I became emotionally cold. I told Gail about my suspicions of possession and this scared the crap out of her. I was not happy about it either and this meant a whole new level to the ongoing, haunting nightmare.

I said the nastiest things to everyone when I was over powered by "It". My words were hateful towards strangers and loved ones alike, including Gail. I loved Gail with all my heart and would never purposefully say anything to hurt her feelings. I felt scared and sad about my cold-hearted words. I explained to her that it was not really me and that something else had been speaking through me, but that did not heal the emotional blow. I did some things that I would never have normally done; getting a ridiculous hairdo for one. I did not feel like myself the whole time I was walking to the beauty salon or when I asked for a perm and a hairstyle I saw in their magazine. I paid the same as a months rent for a hairdo that made me look like a poodle sweating in the heat. The new hairdo was so against my "Look" and more street hussy than tomboy. Now I needed some serious help as the situation with the evil spirit that was making a home inside of me worsened. I showed Gail my eyes when I felt "It" inside of me and she saw the difference and felt the change in my energy, as well.

I was going insane over knowing that I was being frequented by some force that made me say and do hurtful things to my loved ones. I was afraid that "It" would destroy of all my friendships and support system. I felt totally alone in this personal horror movie and wished my mother was with me. Gail was worried about the outcome and so was I, enough so, that I found the faith healer woman at the bookstore. I went to the bookstore that my friends had told me about and asked the clerk when the healer held her classes. Her class happened to be in progress at present, so I quietly walked in and sat in the back. I hoped that nobody would notice me come in; unfortunately all twelve people in her class turned around immediately and looked at me. The teacher was an older woman around sixty-five years old, with a slight build and wearing glasses.

I did not say a word and sat listening to what she was telling these people that was so compelling. The students were mostly middle-aged women, except for one young woman and an old man. I knew, with every cell in my body, that the students and the teacher sensed the evil entity around me. The teacher finally said, "Oh, there you are, an Angel told me that you would be coming." Since my life was filled with the miraculous I did not think that her statement was weird, even though it was.

The faith healer woman, Gloria, continued teaching and spoke about the benefits of thinking positive thoughts, always. Gloria said that if you thought about things in a negative way that you were fueling a bad outcome. She went on to say that if your thoughts are positive that they would repel bad outcomes and attract good ones into your life. I thought that this philosophy was the biggest line of crap I ever heard and said so. I blurted out, "If you believe that what I think has anything to do with me being hit by a truck, or not, you are cracked." The whole class turned around and glared at me, standing there in my black leather jacket and decorated in chains and rhinestones. Gloria said, "Oh yeah, I dare you to think only positive thoughts for one week and then come and tell me about it." I took the dare, saying, "I will be positive for a week and show you." The class ended and I walked up to pay her the class fee. Gloria said, "No, I was told by an Angel to not take a penny from you." She really was different than anyone I ever knew and I thanked her very much.

While on my walk home, I noticed that I was vibrating more and aware of a lightness surrounding me. I knew that the energy filling me came from being around Gloria and my need for her help was crucial and mind-boggling. I held an over-current of fear that the blackness would come into me at any time, and kept relentlessly on-guard.

I was serious about Gloria's dare and set out being positive for the week and extremely happy that I found her. I hoped to have a moment alone with Gloria the following week so I could ask for her help with the haunting. Being positive was a challenge because that turned out to be a week from hell; Gail decided to move back to her parents home and return to college, without any notice or discussion. I had the feeling that my spiritual problem finally became too much for her to cope with. I knew that dealing with a heavy blackness that groaned a blood curdling, wall-breathing, tone was difficult enough. Possession fell into a different category of spooky and I couldn't honestly blame her in the slightest. I was looking at the move in a positive light and wanted another chance to leave the evil spirit behind. The change would relieve a lot of the intensity going on in our friendship: we needed the break.

The timing of my next visitor was perfect. Ricky came over to the apartment and proclaimed his success in getting off needles. He told me how much he still loved me. Hanging onto his every word, I fell for him again. He was as sincere as anyone I had ever heard, plus cute as all-get-out! Ricky won my heart again and we moved into an apartment together. The new apartment was perfect: spacious, with big windows and felt good. I was floating on clouds being together with Ricky again. I wondered how he might react to the problems I am dealing with, however. Observing my every thought and keeping them positive through the bad memories of Ricky's addiction tested me. My happiness to be living with Ricky again helped me reflect on my thoughts as they surfaced. I was committed to the dare to be positive for the week, and wondering if Gloria was right. 'Did her dare have anything to do with the fact that I moved within the coming days? Are Angels watching me?' I thought.

Ricky had two big house painting jobs lined up. He was painting the summer homes of his family's friends, out at the lake. The drive was at least two hours away so he spent the weeknights at the lake. Having the apartment to myself gave me the peace I needed to think positive thoughts. I was thankful for the quiet time to wonder about how I would approach Gloria with my spiritual problems. I concluded that being straightforward with her was the only way and that she was probably already informed by her Angel friends, anyway.

Gail phoned and wanted to come by for a visit which sounded great. I reminded her that she had to be positive while she was here. I missed Gail enormously and was overjoyed about her coming to see my new place. She arrived and we gave each other a big hug. I showed her around the apartment, then we sat in the living room with a bottle of wine. Gail was glad to see me being positive and saw how important it was that had I met Gloria. She told me how good I looked and was shocked to find out that I did not have any cocaine. I believed that the lightness surrounding me and powerful vibrations running through me affected my drug addiction in a great way. I was, seemingly, automatically loosing interest in cocaine and it had less power over me.

The conversation with Gail turned from nice to frustrating as she was harassing me about being positive. She assumed that I was bluffing and going to bullshit Gloria about being positive for the week, and really maintain my negative, druggy ways. I became irritated with Gail for saying negative things and I felt the energy shift around me when she did. There was no denying that I had become more sensitive to energy and needed all the good vibes I could get.

I warned Gail about my need for being positive when she called me in the first place. So, I reminded her a few times but she still wasn't taking me seriously. Finally I could not stand what was happening to my energy any longer and asked Gail to leave. I showed her out the door and told her that I would call her the next day. I assured her that I was committed to the positive dare and reminded her of the horrible problems that I needed to solve. We were not mad at each other; it was what I had to do for myself at that moment. The new apartment had a feel of healing and safety, and I wanted it kept that way. I was so scared of the evil spirit possessing me that my main focus was Gloria's challenge and I took it to heart. After only five days of thinking and speaking in a positive way made me consistently happier!

The next week at class Gloria greeted me with a big hug and told me how glad she was to see me again. I explained to her that I was sorry for disturbing her class and how daring me to be positive has changed my life. Gloria was not the slightest bit surprised. Of course she already knew what I was going to go through. I let her know how hard it was for me and that I had to change almost every thought that went through my mind. The class was interesting and way "out there" for me, even with my psychic experiences. Gloria spoke about some information that was from an Angel, channeled by a woman. Gloria spent half the class speaking about the information coming from Angels through various people who are channels. Basically the Angels told us, humans, to love everything, meditate and be positive.

I was able to spend ten minutes speaking with Gloria after the class and she blew my mind! Gloria looked directly into my eyes and told me that her Angel friend had told her that I was coming, and for her to help me. I briefly told her about the scary entity problem and she acted as if she already knew. Then her tone turned firm when she said, "You must stop selling drugs right now and raise your energy level up, dramatically, or you will lose this fight." A chill like none other ran through my body while I listened to her.

OK, this rocked my world because I thought my drug dealing was my secret; but she knew all about it. Unquestionably, Gloria saw right through me. I knew that I had to be honest with her if she was going to save me from the demon, so I didn't try to jive her. Gloria reached out and took my hand, gently placing it between her palms, and said, "Do not worry. I am going to help you." I thanked her and we made a date for the next week, then she could instruct me in getting rid of the evil spirit. I skipped all the way home and had no doubts that Gloria could easily take care of it. Her words catapult me right out of my trade and I stopped selling drugs immediately. Positive is the name of the game and I had to do my part in saving myself.

The next day Gail phoned and asked me if I would use my psychic gifts to pick the winning horses in a race. She met some guy and told him all about my powers and he wanted my help. I agreed to try and the two of them came over with the horse race betting cards. I opened up the race information and, with my eyes closed, slowly ran my right index finger down the page. I felt energy bursts as my finger glided down the page and I looked to see which horse my finger was over. I told the man the 1st, 2nd and place horse's names.

This man looked like a mobster-city slicker and was elated to have had my help. I told him to bring me a case of great Chardonnay if he won. Two days later, the man shows up at my door with a case of wine and wondered if I would pick some more horses for him. I refused and don't know why I didn't take him up on it, since I couldn't sell drugs anymore. I thanked the man for the wine and told him that I couldn't use my gift for gambling anymore. He begged me for a few minutes and then left, after asking me to call him if I changed my mind. Maybe Gloria was having a bigger effect on me than I thought. It wasn't like me to consider the integrity of anything like gambling with my new powers before.

I became a tarot reader and enjoyed it very much: keeping tabs on my life and being connected to the "other-side." I was reading the tarot cards one evening, while Ricky was out of town working, and decided to check up on my family in Africa. A brutal military coup was presently underway in Liberia and communications from the country were all but shut off. The news reports were horrifying and I needed to know what my family was feeling. I laid out five readings to narrow down the details of what I picked up on, initially. I came to understand that my mother was terribly worried about the whereabouts of my father. I knew that my little brother was fine but was also painfully concerned about my father. I learned that my father was alive and fine, yet not with the family.

I had plenty of time to realize the reality of what might happen to my family and there was no way to speak with them. The Clergy were the prime targets for murder during this violent coup. My gut feeling was one of loneliness and pity for myself if I never saw my parents and brother again. I wished they would find a way to leave the country and suddenly show up again, safe.

I put my positive thinking to work and sent my family thoughts of their protection and safety. Amazing how I became calm and peaceful, opening my chest for air and breathed the worry away. This experience made my enthusiasm grow for learning what else Gloria could teach me.

Positive thinking was working wonders for me and I started a new job. To be hired at this restaurant I had to pass a lie detector test and knew they would question me about stealing and drug use. I bummed a Valium from a friend and hoped for the best. I focused my attention on a frog statue that sat on the bookshelf, while breathing consistent and kept relaxed. I answered the questions with equal reactions and passed the test.

I, shortly thereafter, began waitressing at the restaurant that was located inside of a hotel. The mile walk to work did me a world of good and gave me time for reflection on being healthier. I met a woman bartender at work and we immediately liked each other. I was a breakfast waitress and enjoyed being finished with work early in the day; having plenty the time to prepare dinners, peacefully.

Working helped keep me out of drug trouble and I surely needed the money. My boss told me that I must wear my hair in a ponytail; making me look even more like a poodle. The hairdo I asked for while possessed by the demon included having a perm, taking months to grow out. At least I worked in a restaurant where nobody I knew would ever come.

I counted the days until the next class with Gloria, when I would hear her advice for me. Gloria had a disturbing story for the class, all ten of us, and we wondered why? Gloria told us that the previous day she was thinking about what to teach me while she was praying for me, when suddenly she could not breathe. Her mother rushed her to the hospital emergency room, where she was treated and released this very same morning.

I freaked out at hearing the story for many reasons. My first reaction was selfish; thinking, "I am doomed if this evil spirit bumps her off." Then I thought, "Holy Shit, what if I kill this sweet lady by bringing an evil spirit to her." We all calmed down and Gloria taught a light channeling class that evening. She told me that we would have to speak the following week because she was too tired to go into the details with me. I walked home feeling vulnerable and scared by knowing the power of the evil entity and it was truly after me.

The next week Gloria's mother and another senior student led the class because Gloria was in the hospital because she had stopped breathing again. My walk home felt lonely to my core, empty. Even with thinking as positive as was possible, I knew I was in real danger. I prayed to the Angels of the Light for Gloria to recover fast and fully so that I could stop shaking with fear. I really did shake with terror knowing I had no place to turn for help except to her.

Midweek Gloria phoned me and I almost fainted with relief. She decided to tell me how to protect and rid myself of this evil entity then, over the phone. Gloria explained that this entity is strong and evil. She also warned me that it would return one last time to test me. I was told to say this, "Jesus Christ, please open me up to your white Christ light and keep your ring of protection around me" and to repeat it three times. I said the prayer and actually saw white light surround me and instantly had a feeling of comfort, safety and love.

Gloria then told me about the importance of energy with what was happening to me and how to keep my vibration high. She went on to say that fear pokes a hole in the protective force field. Therefore, I need to have unwavering faith, even belief, in that the white light is more powerful than this dark spirit. OK, I got it! The key to me surviving this ordeal is knowing, without any doubts, the white light is always protecting me and have no fear when this evil spirit shows up. Gloria repeated herself saying, " The dark spirit will visit you, at some point, to test your faith so be ready." I was told to say the prayer, stand strong in the face of the evil spirit, and to sternly tell it to go away forever. I liked experimenting with the white light and was amazed at how quickly it arrived. The light surrounded me and brought immense comfort, whenever I asked. I believed Gloria about the protective power of the white light so I had complete and fearless faith. I thanked Gloria with all my heart and words could express: she saved my life as far as I saw it.

It was early in the evening and I was sitting on the couch watching the television, without a worry in the world. Suddenly my vision made a bizarre shift; I was seeing the bedroom except, I was still looking at the TV. My field of sight showed the bedroom but I was still sitting in the living room--too wacko. I saw what looked like the depictions of the Devil himself standing in my bedroom. I knew what I needed to do. I stood up, walked into the bedroom, and stood in front of the demonic creature. The demon was as tall as the ceiling was high, black and scaly like an armadillos shell, and steam rose from it's seemingly moist body.

Fearlessly I surrounded myself with the white light, while praying to the Angels of Light and Jesus Christ for their help. In a loud and forceful tone I said, "I am protected in the white light and you can not do anything to me anymore so go, Now!" The Devilish manifestation stood firm and stared at me. I loudly repeated myself and felt powerful with the white light around me, and did not waiver in my faith.

The Devil looking creature disappeared into the ether! I was ecstatically happy knowing this evil spirit was gone for good! I ran to the telephone and called Gloria with the great news. I could not thank her enough for saving my life. She was overjoyed, saying, "You make me very happy." I love Gloria! I felt like the sun returned after a long, dark trip to Hell and back.

The next day, Ricky returned home after finishing his painting jobs at the lake. I was overjoyed when telling Ricky what happened and that I was no longer going to be haunted or possessed. Our life together was going wonderfully and I was glad that he was back. I missed him very much. He was also thrilled about my new job and doing less drugs. I told Ricky about the tarot readings I did on my family and about the mess they are in. He consoled me he wanted the best outcome for them. I couldn't exactly put my finger on it but, something about Ricky's behavior did not feel right. I thought, 'maybe we'd grown apart already?'

Gloria taught me "crystal gazing" at her next class and I was able to meet two of my spirit guides. The whole class, each, picked a crystal from a big box full that Gloria brought. She had us all relax and talked us through energetically entering the crystal and being able to meet our spirit guides; first a man would appear and then a woman. Two Angels did show up in my crystal gazing, a man and a woman, both were breathtakingly beautiful, caring and quite helpful.

I carried the crystal in my pocket for good luck and entered it for energy cleansing when I needed to. Gloria said that crystal gazing would raise my energy level substantially higher and help protect me. I believed anything she told me for my protection, due to my belief that serendipity through Angels brought us together, initially. I don't know what would have happened to me if I was not led to Gloria, I suspect it would not have been good.

During the next class with Gloria I felt a gigantic energy surge and knew that a powerful entity had just entered the room. At the same time I felt it, Gloria said, "Excuse me class, but there is an Angel in the room and I must ask it why it has come." A big, blinding bright, white light ball appeared in the middle of our circle. The white light ball came over towards me and a large, white light hand reached out from it. This hand placed itself on my head and I almost blew up. I heard a deep male voice say, "Never worry about the things you need."

Gloria heard the white light ball tell her, "You are All Love." Everyone in the class was awestruck and could only look at each other for the moment. Gloria instructed us to take a big relaxing breath, appreciate the blessings from our healing guest, and give thanks for its coming. I was a little uncomfortable because some of the students saw the hand of white light reach out to me; I could feel envy mixed in with their love for me. After all, I had no control over the Angels and if it was my evening to be blessed, then so be it! I hugged Gloria after class, while telling her how thankful I am for her being in my life.

I was right, there was something very, very wrong with Ricky and it wasn't us growing apart. That night Ricky returned to the apartment wasted and told me he was out drinking with Sam. Sam was a scumbag, drug dealer and supplied Ricky with the dope he previously shot up. Sure enough he was back at it, and I immediately became outraged. I went off; yelling about how baby-sitting him had made my life stop and how I never should have gone back with him. I was extremely clear when I then, said, "Ricky if you see Sam or Martha again, I will leave you forever." Ricky promised me that he wasn't shooting up anymore and how he accidently bumped into Sam so they decided to have a drink together. I am no push-over and didn't believe a word he said. I sensed dishonesty and had a gut knowing that he was seeing Sam while he was staying at the lake. The new boost in my intuition was becoming my saving grace.

The next day, I went downtown to the police department and had a visit with the chief of police who was a longtime friend of my father. I stretched the truth considerably when I told him why I was there. I told the police chief that I had a terrible problem with a man coming to my house and trying to make me into a junkie. I asked him, "What could I do to keep him away and protect myself?"

The police chief escorted me to the district attorney's office down the hall and we filled out some forms. The police chief said, "Now, if he comes within ten blocks of your house, he will be arrested on the spot." I thanked him and went directly home, feeling much better. I told Ricky exactly where I had been and what I did. I was pissed-off and told him to tell scumbag Sam too.

There was a knock on our door and I ran to get to it before Ricky could by jumping in front of him. I opened the door and there was Sam. He looked bummed out because I was home. I told Sam, "I was at the police chief's today and there is a restraining order on you. If you are seen within ten blocks of here you will be arrested." Sam did not say a word, turned around, and ran down the stairs and out of the building. Goodbye Sam! Ricky was furious with me and I then realized that he had been waiting for him. They thought I would be gone long enough to drop off drugs, except I sent it away instead. Well, too bad for Ricky and Sam.

I told Ricky, "I am not having anything to do with you shooting up anymore." Ricky could hear it in my voice; I was going to leave him. He sat quietly on the couch for about an hour before he wanted to have a conversation about what happened. The bottom line was that he did not want to see Sam or shoot up drugs again. He cried as he told me that he wanted to stay with me, more than anything. His words bored me at this point. Ricky went on to say how deeply sorry he was for letting Sam and his friends visit him at the lake, and for shooting up again. He begged my forgiveness for two hours before I gave in. I told him I would stay with him only if we move and he keeps our new address a secret from Sam and Martha. Ricky agreed to start our new life together, in privacy, away from his junkie friends.

I wonder sometimes if this was a coincidence in timing or he was simply a scapegoat? Sam was arrested for murder two days after I was at the police station. Some of Sam's friends said he was framed, and went to jail nonetheless. I was happy that Sam was out of the picture and he couldn't ruin my life from behind bars. I would not have put it past him to have been involved with low-life murders, either.

Our present apartment was on a busy street and we decided to move into a quieter neighborhood, and closer to our healthier friends. We moved into an attic apartment in a very big, old house. This was a one-bedroom apartment with all the wonderful cubbyholes and alcoves of an old attic. The apartment had plenty of sunshine and was only a few blocks away from a beautiful park and Gail's house.

My sister and I found the chance to catch up over the phone. Wow, did we have lots to speak about. I filled her in about Gloria and how she saved me from the evil demon with white light and angelic help. My sister did not know what to think about me; knowing what a druggie I had been. With that said, this was the best news I'd given her in a very long time. She was doing great with her boyfriend and their restaurant. We spoke about how much we missed our family and how we hope to see them again, someday. She was deeply supportive of my being as positive as I could, not dealing drugs anymore, and working. After the haunting stories and telling her about some of my party times, our conversation was music to her ears.

At the next class, Gloria taught us TM, "Transcendental Meditation" and I loved it! Each week Gloria read to us from the *Universarius* pamphlets she subscribes to. She gave us the latest "channeled in" information from Angels and spoke about the other dimensions. TM was a method I could use to meet with my spirit guides and rejuvenate myself with relaxing inner travel. Having the ability to drift off to a replenishing inner paradise was a blessing. My inner world included flower-filled gardens, lush forest paths, and beautiful sunny beaches. I was becoming more positive as time went on, it had become easier to repel any negative thoughts, and low energy people were more obvious to me now.

My drug use went from smoking half an ounce of cocaine and snorting three grams a day to snorting less than a gram a week and smoking less pot, yet still every day. This still might seem like a lot of drugs but was nothing in comparison to my past, plus my cravings for them decreased by eighty percent. I was fine if I stayed away from the people with the mirrors lined with the tempting powder.

I began thinking more about my future in a realistic way and looking into a few career training programs. 'My parents would be proud of the changes I had made' was one thought that helped to keep me on track. I still went to hear my favorite bands play and danced with abandon, just not as often as when I dealt drugs. Ricky was hired at an auto body repair shop and woke up early, helping me to keep a regular schedule. Ricky and I were getting more serious about our relationship; we often spoke about marriage and starting a family. The idea of settling down with Ricky, being a wife, and becoming a mother all seemed heavenly. 'A logical relationship progression', I thought. I don't know where the idea started, 'if you are together for a long time and in love then the normal thing to do is get married and have kids'. I went as far as buying an antique, wooden rocking basinet at a garage sale.

There was, and is, no other way to put it, I was blessed with finding the white light and becoming more positive. I knew that these were the keys to my getting off freebase and saved me from the dark forces. My experience was so powerful that I felt it was necessary to share it where I could help other youths going through the hell that I did. I decided to contact a halfway house for drug addicted teenagers, down on the Southside. The rehabilitation program was run by the United Way foundation and I thought they might let me tell the teens what happened to me. I hoped that by teaching them some of the skills I learned might help them to beat their addictions.

I called the halfway house for adolescents and made an

appointment to speak with the director. He was a large, black man, with some grey in his hair. The vibe he gave off was comforting and his smile made me feel that I was in the right place, with the right friendly man. The director of the halfway house patiently listened to my story and the information that I wanted to share with the teens there. He smiled at me and nodded his head up and down the entire time we spoke. I finished my story and then he told me that I impressed him, and he was happy for my success.

He led me back to the entry room, asking me to wait for him there. He said that he needed to make a phone call about our meeting. I sat in a chair against the back wall and waited, while observing the counselors and teens interact. The room was big, with three desks, and each one having two chairs. A black man who was probably in his late thirties and handsome was sitting at one of the desks. He asked me, "What are you waiting for?" I told him that I was seeing if I could help the teenagers with their drug addictions. He asked me where I went to school and I told him. He glared at me with obvious irritation. "That's a high school and you need a Master's Degree from college to work here", he declared.

At that awkward moment a teenager came in for his counseling and sat down at this man's desk. I was saved from having to speak with the arrogant jerk. I listened to every word of the therapy session and, I became angry and frustrated by what I overheard. Basically, this man told the teenage boy how his life is shit and will always be shit and, how he is not capable of doing anything he talks about; and treated the youngster like a criminal. The teenager entered the room bouncing with happiness and having a plan to better himself. He was enthusiastic about his goals and filled with hope. The counselor emotionally ripped him apart and I watched the teenage boy's posture change into a cowering, failure pose.

Their so-called therapy session ended and the boy stood and began walking away. I couldn't help myself and said to the teenager, "Hey, come over here. I might be able to help you." The young man came over and I shared a little about my drug survival story. He was looking in my eyes and paid close attention, so I added, "Where there is a will, there is a way. Pray for the white light to surround you, protect you and to give you enough power to keep off the drugs. Be as positive as possible, always, and good things really will happen in your life. You can do it and do not listen to anybody, unless they truly love you." The statements rattled out of my mouth and he latched onto every word. The teenage boy believed me and his eyes became teary with joy.

He knew I was telling him the truth and it resonated exactly with what he was going through. His posture shifted; he stood tall with an opened chest and was smiling. He thanked me and walked away, and up the stairs. The counselor growled at me to go along with his mean glare.

My wait was going slowly with the man sending me bad vibes from across the room. The director finally came and ushered me back into his office. He was happy to say they were going to find a way to incorporate me into their program. He said he was thrilled that I showed up and, that he will call me within the next two days with the details. He saw me out and we hugged at the door, with the angry counselor staring on. I was elated and could not wait to tell Ricky about my day.

The news came the next day with his phone call, that I will be paid $60.00 a week but, I knew that I needed $70.00 a week to barely survive. I told the director that I need $70.00 just for the bare essential and not counting my bus fare to work. He said, "It's all the money I could get for you", sincerely apologizing while asking me to please come. I declined the job because I needed an extra $10.00 a week. I wish I used my faith and Angel guidance then because I am sure the Angels could have found a way to make another ten dollars for me. Living by faith alone was new for me and the numbers didn't crunch. I know better now.

I still wanted to share what information I could to help people suffering like I was. I called the male psychiatrist I saw years ago, during the court-ordered, family therapy sessions. I reached him and we had the best conversation. He expressed how proud and happy he was with me. The psychiatrist learned something from what I shared and I felt wonderful about that. Surprising me that he was a real friend, after all.

✦

The Spirit Guides whom I met while crystal gazing were John who represents love, and Elizabeth, who represents truth. I crystal gazed almost every day and decorated my inner world into a jungle, with macaw parrots and beautiful butterflies. My jungle within the crystal felt tranquil with a mesmerizing, gentle steam running through it. My Spirit Guides, John and Elizabeth, joined me at an enormous, sparkling rock and we spoke about some ways of approaching my life quests. I made a magic waterfall of the brightest light imaginable and bathed myself under it; cleansing my energy. I used the crystal gazing for recharging myself, healing, and felt my energy increasing.

The nightmare I went through, when the evil spirit was after me, frightened me out of my wits, for months. Keeping my energy high enough to repel dark spirits became my daily priority. My awareness of the energy fields of people and places filled my every sense. I wanted my energy field high enough to protect me, more than anything else in the world!

I was laying on my bed and practicing Transcendental Meditation, and asked my Spirit Guide, Elizabeth, to visit with me in my inner meditation world. I was sitting on a lush lawn that blanketed a high bluff, overlooking the ocean. The bluff was my healing place and the day could not have been more splendid, like always. In my meditation the bluff is always sunny and warm, with a gentle breeze for the butterflies and ladybugs, the sky is clear and bright blue. Sitting on the bluff filled me with such huge amounts of happiness that I could have blown up!

My Spirit Guide, Elizabeth, arrived and stood in front of me, a little towards my left side. She is beautiful. I asked her if she could take me on a journey to visit somewhere I'd never been before. Elizabeth smiled and reached out for my hand and, in less than a second, we entered another realm of existence. This realm looked grey, with a dreary feeling hanging in the air. I saw grey colored entities with human shapes wandering around aimlessly. I sensed that these spirits weren't happy; sobbing and moaning while they roamed. I asked Elizabeth, "Where are we?" Elizabeth answered, "We are just outside of what humans on Earth can commonly see, the closest other realm to Earth." She told me that this realm was full of many kinds of spirits. Some are those who did not believe that anything except the Earth exists and making their educational transition and, other spirits here were not completely aware that they even died, yet.

I asked Elizabeth, "Can we go somewhere else?" She said, "Yes" and we drifted to a wonderful place, in less than a second. This place filled me with a complete sense of peace and, with more joy than I ever felt before. This realm was light green in color, like a pastel emerald. Balls of white light, which I knew were spirits, were dancing around in the air. I could feel this was a happy place and knew the balls of lights were communicating to each other. I asked Elizabeth, "Where are we now?" Elizabeth said that we were further from the Earth realm and, if I left my physical body (died) today, this is where I would vibrate to. I was thrilled that I would be going to a place that felt this thoroughly happy!

Elizabeth never let go of my hand for the whole trip and never once did I doubt my safety. We drifted back to my beautiful bluff overlooking the ocean and stood in the sunshine together. I thanked her for the adventure and memorable trip. We said our temporary goodbyes because I was exhausted from the experience and needed to sleep.

Life was not as easy as flying around with my Spirit Guides; Dan, the drug dealer I owed, was spreading the word around the city that he will kill me when he finds me. I heard the frightening news from Gail but I thought, 'if I could speak with him then I could calm him.' Dan and I shared a long history and had many mutual friends. He made lots of money from me already so, I thought a meeting was worth of a try. I went to Dan's house for our talk, where he was acting completely out of character; like a man I had never met before.

Suddenly, Dan pulled out a gun and pointed it at me and said, "I will not shoot you if you undress, now." Dan had two German Sheppard, attack dogs at his side so, I was helpless. He wanted to take nude photos of me and that he won't touch my body at all. Under the circumstances it seemed like a good offer, so I stripped down. I stood naked and scared in his living room while he snapped two photos. Like he said, he never touched me or asked for porno-type poses. I jumped back into my clothes and ran out of the house, thinking I cleared my debt. No doubt I looked under duress in those photos so, they must have looked like they were from a criminal origin. Dirty was how I felt after leaving his house, but relaxed that he was off my back and might even front me more drugs.

✸

I wanted a new waitress job that paid better and decided to go downtown to the employment office to see about any leads. The employment specialist looked through her files and suggested some waitress job openings. The restaurants she suggested were sleazy. Then I asked her, "Do you have any real waitress jobs?" The employment specialist changed the way she was looking at me and said, "Yes." She called a fancy restaurant downtown and arranged an interview for me. The interview was at the swankiest French restaurant in the city. The waitress job actually excited me and the money I would make could be five times more than at my current job.

I bought a new, full length, cashmere coat and a pantsuit to look my best for the interview, and I felt very positive about it. The manager stunk of cheap cologne, was a chubby flaming Queen, and dressed in a tuxedo. We liked each other immediately. I was hired, and I started my new job the next day. I followed behind the senior waiter for the first three days, before I was given my own tables. The restaurant required that we serve in teams: a front person and a back person. My life seemed like it was all coming together and flowing calmly. I had lots to be thankful about, except one big hole; I wanted my family to return safely from Liberia!

CHAPTER 15
LAST CHANCE ANGEL, "LISTEN OR DIE"

This was "It" the final lies, and I left Ricky forever. My heart was broken beyond repair this time! We planned a wonderful future together and I thought he was my partner for life. I discovered he was seeing Sam and Martha again, shooting up drugs and had spent our rent money on his habit. He was forced into telling me what he did only because we were evicted from our apartment for not paying. I could not cover the entire rent myself and did not want to live with him for one more minute, anyway.

He told me the "junkie" news at around nine o'clock at night and it completely devastated me. I yelled and screamed out every curse word that exists, with tears pouring down my cheeks. Not knowing what to do, I stormed out of the house for a walk. I needed to cool off and emotionally regroup since my plans for the future had crumbled.

I gave Ricky all my money to pay the rent, and just began getting paid for work; I was broke. With only enough money for a beer and a pack of cigarettes, I walked to the store. Instead of returning home, I cried my heart out while walking streets. An emotional dam broke that had been holding in all the disappointments I ever felt with Ricky and the flood of tears seemed endless.

I walked up to a home with a huge front porch and sat on the stranger's steps. While I gazed up at the moon, I prayed, for what seemed like the first real time in my life. I'd asked the Angels for help with protection from the evil spirit, but never prayed like this before. I yelled, "Jesus, if you are up there, then get your butt down here and save me! Please tell Pat from class who my Master Angel is, so I know you are really there." Pat was one of the students in Gloria's classes and she proclaimed to hear Angels speak, so I figured Jesus could tell her the answer. I returned home and was glad to find that Ricky had gone out because I could not stand the sight of him.

Frustrated, I kicked the baby basinet across the bedroom floor, got into bed, and sobbed myself to sleep.

At the end of Gloria's next class, Pat walked up to me and said, "I don't know why, but I need to tell you that your Master Angel is..." (I'm not disclosing the name, here). Instantly I almost fainted, really, I forgot that I'd asked the question to Jesus in prayer a few nights before. A jolt of energy, like I'd never felt before, shot through my body and I became speechless. I was barely able to mutter, "Thank-you Pat." Hearing my question answered threw me into shock and I needed to quickly get outside. My body felt electrocuted again, but mellow in comparison to the first white light blast in Gail's basement.

Now that I knew there was a powerful Angel out there, someplace and listening to me, caused me to rethink a lot of my beliefs. While walking home, I noticed that I was whispering to myself and tiptoed, as if trying to be quiet for some reason. Looking up at the night sky, I repeated in a whisper, "I know you are out there now and this is shocking for me." Experiencing and knowing that I am not living alone, after all, truly did blow my mind and needed some getting used to. Being watched and listened to by Angels was enough, but I also felt like a high-voltage wire was running through me. Yes, it really was too wild for me to readily fathom! I vibrated and glowed for a week, while I got used to my increased intuitive hunches, my unnerving energy zings and more clarity with my life.

✹

My drug dealer problem was getting worse and, he said that I still owed him money, that the naked photos were an interest payment. "That Fucker", I screamed! With my new job and consuming less drugs, the chances of me paying Dan were higher. Just before the final day when Ricky and I had to be out of the apartment, Ricky invited Martha over. She came over to shoot up drugs with Ricky while I was out working. Martha loved making trouble and told Dan where I lived and my phone number. One upside to being evicted was that, I moved out before Dan could kill me.

Thank goodness for my new job paying me much better than the ones in my past. Although, one big bummer with my new job was that I was working during Gloria's classes and stopped going. Missing Gloria was sad enough, but I did not realize how important those classes were for my spiritual health until later on.

Gail invited me to stay at her parents house until I decide on what I would do next, now that Ricky was out of my life forever. Drifting into the day-to-day flow with my new life phase, things were spiced up by seeing my old boyfriend again, the "city-slicker". The thought that I ever went back with Ricky in the first place left me feeling like a dunce. My relationships with Gail and our lovers picked up right where we left off. Gail and I decided to move into a bigger apartment than we had before, where we could make more noise. We were not quiet by any means, especially with resuming our nightly, party lifestyle.

Our new apartment was on the top floor, in an older home and another two bedroom, but these rooms were huge and with high ceilings. I traded drugs for a stereo system and my life was looking up. Gail and I were overjoyed with our new digs, just in time for the winter snow storms. We only saw our boyfriends three days a week and loved every second of their company.

It took no time for me to make friends with my new co-workers and they were a fun bunch. Within a month, I began selling drugs to three of my co-workers and liked the extra money. Gail and I became especially close friends with one waitress, Shelly. She was a streetwise woman, married with a young son, and living on the rough side of the city. The three of us went bar hopping almost every night after work and the drugs flowed again.

My classes with Gloria seemed like a world away, except the knowledge she gave me was alive and still working inside of me. No question that I had relapsed and was unaware of how easily it could happen. Little by little, my addiction to cocaine resurfaced--rearing its ugly head.

My intuitive gift was quite strong as far as knowing the future of others; yet when it came to me, I found it difficult to get a clear picture. I found a new gift! I could think about someone and envision them doing something, and then they would do it. An example was when Gail and I ran out of coke and desperately needed more. I closed my eyes and saw where our boyfriends were at that moment, then I repeated, "Call, Call, Call" over and over, while I envisioned them getting off the highway, going to a pay phone, and calling us. I only did this on a few occasions, mainly because of the kick I got out of showing Gail how I could. Each time I did the visualizations and repeated my desire, my boyfriend called us within ten minutes. He always said, "I was driving and had a sudden urge to call you, how are you?" I explained how much Gail and I needed to see them and they drove directly to us. This proved the power of prayer, yet not intended for scoring cocaine, I'm sure. Gail and I got thrills out of my tricks and they gave us plenty of reasons to laugh.

Gail knew about my way of reading the tarot cards that let me narrow down the specifics, when the initial card layout looked vague. There was no word from our boyfriends since the previous weekend and I wanted to check it out. That night during a tarot reading, I told Gail that her boyfriend was going to arrive at 3:17 am. I was 100% certain and advised Gail to sleep by the door, so she would hear him knock. She believed me, placed her sleeping bag at the door, and set her alarm clock. I woke up to the sound of her boyfriend knocking on the door and Gail's alarm clock. I came out of my bedroom to find Gail screaming in the living room. Apparently, when her lover knocked on the door she was so surprised that all she could do was scream, so I pushed her into her bedroom. I said, "calm down, I will answer the door."

Gail's lover promptly asked me "Why did she scream?" I explained to him about the tarot card reading and the suspense made her scream. He became very interested in my intuition and being able to know what he was doing, plus other things I could know. His thoughts began running freely and I enjoyed the extra attention. Only a handful of our friends knew about my new powers, the haunting spirit, and my being saved by Gloria's wisdom.

Keeping up with my renewed addicted ways, I found a second boyfriend that had plenty of cocaine and loved cooking up freebase for me, hour after hour, day after day. Gail witnessed my behavior in awe; watching me drop off one boyfriend, while on my way to pick up the other. I was a successful drug addict if one exists. Having both of these boyfriends in my life kept me very satisfied, I must say. Seriously, running out of cocaine was not an option for me. My saving grace was that I loved my job and had to keep myself 'together' enough to keep it. On the side, using the tarot cards, I helped one of my boyfriends with his business; he had an inside scoop and I earned some of the cocaine that I consumed. I read the tarot cards daily to make sure that my boyfriend's deals went smoothly. I asked the cards many questions: whether he should trust a particular person or, if a drug shipment was going to be top quality or cut, and always, if the police would catch them. The tarot card readings were basic and to the point. I loved reading the cards; it had a special appeal by being spiritually fascinating to others.

One day I laid out my usual card spread for the drug dealers and it did not look so good. After some additional readings to narrow it down, I had some disturbing thoughts about their dealings. With the information I got from the cards, I figured that these dealers were about to go to Florida for a deal and that someone was going to be busted, and go to jail for a very long time. Immediately, I called up my boyfriend and stressed the point of his needing to speak with me, right away. Sweetie arrived quickly and I told him straight out, "Whatever you are planning to do right now, do not do it!" I explained to him the details behind my forceful statement; telling him about someone getting busted and going to jail for a long time. "It will turn out horribly", I said. He absorbed my warning and was listening carefully to every word. He assured me that he wasn't planning anything of the sort and not to give it one more thought.

As if I was a total moron, Right? I firmly told him, "You are full of shit, I know this is the truth and you are warned!" Conveniently, he needed to rush off to somewhere and left. The very next week, he went to Florida for a deal and, indeed, he did end up going to jail for a long time. Greed does it every time! Knowing that he was sitting in jail for the next, many years, with the knowledge that he was forewarned was really sad. What a bummer it was that he did not take the advice he'd asked me for.

I loved my waitress job, WOW! I partied heavily with my co-worker cohorts. Four of my co-workers scored their cocaine from me, and my boss suspected as much. Although I never admitted to his murky accusations, he was actuality wanting cocaine from me too. Never! I refused to sell drugs to my boss, so he began treating me as poorly as was still legal. He told me to do messy, tedious jobs that were outside of my job description set by the union I belonged to. It was a pleasure reminding him about my job description and my rights. Tension between us rapidly grew and I enjoyed annoying my boss; he stomped, fumed, and his face turned red with anger.

My boss was an arrogant man that used his job position to seduce young men into having sex with him in exchange for the best customers. Personally, I didn't understand how he managed it, him being so seedy. Worst of all was the aroma from his choice of cologne, it still turning my stomach just like it did the first time we met.

Gail also became good friends with my co-worker buddies and we frequented the bars together, partying our butts off. Before too long I became a serious freebase addict again and returned to dealing larger quantities of drugs to support my habit. Three of my co-workers were hardcore drug addicts, especially Shelly, my dearest friend from work. She liked shooting up and knew that I worried about her, and wanted her to stop using needles. She insisted that she only did it a few times a year and I shouldn't be concerned. This night, I found her in the bathroom trying to shoot up and having trouble doing it. She asked me for help and I was against it, but I helped her anyway. A calm smile filled her face as soon as the cocaine entered her vein. I was creeped-out by the needles and wanted to leave, rushing her out the door and into the car. 'Unbelievable and horrible that I was back into the drug scene and a full-blown, coke addict again', I thought. As crazy and terrifying as it was, my recent demon troubles were not powerful enough to stop me.

Life seemed sleazier by the day and being in the middle of a freezing winter didn't help. Focusing on getting through my work shift and being with one, of my two, boyfriends was all I could handle. My boyfriends cooked me up, non-stop, freebase and I loved their jovial and intimate company. I kept no secrets from either boyfriend, so they knew about each other and didn't give me any grief over it. Both of my lovers had chemistry degrees from college and an interest in experiencing with mind-altering drugs.

One of my lovers had some DMT and my other lover wanted to try it, so I invited them both over for dinner. Gail could not believe that I invited both of my lovers over to meet each other and thought I was nuts to go through with it. The two men enjoyed each other very much, discussing chemistry for hours on end. The three of us decided to smoke the DMT together and loaded the pipe. I took a big puff, held it several seconds and then exhaled. Instantly my head fizzed and tingled, accompanied with a buzzing sound that rang through my brain for a few seconds. The "high" was different, like never before, and I did not like it. I had a little good sense left and knew not to smoke anymore. My reaction surprised my lovers when I told them, "No more DMT for me, the sensation felt like my brain cells died off." They both enjoyed their experiences and continued smoking it. I added that, "the buzzing and fizzing I felt must have been trillions of brains cells exploding at once." They enjoyed their visit and smoking the DMT, and I was glad to have introduced them. Now, I knew that this was one drug to avoid.

During my daily tarot card reading, I saw that Dan (the drug dealer I owed money to) was closing in on me. I was earning enough money for my rent, keeping my cocaine addiction fed, and my bar-hopping tabs paid. It seemed impossible for me to save enough money to pay him and I was broke most of the time. However, my priorities were warped: drugs, rent, bar fun, and food, in that order. If the drugs allowed me to have self-discipline, than I could have saved the money for his payment a year ago, but that did not happen.

One afternoon, Dan showed up at my apartment door, just before I was leaving to go to work. I opened the door and was suddenly horrified and frightened to see him there. Being alone was dangerous and I knew I needed to do some fast talking. He pushed his way past me, barging into my apartment. He walked around looking at the place, but I was frantic to leave for work. While he roamed around the apartment, he reminded me that I owed him money, as if I'd forgotten. He said, "I am going to get something from you." I walked into my bedroom to get my purse and quickly leave, but he followed behind me. This situation required drastic action, fast. I reached down grabbing a stiletto-heeled shoe and launched into a very loud threatening craze, with nothing to loose. My fury startled him into backing up until I had him cornered in the bathroom.

Standing in the doorway and holding the stiletto heal ready to dig into his face, I shouted "Leave Now!" I held that heel as if I were trained to lethally use it. He said, "You had better get my money" and he walked out the door After calming down for a minute I left for work thinking, 'Now he knows where I lived and this changes everything.'

I thought up a great protection plan to have in place in case he ever came to our front door again. My plan would take care of him effectively, instantly, and maybe even fatally. I told Gail what happened and explained to her what to do if anyone scary was ever at the door. I placed my bowling ball bag on the floor by the door within arms reach of answering it. Our apartment door was at the top of a very high, steep staircase. I told Gail "Just simply throw the bowling ball to the person and their reaction would be to catch it, certainly sending them falling backwards down the flight of stairs. She thought the new protection plan was brilliant and we both slept in peace.

I mentioned my concerns about Dan to one of my boyfriends and he brought me a gift. My boyfriend gave me 22 caliber pistol just in case Dan returns and told me to let him in the door and shoot him if he tried to hurt me. My lover said, " Do not let him start talking or get near enough to take the gun away from you. The police will let you off for shooting him, because you are a single woman defending yourself." I felt more secure by having the gun, never asking about a gun permit, I didn't care.

My boss was increasingly irritated and mad with me; saying threatening and venomously hateful things to me during my work shift. He told that me he was making my time at work sheer hell and torturing me until I quit. We were at war and I had the AFL-CIO Union behind me. I learned a couple of things by observing my father fighting for the rights of black people, and stubbornly stood my ground. I did my job with perfection so my boss couldn't reprimand me about my performance. I had real concerns about him setting me up for a drug bust though, and kept my feelers out. Selling drugs to my co-workers meant that I often had drugs at work. On one rare occasion I needed to stash a liter of ether in my work locker for a day. The ether fumes gave off a strong, distinct odor even through the container that was tightly closed. That was nerve wracking and dangerously combustible, I never did that again. Nevertheless, my boss was starting to stress me out and I sensed that he was up to something besides his usual no good.

A gorgeous, young man was hired as a new waiter, he was tall, slender, and recently moved here. Wasting no time at all, my boss began flirting with him and acting pathetic. My boss had a twisted twinkle in his eye while he stared at the new waiter's butt. The new waiter fit right in, and soon joined us for our after-work partying. My boss became angrier with me by the day; as if it were my fault he was not invited to party with us, when his "new crush" was.

Holiday time arrived and our work schedule was posted for New Year's Eve. The restaurant was located inside of an historic hotel and the Grand Ballroom was the swankiest place in the city to ring in the New Year. Working in the Grand Ballroom on New Year's Eve meant making a thousand dollars in tips. I was the third most senior waitress and quite comfortable that I would be assigned to the Grand Ballroom. My comfort was unwarranted. Rage flooded through me when I saw that I was assigned to work in the worst restaurant in the hotel for New Year's Eve, and that the new waiter, with no seniority, was positioned in the Grand Ballroom.

I knew that the newly hired waiter had been hanging-out with our boss. Now, I assumed they were lovers after the schedule was posted. Spewing anger, I stormed through the hotel lobby and into the office of the senior manager, ranking much higher in power than my boss. We regularly flirted with each other whenever we met in passing. The kitchen staff called me "Hollywood" or "Tinker Bell" and treated me like a treasure. The senior manager loved my legs and made sure I knew it. He was shocked to see me this upset, cursing, stomping my feet, and crying. I yelled, "My boss is mistreating me, assigning me to the basement restaurant during New Year's Eve!" Telling him about the new guy having the Grand Ball Room position let him know the sleaziness my boss was up to. I was so angry that my arms were swinging in every direction while I boiled. He said, "I'll take care of everything, so don't worry over this any further." By that evening, the servers chart for the Grand Ballroom was changed; the new guy was placed in the basement restaurant and I was moved to the Grand Ballroom! Job satisfaction peaked with my boss being scolded for playing favorites and seeing that I prevailed, again.

Working in the Grand Ballroom was truly a ball and I earned a thousand dollars in tips, plus had all the champagne I could drink. Many of us on the wait-staff met in the hotel bar for cocktails after working until 1:00 am. We all snorted plenty of cocaine, and I danced with wild abandon after drinking too many "Long Island Ice Teas". Then my eyes landed on the most elegant man I had ever seen. I wanted to meet him. Being pleasantly high and very drunk, I still managed to speak with him for a few minutes. Wow, he had my attention, even though he walked away and was speaking with other partyers. The bar was extra boisterous, with most of the revelers being guests of the hotel and not having to drive anywhere. Knowing that I was catching a cab home, let me be extra celebratory on this New Year's Eve!

One friend of the elegant man, I was attracted to, walked over and invited me to a party in the gorgeous man's hotel suite. He seemed nice enough, was wearing an expensive tuxedo, and assured me there was lots of cocaine and festivities. I decided to go with him to the party, but found nobody was in the hotel suite. Then he said "Oh, we beat them. They are on their up here", as he motioned for me to have a seat. He poured us some champagne and sat down on the couch next to me. I wasn't so drunk that I could not sense that something was wrong. Without any niceties, he grabbed me and then jumped on top of me. Simultaneously he pulled up my dress and down with my pantyhose as I tried to push him off of me. He kept trying to mount me and was too big and strong to fight him off. He was drunkenly pressing his penis around to find his way in my butt, as I fought him. Suddenly out of nowhere, I yelled "No, my operation!" After he heard what I yelled he got off of me, stood up and asked me, "What operation?" I told him that I just underwent surgery in my intestines and still have the stitches in me. The look on his face turned gentle and showed a caring side of him. Although, he was very apologetic and begged for my forgiveness, I needed to get out of there fast! The amount of thankfulness I felt for not being raped was so huge it is indescribable. I was thoroughly exhausted and I took him up on his offer to drive me home. Without conversation we rode in his big, black Lincoln until he said, "If you ever want to have sex just call me and I will pay you five thousand dollars." I couldn't believe how nuts this guy was! Finally arriving at my house, I said "Goodbye" and got out of the car.

What a close call! I learned some important lessons this night; I could have been raped or even killed. 'No going to hotel rooms with strangers no matter what they say', 'Never get so wasted that I can't defend myself, or be lured away from the safety of my friends', were two of the personal vows I made. I came within an atom's width of being raped when an Angel saved me! Angelic help was the only explanation for me yelling out about an operation, which never happened, and at the critical last second. The perfect words popped out of my mouth without any thought; both weird and wonderful. Something powerful was protecting me on that first day of my New Year, I just knew it.

My boss made it apparent that he hated me and relentlessly threatened me. I only wanted him to leave me in peace to do my job. My harassment included him whispering threats of violence into my ear as he walked by. Finally, two of my co-workers talked me into attending the next meeting of our union local. The two co-workers had complaints of their own and thought I should join them in voicing our grievances to the union.

We arrived to a packed meeting room, filled with at least a hundred people and the panel of union officers sat facing us in the front. Each attendee was given the chance to speak. I explained to the full room about how my boss was not following the "seniority" rules and he was making my life hell by threatening me. I went on to tell them, he said, " I am going to torture you until you quit." Tears were flowing down my face by this point, even though I tried to keep up a stern composure. I have always cried at the drop of a hat and it was embarrassing at times like these. Then I was in shock, after hearing my waiter friend address the union local by saying, "He told me to give him a blow-job or he was going to fire me and hurt my wife."

The union hall murmured with all the members talking among themselves after hearing our accusations and testimonials. After the meeting room quieted down, my waitress friend had her chance to speak and said, "I witnessed the harassment of her, pointing at me, and he does drugs at work." Aghast, the president of our union local said, "These grievances will be investigated immediately." I was happy with the meeting's outcome and felt like the union really does care for its' members.

The three us were walking across the parking lot when I asked the waiter "Did he really order you to give him a blow-job?" He replied "Of course not. I lied to get him in trouble because he is an asshole" and then he laughed. The waitress said that the 'drugs at work' accusation was a lie, too. These two co-workers of mine hated our boss and were joining in my angst for their own revenge. I was surprised by the extent of their harmful intentions. Still, I did not care about them lying and actually thought it was funny.

Days went by with nothing being done to restrain my boss, who never let up with tormenting me. He informed me that he has friends in the Mafia and could have me snuffed at anytime. Oh, now how comforting is that? Not!

So I decided to take matters into my own hands and went downtown to the union office. I met alone with our president of the local union chapter in his stately office. He got an earful and saw that I had a big problem with my boss, and letting him know that nothing got better since he had been informed. I had a big mouth and have often wondered where I got my audacity. "I know my boss arranges hotel rooms, and provides prostitutes and drugs for certain VIP customers. If you do not fire my boss for his threatening and abusive behavior, then I will take you down with him." Then I stood up and pointed my finger in his face, like a real bad ass, and walked out of his office. I have no idea why I spoke with such authority to him, as if I had the final say. What a little punk I was, with no backup for messing with the local union president, and a bigger mistake than I realized.

Two evenings later, three men entered the restaurant and were all wearing expensive black suits and were seated for dinner. For some reason I got a bad feeling from these men and was thankful that they were not seated in my section. I caught one man pointing at me and telling the others, "There, that girl is the one." Mysteriously, I was left a dozen long stemmed roses that same night, with no card. Life was becoming stranger with each passing day.

My mind was made up that I was going to take my boss down! As far as I saw it, the president of our union local and the hotel management were allowing the injustices towards me to take place. I also have a pet peeve about any racial discrimination of any kind and

I saw that the minorities were mistreated at the hotel, as well. After a lot of thought about a strategy, I came up with a grand plan to rid myself of my boss forever. I began to implement my plan by thumbing through the phone book, picking out a few law firms that I thought might be interested in taking my case. I spoke with two law firms that, flat-out, said that they could not take my case due to personal relationships with the hotel management. The cat was out of the bag!

Another law firm was a husband and wife team that rocked! Over the telephone, I explained my issues with the lawyer duo, and how I want to stop the unfair labor practices and racial discrimination at the hotel. These two lawyers were all over it! They were both, energetic black activists and she was as dynamic as it gets. I advised them to enter the hotel through the employee entrance at three o'clock, make a left turn, and go into the laundry room. The two legal dynamos were planning to interview the employees about their treatment by the hotel management.

Then I telephoned my flirting buddy, the senior manager, and said, "There will be press coverage of two lawyers who are gathering information about the racial discrimination and unfair labor practices going on at the hotel." Undoubtedly, he must have turned purple and had heart palpitations. I heard purple, if one could. He screamed, "Who the Fuck called them?" I took joy in fessing-up, "I was the one who called, because the abuses have been reported, nothing gets done about it, and the hotel and union allows these crimes to continue." As expected, he freaked out and asked, "What do you want from me?" "I would call the whole thing off if my boss's resignation is on your desk by 2:00 this afternoon" I answered. He told me, "You have it." That's exactly what happened and my boss's resignation was signed and he left the hotel for good. In keeping my word; I called off the lawyers. I never did call the press and phoned the lawyers, telling them that I changed my mind about filing a case and apologized for troubling them.

Going to work had a spooky vibe to it now. I knew that my ex-boss was extremely pissed off at me and lurking out there, somewhere. The danger I was in was so thick in the air that my co-workers picked up on it. So much that the head-waiter, for room service, offered to buy me a plane ticket out of the state, but I declined his gift of concern.

I did threaten the president of our union local who knew my ex-boss very well, as it turns out. It was true that my ex-boss actually does have close friends in the Mafia, and their prevalence was well known in the city. Word was out on the street that my ex-boss put some sort of a "Hit" out on me. He had connections all over the city so, I had to closely watch everything going on around me; bartenders mixing my drinks, speeding cars, bumps in the night. I was on edge but did not give much thought about how I could remedy my dangerous life. I became content with always looking over my shoulder, and partied on, as usual.

The next week, I made an unfortunate mistake of picking up a man from the bar and invited him home with me. I had known him for a few years and always thought he was cute and funny. We had a few drinks and snorted some lines before I got the nerve to ask him over. He thought this was a grand idea and followed me back to my house. The night was sweetly rambunctious and he left early in the morning. It so happens, the man I invited over was followed to my house by the FBI. Evidently he was wanted for questioning about his involvement in a burglary-gone bad, and ending with a murder. I knew nothing more about this man than he went to high school with Ricky, and nothing about a any rip-off. Having a fun night with him wasn't worth the huge trouble I found myself in.

I knew to not ever let the police catch up with me because I could not afford to prove my innocence. It would cost a lot of money to prove my innocence and I certainly didn't have it. I thought, 'big trouble this time, I could have too much pinned on me'. Trusting that the investigators would understand that I had nothing to do with the murder was too risky. Almost every judge in the city knew and hated me. I was a broke drug addict, waitress, and I looked like crap after the many years of abuse. No longer being a juvenile; this might mean prison time even though I was innocent. I made myself scarce by avoiding that bar I picked him up in, which had been my nightly stop.

It wasn't enough to have the FBI after me, my boss trying to kill me, and my drug dealer also wanting to hurt me; I became painfully sick! My diet was sporadic and insufficient at best. I still was not eating meat or poultry, and had taken a liking to drinking herbal teas since I met Gloria. I developed a pain in my abdomen that hurt so much it made standing up straight impossible. I was passing blood in

my poop and knew I dreadfully was sick. Gail's mother saw me
hunched over that evening and became seriously worried about me.
She knew enough about my lifestyle; she made an appointment with a
colorectal doctor for me, the very next morning. Gail's mom drove
me to the appointment and waited with me, in concern. The doctor
recommended I get a barium GI series in two days, with the
preparations beginning then. I did the fasting by eating nothing, and
then drank the nasty stuff that made everything, literally, come flying
out of my colon. I stayed at Gail's moms' house that night and spent
most of it sitting on the toilet.

In the morning I went to the hospital for the GI series and
promptly fainted on the table from low blood sugar. I overheard the
nurse say, "Try and give her a sip of orange juice." Two nurses sat
me up and I was able to sip some juice, then they laid me back down
and gave me a straw to sip a little more. My awareness started to
come back and, was then, told that I have ulcerative colitis and the
doctor recommended that I have a part of my intestines removed.
Hearing this made me almost faint again but, I understood what was
being said. No way was I going to let these people cut into me! I
wished my mother was here and I didn't know what to do. I jumped
up and grabbed my clothes, still dressed in the hospital gown, I ran
out of the hospital. I yelled, "You are all butchers", and kept going
as fast as my legs could carry me. I squeezed between some bushes
and a nearby building for the privacy to put my clothes back on.

I was not sure if the hospital staff would send someone to look for
me or not. The thought was probably a carry-over from my being
chased throughout my runaway days, but nevertheless, I hid. At dusk
I walked to a pay phone and called my sister, who came right away
and picked me up. She drove us to her house and I explained to her
what the doctor said, while she nursed me with a bowl of healthy
soup. I slept great and felt safe being with my sister. She also
understood about missing mom and loved me, no matter what stupid
crap I was involved with. I worried her when I spoke about the "hit"
my ex-boss has on me, and the drug dealer after me. What else could
I say? OK already; painfully sick, wanted dead, a drug addict, and
needed to quit my job because of danger.

The next day she dropped me off at home and I told Gail what
happened at the hospital. She worried herself sick about me because
her mother told her that the doctor called her with my diagnosis and

said that I had ran out of the hospital.

My cocaine addiction was screaming at me, "Now!" The only thought in my mind was snorting a line. Gail and I began our nightly ritual of going out on the town to be wild. We went to a nightclub and were listening to the band play, when I met a gentle mannered, healthy looking man, Ray. His giant smile and suntan drew me in. He was uncommonly polite and quite interested in me. Ray asked me a number of questions about myself and I ended up mentioning my ulcerative colitis condition. He said, "I can help you heal from it and am willing to be of service." We agreed that he would come to my home the next day and educate me on basic dietary needs, especially whole grains and complete proteins.

Ray did arrive, just as he said he would, and I listened carefully to what he was telling me. What he said about my lack of dietary fiber made logical sense to me. It's no mystery that I had colitis after my lack of healthy foods: growing up on Wonder Bread, refined pasta, and white rice. Ray praised me on my decision to stop eating meat and poultry, having me add refined grains and rancid fats to my list. I began eating oatmeal twice a day and the recommended herbal teas for the infection, cleansing my blood, and general colon care. After just two weeks, I felt renewed and comfortable with my intestines feeling happy again. Thank goodness that I did not let the doctors cut me open. It would not surprise me if the Angels arranged for Ray and I to meet because, I certainly needed his valuable knowledge to live by.

In more ways than one, Ray was a blessing in my life, besides being a kind hearted, gentleman, he gave me the exact information I needed to saved my guts! He stepped out from the shadows in the club and helped me. Yes! We had a short, yet intense love affair. He was just in the city for two weeks, visiting his parents for the Holidays. Ray was a student of music and living in northern California. I was well loved and healed by this beautiful man, who left on one bitter cold day. The dietary wisdom worked its way into my life and I ate much better, grew to appreciate herbal teas and noticed that I was drinking less alcohol. The amount of put-downs my friends gave me for changing my diet was unexpectedly enormous. My friend's reactions to my new diet were silly and they had wondered if I had lost my mind. When my friends heard that I stopped eating meat, they thought that it was weird and shook their heads. Being seen as "odd" appealed to my rebellious nature and made it more fun than ever to eat for the shock appeal! Health food equated with being some kind of religious freak in the city I grew up in, back in these days.

Dan, my drug dealer, showed up at my door and totally surprised me. I had been focused on my ex-boss and health and I wasn't thinking about him. Dan was super wasted on something, angry, and looked frightening. He attempted to rape me by grabbing me but I fought him back. He said, " You owe me money and I am taking your ass for the payment." I quickly grabbed my gun and pointed it at his face. He backed up and raised his arms like he knew the routine. I yelled, " Get the fuck out or I am going to shoot you and I can get away with it!" Dan knew this was true and walked straight out the front door saying, "I'll get you!" I knew that he would return shortly with firepower of his own and I did not stick around for him.

When Gail returned home, I let her know that my life was closing in on me and I needed to spend the night at my sister's, in case Dan returns. She knew all the details about Dan and agreed that I did, indeed, need to escape. We hugged many times while I packed my few, favorite possessions. I did not leave that apartment; I ran for my dear life!

My sister was trembling at hearing about the trouble I got myself into. I told her everything; the "hit" out on me from my ex-boss, the drug dealer who was trying to rape and kill me, and the FBI wanting me for questioning about the murder. As if that was not enough, I reminded her about my toxic health situation, but was less worrisome now. I admitted to still being a serious cocaine addict and to quitting my job, because it was dangerous for me to go there. She had heard enough after I told her about my boyfriend getting busted in Florida and how I dreaded each day. The only thing my sister and I could do was to share a bottle of wine and try to figure something out. After such an exhausting day and drinking the wine it was easy to fall asleep, putting my many problems to rest.

I was accustomed to waking up around 11:00 am, but I was awakened at dawn by a gigantic energy surge. It was powerful enough that it jolted me into sitting straight up in bed. I popped up in bed and saw a big, red light glowing in my bedroom. The magnificent, bright light spoke to me with a very deep, masculine voice. The radiant, red light told me, "Get on the 3 o'clock bus today, or you will die, be killed, or be locked up in prison for a long time." Each word spoken by the red light vibrated through my body and making the hair on the back of my neck stick up. I was riveted to the bed with the power surges and my whole body was trembling. I could not explain this one away; impossible to ignore the otherworldly phenomenon. The entity's message was a drastic and confusing one, so I asked the radiant ball of light, "Excuse me, but a bus to where?" The bright, red light replied, "San Francisco."

I leapt out of bed and called the bus station, to check if there was truly a 3:00 bus going to San Francisco and there was. I woke up my sister, screaming to her about what the bright light said. She was visibly shaken up. I was excited, amazed, electrified, and in shock-all at once. My sister calmed me down the best she could, but I was blown out of the water with my life suddenly changed forever. I asked her if she would drive me to the bus station and she reluctantly agreed. It was clear that I had an Angelic visitation that sternly warned me with information that sounded too feasible to distrust. This bright, red light knew more about the trouble I was in than I did, and my entire Being felt it. My sister didn't have any better idea for getting me out of the trouble I was in than leaving, agreeing to store my few things. I called Will and Gail to say "goodbyes" to them but couldn't reach Gail. Will told me to stop messing around and that I was full of shit. I said, "Think what you want, I love you and will see you someday." After buying the one-way bus ticket, I had $235.00, a notebook and pens, snacks, a light blue, vinyl suitcase, and an ounce of "Acapulco Gold" pot.

My sister walked me to the door of the bus and said, "I love you and am mad at you because you are going to have an amazing adventure." I thanked her for everything and told her how much I loved her. We agreed that I would phone her when I arrived someplace, then I hopped on the bus. I felt completely safe and thrilled while we waved goodbye to each other through the window.

I sat five rows up from the back of the bus and made myself comfortable for the very long trip ahead. Dreamlike, I stared out the window and watched the city become distant. In more ways than one, I felt thankful that I was still alive. Then the thought occurred to me, 'I was at the beginning of a serious drug withdrawal' and I broke out in a clammy sweat. Luckily the bus was under half full with nobody seated next to me, so I stretched out and zoned inward. Just as I needed it most, a blissful feeling of deep serenity filled my body, and I knew it was the protection from the Angel, who told me to catch the bus in the first place.

The bus stopped in many places but in Cleveland and Chicago we started to fill up with some very entertaining characters. Thank goodness the seat next to me stayed vacant. My first night of sleep was easy because the detox from cocaine and Quaaludes, and shedding my "Old Life" was exhausting. I woke up feeling replenished and eager to start fresh. After the bus stopped at a diner, I freshened up and got myself a cup of coffee. It was a beautiful, warm sunny day, and perfect for the stretching I needed desperately. Happily back in my seat, I began writing in my notebook.

The bus ride gave me plenty of time to realize how deeply my parents loved me and how I had put them through Hell. I spent most of the day writing a lengthy letter to my parents; over ten pages of apologies for my inconsiderate behavior. I realized that the amount of worry I caused them was tragic and how no family should have had to go through that. Also, I understood that there was an upside to my parents' and brother being in Africa; they did not have to witness me going through my drug addiction and all the subsequent trouble. I was at the point where there was almost nothing else that could be done for me, except to reserve me a coffin. I wrote about the fact that I had no idea what was going to happen to me next and felt pulled out of my world, in the flash of a divine, red light. Writing gave me the opportunity to reflect on my past and find forgiveness for my father and even some for myself, as well.

My Father tried everything he could think of to break me down emotionally, yet spent an equal amount of time saving me from the court system. My loving mother was the most injured of all the victims because, I wanted to be with her, but I was at "War" with my father. My mother and siblings were robbed of a happy household and I sickened them with worry. OK, there was a life long feud with my father but, at the same time, I was a selfish asshole. In the letter, I begged my mother for her forgiveness and promised to not worry her in the future.

Yet, I knew I would already have lived in California for at least a month before the letter would reach my parents, so I reassured them that this was the safest choice I could have made. Being able to have the long bus trip to gain a better understanding about what happened to me, and what I did to help cause my problems was both: good and alarming. It became clear why I needed to be sitting on a bus that was heading all the way to the other side of the country.

Sitting with the notebook opened and pen in my hand, while staring out the window and counting my lucky stars, it dawned on me what a thoroughly life-changing journey this was. Every time I looked up at the sky, I saw a bright star shining, whether it was in daylight or nighttime. The bright star gave me a sense of comfort and, seemingly like magic, kept me from becoming anxious. Divine intervention must have been at work within me because my drug withdrawal was, thus far, unbelievably gentle.

The bright light, that I now called, "My Angel Friend", advised me during the bus ride by showing up and speaking with me. My Angel friend had a deep voice that I could feel inside of me, as well as hear. I recognized the Angel's words as being the truth, like a heart-centered intuition that I could feel in my spine. The Angel said, "Write down everything about yourself that you want to leave behind, then write all the qualities within that you that want to take with you into your new life." Without hesitation, I started on what I was instructed to do and soon found the thought process to be a life's journey in itself.

The seventy-two hour bus trip seemed like it was closer to three weeks long and having short hair was a blessing. I could fit my head under the water faucets at the greasy spoon restaurants we stopped at and washed my hair. Having clean hair made a huge difference in being comfortable enough in my own skin for my task; my soulful character assessment. Refreshed and completely enthralled with my angelic assignment, I decided which parts of my personality I choose to discard forever and which of my qualities I value, and will nurture.

One afternoon my Angel friend spoke to me, reminding me that it is simply keeping my energy high and vibrating with love that is ultimately my most powerful protection. During the long bus trip, the Angel and I spoke for hours about the decisions I was then making and he made sure I was thorough about it.

By being accompanied by the Angel, and feeling replenished despite my drug withdraw, and not knowing my future; I still seemed fine. Over the course of the trip, I became crystal clear about what I must do, Now! I am discarding the parts of myself that are low energy, unhealthy, and any character traits that I could think of that are other than "Good".

I chose to flourish and knew that the Angel was with me for my protection, as well as education, and kept me oddly calm, given the circumstance. The qualities I decided to live by are: to always be loving and caring, be honest, be as positive an asset to the world as I can be, earn my money from doing good things, never smoke freebase again, keep aware of the types energy I am around, have a joyous time on Earth, and to keep my life mission in the forefront of my thoughts--no matter what! My mission to be a good person became clear that day.

One morning as I watched the landscape whiz by from my window, it dawned on me that the Angels of the Light are the most happening thing on Earth! Enormous thankfulness to the Angels for saving my life, and so many times, flowed through me. I was aware of a loving, white light that surrounded me. Looking in the mirror, I could notice my appearance was changing with each passing day; I looked healthier, more relaxed, and younger. The biggest emotional change I noticed was the amount of happiness I felt; being "high on love" was a better feeling than any drug I ever tried. The best drug ever is "love" and it was right under my nose, it's free and priceless at the same time.

I got up enough nerve to ask my Angel friend, "Can I work for you while I am here on earth, it seems like you have the best jobs that exist?" My Angel friend told me, "Yes, you can work for us", meaning the Angels of the White Light. 'How simple' I thought. I just do what the Angels tell me to do and my life will be wonderful. I believed that my choice of careers was a brilliant opportunity to be helpful to the world and have fun while doing it. Even though I was clueless about what this new career actually meant, I knew that my life was going to be wonderful and positive from this moment onward! Just as I surrendered to the Angel, he reprimanded me harshly and used no uncertain terms. I was scolded for using my psychic gifts to get drugs and win at gambling. My Angel friend continued, telling me that my gifts are to be used for helping and healing others. My powerful gifts were, then, taken from me until I learn how to use them properly. I was not told how or when the

Angel would reinstate my psychic gifts, and made it understood that I conducted myself very poorly. I apologized and pleaded ignorance and drug-induced mistakes. My Angel friend assured me that I was loved and forgiven, and knowing that was all part of my unique education. The drugs helped push the doors to other realms open, further than by my being born with a spirit world sensitivity. With the un-closable door opened, I was needing to learn how to best live with this fact.

Passengers got on and off the bus with each state we drove through, but I did make friends with a young man who was sitting behind me. Cliff is the man's name and he boarded the bus in Salt Lake City, Utah, and was cordial and respectful of others. He was tall with long wavy brown hair and wearing a tie-dyed t-shirt. We shared a few meals together and snuck into the corners of buildings to smoke joints at our rest stops. He was returning to his home in Berkeley, California after visiting his fiancé in Salt Lake City.

Cliff was a highly intelligent man, who was the soundman for a rock band, and obviously still embraced "The Summer of Love". I kept my new Angel friend a secret and didn't tell Cliff very much about why I was going to California. He gave me a few tips on where to go and where to avoid; cautioning me to stay on the bus through Oakland. I liked him and was comforted by having a buddy.

Back in Cleveland, a hairy man boarded the bus and he was still with us too. As it turned out, this hairy man was also wearing a tie-dyed t-shirt and going to Berkeley. He was extremely happy and excited about his adventure; he was going to live with the "Rainbow People". I told him that I never heard of the "Rainbow People". He explained to me how love filled his life is going to be with them, "It will be groovy." I gathered that the "Rainbow People" are "Hippies" and lived a free lifestyle. He was cool enough and joined Cliff and I for a few joints along our route. He was amazed that I had no idea where I was going, or what I was going to do when I got off the bus in San Francisco, and without a worry in the world.

Both of my bus-traveling friends were shocked at my young age and the confidence I had. I was tempted to tell them that I was on a "Divine Mission" with an Angel friend, just to help them understand; my sense of security and calm independence was completely dependent on my faith, but I thought better of it. I already seemed strange enough to them. These men were not worried about me either, and that was helpful because I did not need to hear any fear-based crap. I saw that we were traveling through the beautiful Sierra Mountains and knew that my friends would be gone by early afternoon. Blessed is how I felt, as we drove through the mountains, more glorious than I could ever have imagined them. This was my special morning! I washed my hair and changed into my floral skirt, white t-shirt, black leather jacket and my combat boots, in preparation to begin my new, love-filled life!

The bus rolled into the Bay Area and Cliff gave me his phone number, telling me to keep in touch with him. I let him know how glad I was to have ridden with his company and we said our "goodbyes". The bus stopped in Berkeley and I wished the man from Cleveland a great life with the "Rainbow People". He smiled big and invited me to join him. I declined and thanked him for the opportunity, keeping on my route. My Angel friend clearly said to go to San Francisco, and so be it. My bus friends were gone and I was in the company of only my Angel friend, who helped keep me relaxed.

San Francisco was a beautiful sight from the bridge and seeing its' enormity sent my heart fluttering. I was overflowing with excitement while we drove over the Bay Bridge and into the heart of the big city. My curiosity about what will happen to me next sent my brain bubbling in fantasy. This is really it! My new life began and it was sinking in. I was saved from a very horrible outcome, and now delivered into "Paradise". Spring was here and the perfect timing for my new beginning. The landscape was ultra delightful in comparison to where I left. As I gazed out of the window, it was clear to me that I did indeed change on the bus trip; enchanted with my Angel friend and new career.

Paradise welcomed me with a surprise, alright! As I stepped off the bus, I was attacked, as soon as my second foot stepped onto the pavement. A filthy woman in her mid-twenties jumped at me and punched me in my shoulder. She began screaming, "See, she hit me, Bitch" and grabbed her own neck trying to convince onlookers that it was me who attacked her. I wasn't in a mood for any crap from her, especially after a 3-day bus ride. My streetwise, invincible streak kicked in, and I screamed as loud as I could, "Fuck you!" The insane woman looked into my eyes and knew that I was going to pound her into the cement if she came any closer. Then she simply ran off into the crowd and disappeared. The immense amount of happiness and love that poured through me kept me from being disturbed by the attack of a sicko-woman.

I picked up my suitcase and strolled around the ugly, depressing neighborhood for a little while, with the bus station being located in a ghetto. I asked my Angel friend, "What shall I do now?" As fast as I asked the question the reply came, "Go in the bus station and ask the ticket agent about the rolling hills." So, I did. The delightful ticket agent suggested that I go over the Golden Gate Bridge if I really wanted to see some beauty and rolling hills. I was aware of my Angel friend being close by and could hear his words, "Go to San Rafael and start walking." I boarded the bus to San Rafael and knew that my life, was now, really on a divinely orchestrated path.

From then on, I never touched freebase again and the buzz from feeling the White Light and Divine Love was all I ever needed. I have lived the rest of my life according to the wishes of my Angel friend and know that I am truly blessed! Since then I have met more Angel friends; all dear to my heart and, every day, I am grateful for knowing them! With certainty, I know that my life would never have been this spiritually fulfilling, adventurous and happy without my angelic friends. I feel like a precious plant that almost died when the Angel watered and nourished me, educated and protected me, and pointed me in the right direction to blossom. I developed my clairvoyant abilities and use them for the highest good of All. For some reason the Angels decided to intervene with me, and love and guide me, so that I may accomplish their desires. I know this might sound hokey but I would never have wished for anything else to live by; as strange as my life is! With the angelic guidance, I have been educated in the "Healing Arts" and blessed beyond belief by having plenty of opportunities to help others. Life has been filled with many bizarre twists and the Angels keep me busy with their plans for me. This is where the darkness ended and my bright future begins to unfold, divinely orchestrated and still wild as ever! The job that I asked for is one that I can never quit and just the thought of ignoring my angelic instructions is too disturbing. I can tell you this, often times the information that I received from my Angel friends was humanly impossible for me to have already known-point blank. I accidently became a NUN, as unconventional as it is, and I could not have picked a better life on Earth! This book tells about the beginning: slightly unusual, yet normal in comparison to my future.

ABOUT THE AUTHOR

I, Anne Victoria, am busy writing the next two books of the *Seriously Light Trilogy* and plan to finish the next volume soon. As always, I am available for whatever my Angel friends ask of me. Of the greatest importance to me is continuing to use my Angelic information resource to assist people with their healing and providing assistance in crime solving. Also, my innate mediumship allows me to easily communicate with spirits who have passed over to the other-side, thus helping people to have more resolve and understanding, often easing their grieving. The unique education and skills that I have are useful in helping others with their own life navigation, healing and finding more joy and inner peace.

Maintaining the balance between my writing, teaching and consulting feels like a rewarding career in itself. After daily meditation, prayer and yoga, I still make the time to enjoy the natural beauty of Oregon, and it's wild mushrooms and organic veggies.

Singing words of "Thanks and Gratitude, and Prayers for the Earth and All Divine Life" pours from me everyday.

Trust me when I say that my Angel friends keep me very busy and there is nothing else I could be living in accordance with, that would be as joyfully fulfilling.

www.ingramcontent.com/pod-product-compliance
Lightning Source LLC
Chambersburg PA
CBHW070341090426
42733CB00009B/1254